In friendly
remembrance from your
Sponsor
   Otto H. Lochs

**PAUL.**

PAINTER AND PUBLISHER NOT KNOWN.

# Paul

## Life and Letters

William Dallmann

Concordia Publishing House, St. Louis, Mo.
1929

Copyright 1929
by
CONCORDIA PUBLISHING HOUSE
St. Louis, Mo.

PRINTED IN U. S. A.

*From the Proceedings of the North Wisconsin District at Wisconsin Rapids, 1927:* —

"Synod acknowledged the excellence of Dr. Wm. Dallmann's 'Paul' by giving him a rising vote of thanks. The essayist was petitioned to edit his interesting and edifying treatise in book form and have it published by Concordia Publishing House.   A. M. W. WAHL, *Secretary.*

## CONTENTS.

| CHAPTER | | PAGE |
|---|---|---|
| I. | Saul of Tarsus | 1 |
| II. | Saul's Conversion | 26 |
| III. | Paul's First Missionary Journey | 64 |
| IV. | Paul's Second Missionary Journey | 99 |
| V. | Paul's Third Missionary Journey | 164 |
| VI. | Paul's Imprisonment at Caesarea | 214 |
| VII. | Paul's Journey to Rome | 239 |
| VIII. | Paul's Imprisonment at Rome | 282 |
| IX. | Paul's Fourth Missionary Journey | 304 |
| X. | Paul's Death and Influence | 325 |

# ILLUSTRATIONS.

| | PAGE |
|---|---|
| Frontispiece: Paul. | |
| Tarsus, Where Paul was Born | 2 |
| The Falls of the Cydnus above Tarsus | 3 |
| Jewish Synagog | 4 |
| A Synagog | 6 |
| The Roll of the Law | 8 |
| Bird's-Eye View of Present-Day Jerusalem | 11 |
| Jerusalem in Her Glory | 12 |
| Herod's Temple | 15 |
| Mount Moriah, Where Abraham would have Sacrificed Isaac | 18 |
| Tablet Warning Gentiles against Crossing the Wall of Partition | 19 |
| Jerusalem | 21 |
| Mar Saba, Valley of the Kedron | 23 |
| The Stoning of Stephen | 27 |
| St. Stephen's Gate, Jerusalem | 29 |
| View from Neby Samwil (Mizpah) | 30 |
| Tiberias | 31 |
| Nablus, the Ancient Shechem, with Mount Gerizim and Mount Ebal | 32 |
| Caesarea Philippi | 33 |
| Mount Hermon | 34 |
| The Valley below Mount Hermon | 35 |
| Rivers of Damascus | 36 |
| Paul's Conversion | 38 |
| Northwest View of Damascus | 39 |
| Street of the Palaces, Damascus | 41 |
| Paul Let Down in a Basket | 45 |
| Wall of Damascus | 46 |
| Jerusalem, from Scopus | 47 |
| Haifa, at the Foot of Mount Carmel | 49 |
| Gorge of Kadisha, Mount Lebanon | 50 |
| The Famous Ladder of Tyre | 51 |
| St. Paul's Gate, Tarsus | 52 |
| Antioch | 54 |
| Syrian Antioch, Where the Disciples were First Called "Christians" | 57 |
| Julius Caesar | 60 |
| Augustus | 60 |
| The Port of Seleucia | 62 |
| Paphos on Cyprus | 65 |
| Paul and Elymas | 66 |
| Pisidian Antioch | 69 |
| A Recent View of Pisidian Antioch | 70 |
| Mark and Paul | 73 |
| Modern Iconium (Konia) | 76 |
| An Older View of Iconium | 77 |
| A Recent View of Lystra | 79 |

# VIII  ILLUSTRATIONS.

| | PAGE |
|---|---|
| An Older View of Lystra | 79 |
| Paul and Barnabas at Lystra | 81 |
| Derbe | 83 |
| Mount Casius at Antioch | 85 |
| Peter and Paul at Antioch | 86 |
| Paul | 94 |
| Peter | 94 |
| Jerusalem, from the Mount of Olives | 95 |
| The Entrance to the Cilician Gates | 100 |
| The Cilician Pass through the Taurus Mountains | 102 |
| Arches in Alexandria-Troas | 103 |
| Neapolis | 106 |
| Cathedral Ruins at Site of Philippi | 107 |
| Site of Philippi | 108 |
| The Place of Prayer by the Riverside at Philippi | 110 |
| Ruins of the Market-Place, Where Paul was Scourged | 112 |
| The Philippian Jailer before Paul and Silas | 115 |
| The Ruins of Amphipolis | 117 |
| Triumphal Arch, Thessalonica | 120 |
| Thessalonica | 121 |
| Berea | 124 |
| The Piraeus, Port of Athens | 128 |
| The Street of Tombs at Athens | 129 |
| Paul Preaching at Athens | 131 |
| Paul in Athens | 132 |
| The Acropolis at Athens | 133 |
| The Acropolis, the Ancient Citadel of Athens | 134 |
| Gate of the Agora, or Market, North of the Acropolis | 136 |
| Pallas Athena in the Parthenon | 139 |
| The Isthmus of Corinth | 144 |
| The Corinthian Canal Across the Isthmus of Corinth | 145 |
| Corinth | 147 |
| The Famous Fountain of Pirene at Corinth | 148 |
| Cenchreae | 152 |
| Ancient Ephesus | 165 |
| The Temple of Diana at Ephesus | 166 |
| Ruins of the Theater at Ephesus | 167 |
| Artemis, the Diana of Ephesus | 169 |
| The "Ephesian Letters," or Charms | 170 |
| Burning of the Books of Magic in Ephesus | 175 |
| Ephesus | 184 |
| Christians Pressing Their Gifts on Paul | 188 |
| Paul Writing the Epistle to the Romans | 194 |
| The Emperor Trajan | 199 |
| Samos | 200 |
| Assos | 200 |
| The Gate of Assos through Which Paul Passed | 201 |
| Miletos | 202 |
| Mitylene, Capital of Lesbos | 203 |
| The Theater at Smyrna, Where Polycarp was Burned | 203 |

# ILLUSTRATIONS.

| | PAGE |
|---|---|
| Smyrna, Where Polycarp is Buried | 204 |
| Paul Parting from the Elders at Miletus | 206 |
| Patmos | 207 |
| Rhodes | 208 |
| Ruins of Ancient Tyre | 209 |
| Tyre | 210 |
| Ptolemais | 210 |
| The Prophecy of Agabus | 211 |
| The Mount of Olives, from Mount Zion | 212 |
| Castle Antonia | 215 |
| Paul Rescued from the Jewish Mob by the Chief Captain Claudius Lysias | 217 |
| Paul Bound by Roman Soldiers | 218 |
| Ancient Caesarea | 223 |
| Paul Before Felix and Drusilla | 228 |
| Caesarea. St. Paul's Prison | 232 |
| Caesarea | 234 |
| Paul Before Agrippa | 236 |
| Sidon | 240 |
| Sidon, with Lebanon in the Background | 241 |
| South Coast of Crete | 242 |
| Paul Exhorting His Fellow-Passengers to Be of Good Cheer | 245 |
| The Bay of St. Paul, from the South | 247 |
| St. Paul Shipwrecked | 248 |
| St. Paul Casting Off the Viper | 249 |
| Syracuse | 252 |
| Syracuse, with Greek Theater in Foreground | 253 |
| Rhegium | 254 |
| Strait of Messina | 255 |
| The Ragged Rocks of Scylla to the East of the Strait of Messina | 256 |
| Capri, with the Twelve Villas of Tiberius | 256 |
| Tiberius | 257 |
| Naples and Vesuvius | 258 |
| Island of Nisida | 259 |
| Hill of Posilipo | 260 |
| Mount Vesuvius | 261 |
| Seashore of Bagnoli, Pozzuoli (Puteoli) | 262 |
| Looking Across the Bay from Pozzuoli toward Nisida | 262 |
| The Bay of Puteoli, Now Pozzuoli | 263 |
| Pier Where Paul Landed | 264 |
| Pedestal of Statue in Honor of Tiberius at Puteoli | 265 |
| The Villa of the Gentilii on the Via Appia | 266 |
| The Mausoleum of Augustus in Campus Martius | 267 |
| The Ponte Molle, Milvian Bridge | 269 |
| The Fifth Mile from Rome on the Via Appia | 270 |
| The Pantheon | 271 |
| Part of Roman Forum | 272 |
| Part of Roman Forum | 274 |
| Agrippa, Son-in-Law of Augustus, Builder of the Pantheon | 275 |
| St. Sebastiano Gateway, Appian Way, through Which Paul Must Have Passed | 276 |

# ILLUSTRATIONS.

| | PAGE |
|---|---|
| Paul Reaches Rome in Chains | 277 |
| Paul Preaching in Rome | 279 |
| Paul Pleading with His Centurion | 283 |
| The Camp of the Pretorians | 284 |
| "St. Paul's Prison," Rome | 286 |
| Messalina, Claudius, Britannicus, Octavia | 310 |
| Nero | 312 |
| The Silent Witness of Nero's "Living Torches" | 317 |
| Nero's Living Torches | 319 |
| Diana or Christ? | 321 |
| The Last Prayer | 323 |
| The Emperor Hadrian and His Arch at Jerusalem | 325 |
| Pyramid of Gaius Cestius | 326 |
| Church of St. Paul at the Three Fountains | 327 |
| Wall of Wailing | 328 |
| Ruins of the Roman Forum | 329 |
| The Earliest Representation of Paul's Martyrdom on the Sarcophagus of Bassus | 330 |
| St. Paul on Top of the Column of Marcus Aurelius | 332 |
| Constantine Promises Victory to His Soldiers in the Sign of the Cross | 333 |
| Nero, Titus | 334 |
| Facade of St. Paul's Outside the Walls of Rome | 335 |
| The Flavian Theater | 335 |
| Interior of Church of St. Paul without the Walls | 336 |
| The Entry of Titus into Jerusalem | 337 |
| Porta del Popolo. Church of Santa Maria del Popolo | 338 |
| The Arch of Constantine | 338 |
| The Emperor Constantine the Great | 339 |
| A Christian Mother Strengthening Her Daughter to Be Faithful unto Death | 340 |
| Spoils from the Temple at Jerusalem | 341 |
| Faithful unto Death | 342 |
| Medals Struck by Vespasian to Celebrate the Capture of Jerusalem | 345 |
| The Archangel Michael's Victory over Satan, or Paul's Victory over Paganism | 346 |

THE CONVERSION OF SAUL

Acts 9:4

## CHAPTER I.

## SAUL OF TARSUS.

*A citizen of no mean city.* — Acts 21, 39.

PEGASUS, the flying horse of Zeus, dropped a wing, in Greek *tarsos*, and Tarsus was the name given the city that grew there on the banks of the Cydnus, as alluded to by Juvenal. Another legend makes Triptolemos the founder during the wanderings of the Argives in search of Io. Athenodorus, friend and teacher of Caesar Augustus, says the founder was Parthenius, son of Cydnus and grandson of Japetus, or Japhet. The Jews, however, held the founder was Tarshish, son of Javan, or the Ionian, mentioned Gen. 10, 4. They are supported by Strabo, the old Greek geographer; by Josephus, the old Jewish historian; by Prof. A. H. Sayce, the Oxford archeologist, and by Ramsay.

About five miles below Tarsus the two-hundred-foot Cydnus River widened into the little lake Rhegma with the docks, wharves, and arsenals. Here you could see the rafts of timber cut in the wild, snow-capped Taurus Mountains float down the Cydnus to be built into vessels in the largest shipyard in the world, and in this harbor you could see the fleet of the Roman mercantile marine, the largest of the world outside of Alexandria. These were the ships of Tarshish spoken of in the Old Testament, Josephus and many others think. 1 Kings 10, 22; Ps. 48, 7. Strabo says the Cilicians were great travelers and traders. In order to bring business, the shrewd Tarsians, about 1000 B. C., built the famous Cilician Gates through the solid wall of the Taurus Mountains, about thirty miles north. It was a wagon-road, only about eleven paces wide, but a hundred yards long and several hundred feet high; an engineering triumph like Roosevelt's Panama Canal. Through this frowning defile passed Xerxes, Darius, Cyrus, Xenophon, Alexander, Cicero, Caesar; Tancred and Baldwin in the first crusade picked their way through here to deliver Jerusalem from the Saracens.

The road over the Taurus is 70 miles; it led to Podandos, Kybistra, Kastabala, Barata, Laranda, Derbe, and Lystra. All the commerce between Syria on the southeast and Asia Minor on the northwest passed through Tarsus and made it prosperous and enabled one to learn the ways of trade

TARSUS, WHERE PAUL WAS BORN.
The Taurus Mountains in the Distance.

and commerce and to know all races and religions that met and mingled in that cosmopolitan city of about five hundred thousand people. Tarsus became the capital of Cilicia, named for Cilix, son of Agenor, the Phenician. Cilicia became famous as the dark and bloody ground of olden days, the theater of many battles of Oriental world history.

The Assyrian King Shalmaneser III took Tarsus in 850 B. C. The rich province yielded to Darius a revenue of five hundred talents and three

THE FALLS OF THE CYDNUS ABOVE TARSUS.

hundred sixty white horses and gave to Xerxes one hundred ships for his war on Greece. About 400 B. C. Xenophon, with his famous Ten Thousand, found Tarsus a large and rich city. In 333 B. C. Alexander the Great came just in time to save the city, for the Persians had already set fire to it. He bathed in the Cydnus, and the icy water chilled him almost to death. The great German Emperor Barbarossa actually died from the icy bath and was buried here in 1190 A. D. And yet they say the water was good for rheumatism and gout in man and beast. When Antiochus Epiphanes presented Tarsus to his favorite mistress, the people resented it and rose in revolt, which forced him to quit Palestine to quell the rebellion. 2 Maccabees 4, 30.

*A Roman City.* — In 103 B. C. Mark Antony, the grandfather of the better-known Mark Antony, took Western Cilicia, and in 92 B. C. Sulla was the Propraetor. In 88 B. C. Mithridates massacred 80,000 Romans, says Appian; 150,000, says Plutarch. Sulla reconquered the province. In 83 B. C. Tigranes of Armenia took Eastern Cilicia from the Seleucids. Cicero favored the Manilian law, which gave enormous power to Pompey, who defeated the pirates in less than a year and made the whole of Cilicia a Roman province in 64 B. C. At that time the worship of Mithras was brought to Rome, Plutarch tells us.

JEWISH SYNAGOG.

Thirty miles north the mighty Taurus Mountains were infested with brigands, who were the terror of the rich plain till Proconsul Cicero subdued them in 51 B. C.

Cleopatra, "the cunning mantrap of the Nile," when only nineteen, met Caesar at Alexandria in 48 and became the mother of his son Caesarion and followed him till his death. On his way from Egypt against the Pontic king, Caesar in 47 reorganized the province of Cilicia, and Tarsus was called Juliopolis. When Cassius came to the gates, Tarsus publicly crowned him; when Dolabella came, the Tarsians shouted for Augustus; when Cassius defeated Dolabella and forced the gates of Tarsus, he sold most of the people into slavery to raise the enormous fine of 1,500 talents, or $1,618,125; when Augustus triumphed at Philippi the next year, 42 B. C., Antony set the sold citizens free and made Tarsus a free city, with home rule.

In 41 B. C. the giddy populace left Mark Antony sitting alone on his tribunal in the forum and dashed off to gaze at Queen Cleopatra of Egypt sailing up the Cydnus in her gilded barge with the purple silken sails and silver oars, keeping time to the music of flutes. With her jeweled hand this Venus led captive Mark Antony, the lord of the Eastern world, though her lips were painted red, her eyebrows penciled black, and her finger-tips stained yellow — certainly a work of art. She was twenty-eight, Mark over fifty. Maybe it was here she dissolved those costly pearls and gave to Mark the most expensive drink in all history at the banquet she made for him.

Strabo calls Boethius "a bad poet and a bad citizen"; yet Antony gave him funds to erect a fine gymnasium. Though Boethius was a grafter, Antony upheld him, having been flattered by the rascal in a poem on the Battle of Philippi. When Antony was overthrown by Augustus at Actium, in 31 B. C., the victor replaced the thievish official with Athenodorus, his former tutor, who ruled the city so well that when he died, about 9 B. C., the citizens voted him divine honors and a yearly festival to celebrate the virtues of this scholar in politics. An altar of Augustus was placed in the temple of Artemis.

In Diocletian's tariff law the fine linen of Tarsus comes in for special notice.

As late as about 240 the Tarsians reared a monument to Gordianus III in the Via Sacra, found in 1879.

The games were played in the stadium. The gymnasium was also the university, where they taught the encyclopedia, the whole circle of instruction — grammar, mathematics, ethics, rhetoric, dialectic, and music.

"The city of Tarsus attained in very early time great eminence in philosophy and all kinds of learning, so that in the love of science and art it surpassed the fame even of Athens and Alexandria," says the old geographer Strabo. The professors were all natives. Among the shining lights were Antipater, the grammarians Artemidorus and Diodorus, Dionysius the tragedian. Demetrius traveled as far as Egypt and Britain to gain knowledge. The Stoic Zeno once lived at Tarsus and caught the germs of his philosophy from the world-wise Orientals there. Athenodorus, the son of Sandon, became the adviser of the Emperor Augustus and tutor of young Claudius; he also aided Cicero with his book *On Duties*. Nestor, the Academic, became the tutor of Marcellus, the nephew of Augustus, and Nestor, the Stoic, the tutor of Tiberius; Athenodorus Cordulio tutored Cato Junior and died in his house. No wonder it is written: Rome especially can learn from the multitude of the scholars of Tarsus, for she is full of Tarsians.

The Cilician poet Aratus was rated so highly that Cicero himself turned him into Latin, and Ovid was sure "Aratus will always be with the moon and the sun." Great learning could not keep at least one professor from stealing oil from the city and another from smearing his rival's house with filth; the battle of wits often ended in bloody encounters.

The great university could not keep the Cilicians from Cilicisms —

A SYNAGOG.

bad grammar. Much less could it keep them from bad religion. The world by wisdom knows not God, and in the shadow of the great university one could see the sword of Apollo worshiped by the people for having by a miracle been kept from rust and decay; for good luck the people looked to Hermes Eriounios, purse in hand, stamped on their coins; in sickness they turned to Aesculapius, who still made known his power in the neighboring Aegae. They even "worshiped Messalina, the unspeakably filthy fifth wife of the Emperor Claudius."

Twelve miles out on the road to Soli was Anchiale, where one could see the alleged tomb of Sardanapalus with his colossal stone statue snapping its finger toward heaven and bearing the inscription: "Sardanapalus [Ashurbanipal], the son of Anacyndaraxes, built in one day Anchiale and Tarsus. Eat, drink, and be merry. Nothing else is worth that" — a snap of the fingers. Lord Byron puts it: "Eat, drink, love! The rest's not worth a fillip." Aristotle quotes a poet holding this epitaph more befitting an ox than a king. Such a creed creates a kindred conduct, and the Saccaea, the festival of the supposedly effeminate Sardanapalus, bred unbounded gluttony and brutal licentiousness, so that Kilikia and Kappadokia and Krete were notorious as the three worst K's. Apollonius of Tyana went to study rhetoric under the Phenician Euthydamus, but so great was the immorality at Tarsus at this time that he begged his father's leave to study at Aegae, a more serious and religious place.

>In Cydnus' clear, but chilly wave
>His weary limbs was wont to lave
>　Great Philip's greater son.
>By Egypt's queen, on Cydnus' tide,
>The Roman, proof 'gainst all beside,
>　By beauty's smile was won.
>But now, I ween, in Christian lays
>Had Cydnus earned a holier praise.
>Where Tarsus, girt with greenest trees,
>Her image fair reflected sees
>　In that fast-flowing stream,
>In childhood's hour was wont to stray,
>Poring upon the classic lay,
>　Or lost in heavenly dream,
>He who should carry far and wide
>The banner of the Crucified. — *Anon.*

Yes, far and away the greatest name connected with Tarsus is that of Saul. He was born in the Golden Age, under Caesar Augustus, about the same time that God sent forth His Son, made of a woman, who wrapped Him in swaddling-clothes and laid Him in a manger because there was no room in the inn at Bethlehem.

On the eighth day he was circumcised, and at the same time he was named Saul; hardly for the king, who was not popular on account of his suicide. Saul means "Desired"; his mother had prayed for him, as Hannah had prayed for her Samuel. Like Hannah she dedicated her boy to the service of the Lord. Gal. 1, 15.

As a Roman citizen his name, forename and surname, was recorded in one of the Roman tribes in the empire's capital far away on the banks of the Tiber; and so he carried two names — Saul among the Jews and Paul among the Gentiles.

THE ROLL OF THE LAW.

His father was a citizen of Tarsus and so a man of standing and substance, according to the law of Athenodorus; more than that, he was also a Roman citizen, and so Saul was a free-born Roman, as he proudly stated. Socially Paul was far above the mere citizens of Tarsus; legally he ranked on the same footing with the great men of the empire. And he was a "Hebrew sprung from Hebrews," a pure-blood Jew, and even of the tribe of Benjamin, little Benjamin, the leading loyal and faithful tribe. He was as proud of being a Jew and a Roman as Lord Beaconsfield was proud of being a Jew and an Englishman. He was brought up in the sect of the Pharisees, famous for strict piety and burning patriotism. Acts 23, 6. Before he could talk, he was taught to touch the "mesusah" by the door, a bright metal box, in which were written the words: "Hear, O Israel; God is one God." Deut. 6, 4.

*Learning to Pray.* — As soon as he was able to speak, the little toddler was taught to kneel with his face turned towards far-away Jerusalem and with raised hands say his morning and evening prayers, the *Shema,* including his birthday text, a verse beginning or ending with the same letters as his Hebrew name. When old enough, the little barefoot lad, on the Sabbath, trotted by the side of his mother to the synagog, where she washed off the dust from the feet and took him with her to a seat behind a stone screen, where the women could see the men unseen of men.

After the service the mother wended homewards by the back streets, as women must do, and answered her bright boy's eager questions; for had not the Reader said she was to talk to her son as she walked with him by the way?

*The Bible and Catechism.* — As she sewed a coat for her boy by an oil lamp of an evening, she would tell him the story of Abraham, and Isaac, and Jacob, and Joseph, and Moses, and Joshua, and David, and Queen Esther, and Daniel, and Judas Maccabeus, who had once freed the country of the Jews from Antiochus, and, best of all, she would tell him of the Messiah, who was surely coming and who would surely again free His country and set up the glorious kingdom of His father David.

When Saul was five, his father became his chief teacher, and the lad began to recite his little catechism, as we would say. Boys like to ask questions, and we feel quite sure Saul was a regular walking question-mark. Why did they eat *matzen* at a certain season, and why did his father, with a candle, search every corner of the house which mother had swept so clean of all sour dough? And he was told all about the Passover. Ex. 12. Why did the children in December carry palms to the lighted synagog and have candles in the house and lanterns outside for eight days? Then he was told how the wicked Antiochus had defiled the Temple and how Judas Maccabeus cleansed and opened it after it had been closed for three years. Why did the men stamp their feet in anger when they heard the name of Haman in the synagog and bless the name of Esther; and why did the children get cakes and candies as they left the service? Then he was told the whole story of Esther at the Purim Festival. Esther 3. Why did the children deck themselves with flowers and carry garlands to the synagog, where stood white willow baskets with fruits of all kinds? Because it was the Festival of First-fruits in sunny June (Pentecost) to thank God for the harvest. Lev. 23, 9. Why did the neighbors all stand in the streets looking east? They were watching for the new moon, and the first to see it ran to the synagog to tell the news. Ps. 81, 3. It was a holiday, and all made merry at the cheerful supper. Why, even the heathen Greeks kept that festival. Besides these monthly moons the new moon at New Year was hailed with cow-horns and trumpets so much that it was called the Feast of Trumpets.

The school was given by the Jews the poetic and picturesque name "vineyard." The Jews thought boys, like young vines, had to be trained to grow in the right direction and bear good fruit in abundance. To help on the training, the teacher sometimes used a strap — nothing harder. At six a slave would take the little lad to school and bring him back, just as Nicholas Oemler took little Luther to school, and from this custom Paul speaks of the Law as "the pedagog, who takes us to the school of Christ." Gal. 3, 24. A school without benches and desks, and slates and pencils, and pens and pads, and pictures, and charts, and blackboards, it was. The pupils squatted right down on the ground and wrote their letters and figures in the sand. The teacher recited, and the pupils repeated, repeated, repeated, till they could recite it. So there was such a noise as in a — yes, as in a Jewish school, for that is where the saying comes from. Josephus tells us: "From the dawn of understanding we learn the laws by heart and have them, as it were, engraved on our souls." The school was connected with the synagog and was called the "House of the Book," the Book of the Law being the only book of instruction.

At home Saul would talk the common Aramaic; at school he would learn the ancient Hebrew; and he also learned Greek, the language commonly spoken by the Jews outside of Palestine.

BIRD'S-EYE VIEW OF PRESENT-DAY JERUSALEM.

When Saul had read all of the Old Testament, he began the study of the large mass of traditions, which were accumulating since the days of Ezra and later, 200 A. D., embodied in the Mishna. A little roll of parchment with the Law hung upon the right door-post of his room — always in sight. Under his tunic he wore his prayer-shawl of thin cloth with a blue woolen tassel of eight threads at each corner, to be kissed during prayer in the synagog and to be a reminder of the Law.

On Fridays Saul's father would quit work early. On entering the

JERUSALEM IN HER GLORY.

door, he would touch the metal box, kiss his fingers, and say, "The Lord shall preserve thy going out and thy coming in," Ps. 121, 8, and then kiss his wife and children, dressed in their best, laying his hand on Saul with the blessing, "May God make thee as Ephraim and Manasseh!" Gen. 48, 20, and on the daughter's head with the words, "May God make thee as Sarah and Rebekah!" Gen. 24, 60. The house had been swept and tidied, and he washed and dressed as for a feast.

As the sun set, the trumpet sounded from the synagog, as the silver trumpets sounded from the golden Temple at Jerusalem to tell the Jews in all the world the Sabbath had begun. The room-door is closed. The family stands around the table, upon which the Sabbath-lamp sheds a mellow light on the supper spread on the snowy table-cloth. The father asks a blessing on every one in the house; he washes his hands in a basin held by one of the children; he pours out a cup of red wine and water and gives all a taste; while speaking a few words about God and the vine and the Sabbath-day, he breaks bread, dips a piece in salt for each, and passes it. Then all sit down to the most joyful meal of the week — fish, and soup, and bread, and milk, and fruit, and raisin-wine. After supper all join in singing a thanksgiving, and then the father reads in the Bible those parts telling of the Sabbath.

*Attending Divine Services.* — Next morning everybody walked the narrow streets, looking neither right nor left, to the synagog, a small, round building, with trailing vine, a bunch of flowers, a branched candlestick, or a pot of manna carved in the stone over the door. The father took off his shoes, tied his phylacteries on arm and brow, and walked slowly to the front, where sat the rulers of the synagog. Through the women's screen was seen the tall brass candlestick with seven arms, the rich curtain of purple, scarlet, blue, and gold, where gleamed the lamp whose light was never quenched, a copy of the one at Jerusalem. Beyond was the Ark with the large rolls of Holy Scripture. In the middle rose a platform with the reading-desk, or "wooden tower," of Neh. 8, 4.

*The Service.* — The door was closed. On hearing the voice of the "angel of the synagog," the Leader, all rose and at the end of the two prayers said "Amen." Next was recited the *Shema*, or Creed, made up of Deut. 6, 4—9; 11, 13—21; Num. 15, 37—41. After a third prayer came the eighteen Eulogies, or Benedictions, all closing with an Amen by the whole congregation. The priestly benediction, Num. 6, 23. 24, ended the liturgical part of the service. The clerk next took the Roll of the Law from the Ark and handed it to the Reader, who read the First Lesson for the day in Hebrew and translated it verse by verse into the popular language. The Second Lesson was from the Prophets, translated after every three verses. Thus was read the whole Old Testament in one year. When the Reader sat down, the people silently waited for some one to address them, which any one was free to do. If it was a Rabbi, he would give a sort of sermon on the lesson for the day, during which remarks from the men in the congregation were usual; also questions at the close of the speech.

*After the Service.* — There was no cooking on the Sabbath, but they had good things to eat prepared before. They were only allowed to walk less than a mile, but they had a good time paying or receiving visits. After the service Jesus accepted an invitation to the house of a Pharisee to dine on the Sabbath-day. Luke 14, 1. As the sun sloped westering and the shadows gathered over the city, the father gathered his family and spoke a blessing upon the sacred Sabbath; and when the sun was down, the Sabbath was done.

*Learning a Trade.* — According to the good old Jewish custom the little lad learned a useful trade, likely his father's, that of making cilicium, a coarse cloth from the long hair of the goats of Cilicia; and that name is still in use to-day for haircloth. Tents were made of this cilicium * and also from the skins of animals, and so it is that Chrysostom calls Saul a "tent-stitcher" and also a "leather-cutter." It was a flourishing business; for the Roman armies alone kept the tent-makers of Asia Minor fully employed. Later this trade stood him in good stead. Acts 18, 3; 20, 34. This work, likely, later led him to write: "We know that if our earthly house of this tent [A. V.: tabernacle] were dissolved, we have a building of God, a house not made with hands, eternal in the heavens." 2 Cor. 5, 1. Saul early learned to practise what he later taught: "If any man would not work, neither should he eat." 2 Thess. 3, 10.

*A Jewish Engagement.* — When Paul's sister was engaged to be married, the house was lighted up with candles, the rooms were decked with flowers and greenery, friends were invited, the *Shitre Erusin* — agreement — was drawn up by the authorities and paid for by the groom, who also gave a coin or a letter to the bride to make the engagement legal, and then the night was spent in rejoicing.

*The Wedding.* — After some time came the wedding, usually on a Wednesday afternoon, never on the Sabbath or on the day before or

---

\* Only poor people used the Cilician stuff —
>   Such hair as from the goats of Cinyphus
>   The crookt shears of Cilician herdsmen crop.

So says Martial, and again of the Cilician shoes: —
>   For these not wool, but rank goat's hair was grown;
>   Cinyphian gulfs, where feet might lurk unknown.

after, lest the Sabbath-rest be endangered. Notice of the wedding was given weeks before in the synagog, and days were spent inviting the *Bene Cuppah,* the children of the bride-chamber, the wedding-guests. The bride sat in her father's house, decked with flowers and covered from head to foot in a thick veil, surrounded by her maidens and a throng of guests in their best, all waiting for the groom to fetch his bride to his house, which was the chief part of the ceremony. Shouting, singing, clashing of cymbals,

HEROD'S TEMPLE.                                                                                           SCHICK.

1. Tower of Antonia, named to flatter Mark Antony. 2. Holy of Holies. 3. Nicanor Gate. 4. Court of Women and Treasury. 5. The Gate Beautiful, where Peter and John healed the lame beggar and where Paul was arrested and taken to the Tower of Antonia, where the Roman soldiers were lodged. 6. The Porch of Solomon. 7. Court of the Israelites. 8. Court of the Gentiles. Jesus drove the sellers from 7 to 8. Between 7 and 8 was the Middle Wall of Partition, Eph. 2, 14, with tablets warning the Gentiles not to cross from 8 to 7. 9. Porch of Herod. 10. Wall built to form a plateau of Mount Moriah. 11. King's palace. 12. Valley of the Brook Kedron. 13. Valley of Hinnom.

clicking of castanets, signaled the coming of the groom with his companions. His gayest clothing was perfumed, his long hair curled, crowned with flowers, and fragrant with oil. With much ceremony he entered the house, led out the bride, helped her on to a donkey, took her through the narrow streets, followed by the guests with torches and lanterns, singing and shouting on the way to the house. On the way they were met by gayly dressed, flower-decked girls bearing lanterns on poles, singing the praises of groom and bride in verses of their own making. On reaching the house, the groom lifted his bride from the donkey, and friends carried her into the house, lest she stumble on the threshold, which, all agreed, would be a sad calamity. All sat down to the marriage supper, the richest and most joyful feast they could afford. The groom sat by his bride, but he could not yet see her face, for she was still heavily veiled. After supper parched corn was showered on the guests and on the married couple. The bride's hair was unloosed. "The friends of the bridegroom" now led them to the bridal chamber. Here the groom lifted the veil and shouted his surprise and delight at the great beauty of his bride, so that the people in the other room might hear the groom's joyful voice and rejoice with him. That ended the wedding-day, but the feasting and rejoicing among the friends was kept up for at least a week to show they were delighted with the marriage and wished the young couple much joy in its new home.

When thirteen, Saul became a "Son of the Law," confirmed, as we would say. When he had passed an examination in the Bible, he was declared fit to receive the phylacteries, slips of parchment with Bible-verses in a small calfskin box with straps. One box, the *Tephilla,* was bound to his brow, the other, called *Tephilim,* was placed on his naked left arm near the heart, and the two straps were twined around the arm seven times and around the hand three times, and at the middle finger tied into a knot. This in mechanical obedience to Ex. 13, 9. 16. The short sermon gave him warning and advice and told him never to enter the synagog without the phylacteries, the sign of manhood and full church-membership. A merry family gathering and joyful supper ended Saul's solemn confirmation day. The mother was proud, but also sad, for her boy could no more walk with her to the synagog and sit with her behind the screen. He now sat with the men. Perhaps he was the equal of Josephus, who lived about the same time and was a teacher at fourteen, as he tells us.

## A TRIP TO JERUSALEM.

As Hans Luther had great plans for his Martin and sent him to the high school at Magdeburg in 1497, when he was about fourteen, so Paul's father had great plans for his boy and sent him at about the same age for higher education to Jerusalem, to the "House of Interpretation," the college, to be taught by Rabbis.

O joy! A holiday trip for Paul! "I was glad when they said unto me, 'Let us go into the house of the Lord!'" Ps. 122. After a farewell supper in his honor, Paul set out, likely in the company of pilgrims going overland to the Passover.

A tramp through famous and familiar fields and storied, sacred scenes. At nightfall he would get his pots and pans and kettles to cook in camp, curl up on his mat, and promptly fall soundly asleep, while stars twinkled down on his tent. Around the Syrian Gates in the Amana Mountains wolves and hyenas would sing him a lullaby; even tigers and lions might attack him. And robbers might prowl around and steal, unless the pilgrims paid tribesmen for protection.

*Entering the Holy Land.* — At Antioch Paul, let us suppose, took the road to Damascus and then south to the wooded hills of Bashan and marched through the land of his fathers, now ruled for the Emperor Tiberius by Annius Rufus, the Procurator. From here he could see the white cap of Mount Hermon and the Lebanon range with its famous cedars. Down the rushing river Jordan to low-lying Lake Galilee, dotted with fishing-smacks and dominated by Tiberias, a Roman city in a Jewish land. There loomed the green cone of Mount Tabor, where Barak and Deborah defeated Sisera with his iron chariots of war. Beyond, the plain of Esdraelon, famous field of many battles, and Mount Gilboa, where his namesake, Saul, the romantic king, had slain himself with his own sword because the battle had gone against him. They kept to the east of the lake, for Jewish pilgrims were often attacked by the Samaritans, who worshiped on Mount Gerizim, at Shechem, where Jacob and his sons had stopped for four years on the way to Isaac at Hebron, and where were the Well of Jacob and Joseph's tomb. Through the deep and woody vale of Jabbok to Gilead, where Jacob wrestled all night with the Angel of the Lord, Gen. 32, while in the hazy hills across the lake lay stony Bethel, where Jacob in a dream saw the angels coming down and going up the ladder to heaven. Gen. 28. Paul bathed in the cold Jordan, at the fords where Joshua had crossed a thousand years agone, Josh. 3, and came to Jericho, in the land of his own tribe Benjamin, little Benjamin. Jericho, taken by the sound of rams' horns! Gilgal, from where the people fetched David in triumph to his palace in Jerusalem. 2 Sam. 19, 15. Ramah, where Samuel lived and taught. 1 Sam. 7, 17. Mizpah, where Saul was crowned.

1 Sam. 10, 17. Yonder hill of white limestone — yes, there 600 men of Benjamin had held out for four months. Judg. 21, 13. Leaving the Jericho valley, Paul climbed up a deep gorge in the hills of Judea, "the Bloody Way"; for here pilgrims were often robbed and even slain. Up, by Bethany, up to the top of the Mount of Olives — there! Paul's eyes sparkled, his heart beat fast, but it was too full for utterance as he saw before him Mount Moriah, where Abraham had gone to sacrifice his son,

MOUNT MORIAH, WHERE ABRAHAM WOULD HAVE SACRIFICED ISAAC.
Site of the Temple of Solomon, Zerubbabel, Herod, and Dome of the Rock.

his only son Isaac, Gen. 22; and where had stood Solomon's Temple and now gleamed the white marble one of Herod with its golden roof and crown of gold spikes burning in the shining sun. And beyond, beautiful for situation, is Mount Zion, the city of the great King David.

The waving of palms! The chanting of psalms! The Psalms of Degrees sung by the pilgrim chorus. Down the slopes of Olivet, on the winding way to the Valley of the Kedron to the bridge from which you can look down into the waters of the brook so loved of David — "There is a river, the streams whereof shall make glad the city of God, the Holy Place of the Tabernacles of the Most High." Ps. 46, 4. Up through the Lion Gate — "Our feet shall stand within thy gates, O Jerusalem!" Ps. 122, 2.

Up the steep street to the great white steps leading to the first marble court of colored columns, with sellers of doves in willow cages and noisy butchers selling bleating sheep and lowing cattle, and money-changers,

TABLET WARNING GENTILES AGAINST CROSSING THE WALL OF PARTITION.
M. Clermont Ganneau of the Palestine Exploration Society discovered it in the Via Dolorosa.

at tables stacked with coins of all countries, bartering and bargaining, chaffering and cheating.

Crossing this Court of the Gentiles, Paul came to the *Soreg,* a wall of ornamental marble the height of a man, with openings having pillars on each side, with tablets of warnings in Greek and Latin: —

"No Gentile May Enter This Gate and the Fence around the Sanctuary. Any One Caught has Himself to Blame for the Resulting Death."

This is the middle wall of partition separating the Gentiles from the Jews. Eph. 2, 14. Admiring the famous Beautiful Gate of fine Corinthian brass, Paul passed the middle wall of partition and stood in the Women's Court, open to the blue skies. Paul could see the houses of the priests and the Levites, the store-rooms for clothing, food, lamps, oil, salt, wine, and other daily needs. The treasury was the safest place in all the land for storing valuables, and it was rich from heaps of presents sent yearly by all Jews all over the world. At the doors stood collection-boxes with openings shaped like a trumpet, and everybody made an offering; one poor widow gave two mites. Luke 21, 2. We may be sure Paul reverently sacrificed. Across this court, up more steps, through more pillars, to the Nicanor Gate, of silver and gold, into the Court of the Men and Priests, with the great white altar of rough stones untouched of hammer or chisel, with the smoke rising from the fire never allowed to die out. Here Paul could see the marble shambles on which the sheep had their throats cut, the gold and silver bowls to catch their blood, the bath like a flower on twelve brass lions, and so large it was called a sea, for the priests to wash in after the slaughter.

Up, higher, a third terrace, great stones covered with gold, white marble pillars holding up a roof of gold with a crown of gold spikes, a curtain woven of blue, scarlet, purple, and white, covering a door of gold shielding the Holy of Holies, entered only by the high priest but one day in all the long year.

At the northwest corner frowned the Castle of Antonia, with Roman guards pacing up and down, looking for the least sign of trouble to call the garrison to quell the riot. Herod had built it for a palace and named it in honor of Mark Antony.

*The Passover.* — On the eve of the full moon Paul bought his little white lamb and brought it to the Temple to have a priest look it over very carefully to see it was perfect. He waited at the Priests' Court till set of sun, when the silver trumpets sounded, and the gate flew open, and the throngs crowded in, and the long knives glittered in the bright moonlight and plunged into the throats of thousands of lambs, 250,000 of them, while their blood was caught up and brought to the foot of the great altar, where it was poured out in a great red stream and flushed away by water brought from the Hebron hills, in an aqueduct built by the splendid King Solomon, into the brook Kedron, while the Levite choir sang psalms on the white steps of the Women's Court and at every pause the people responded with loud shouts of "Praised be the Lord!" The lambs were

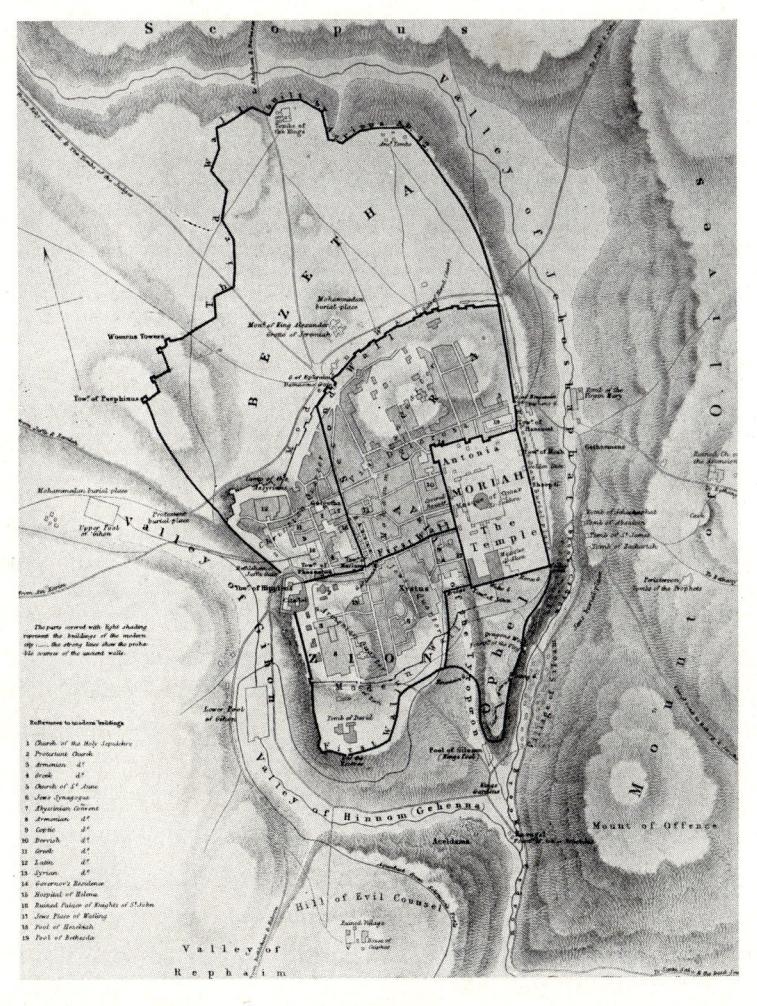

JERUSALEM.

quickly skinned, hung on golden hooks, and cut apart, the priest keeping a part to burn on the altar and Paul shouldering the rest to roast on a spit at home for his Passover supper with his friends, and eating unleavened bread and bitter herbs to remember the bitter days of slavery in Egypt and the Lord's gracious deliverance by the hand of His servant Moses. Ex. 12.

## PAUL AT THE THEOLOGICAL SEMINARY.

The great Temple Rabbis taught in the courts on the north and east and south side of the Temple. Jerusalem had two great schools, one founded by Shammai, the other by Hillel. Though both were Pharisees and taught the Law of Moses and also the tradition of the elders, Shammai placed the Law above tradition, while Hillel put tradition above the Law. So the conservative Shammai was called the Binder, for binding rules on his followers, while the liberal Hillel was called the Looser, or Liberator. The disputes between these rival schools waxed so fierce as to make the proverb: "Even Elijah the Tishbite could not reconcile the disciples of Shammai and Hillel."

Saul entered the theological seminary founded by Hillel and now conducted by his grandson Gamaliel, "the Beauty of the Law," one of the seven who alone had the honored title of "Rabban," "had in reputation among all the people," esteemed even by Titus.

The teacher sat on a platform, and the students squatted on the ground at his feet and "powdered themselves in the dust of the feet of the wise." The teacher would take a text from the Bible, tell what every Rabbi from earlier times had said about it, and discuss the merits of all these opinions. The students would discuss the question with the teacher and debate it among themselves. So it went all day, and every day, for many a weary day and year. The study of the Law was called *Halachah,* that of history, *Haggadah.*

*Saul's Record.* — "I profited in the Jews' religion above many my equals." Gal. 1, 14. It seems Paul made good headway in his studies and soon forged toward the head of the class. He also became a very self-righteous Pharisee and a red-hot patriotic zealot. The great scholar Onkelos, the author of the celebrated Targum, *i. e.,* paraphrase, on the Pentateuch, may have been his fellow-student. So well was Paul grounded in the Old Testament that all his quotations are from memory, as Bleek and others think. He thought and wrote in quotations. He quotes from one hundred and forty-one different chapters and over two hundred single verses, from thirty-three different psalms, and from twenty-nine chapters of Isaiah. His quotations are, for the most part, from the Septuagint.

"Cursed be he that eats pork, and cursed be he that teaches his son the Greek wisdom!" ran a Jewish proverb. Gamaliel defied this popular

MAR SABA, VALLEY OF THE KEDRON.

prejudice. He visited a heathen philosopher and called him his colleague, and he was the first to permit the Jews to write the Holy Scriptures in Greek. His son Simeon says: "The school of my father had a thousand students; one half studied the Jewish law and the other half the wisdom of the Greeks."

*Paul's Knowledge of Greek.* — Did Paul take a course in Greek learning at this time? Zahn says: "Paul writes Greek, not like one who has laboriously acquired a foreign language in his riper years, but like one who has known it from his childhood." J. Rendel Harris says: "Paul was acquainted with Pindar, Euripides, and Aristophanes." He quotes Greek authors, Epimenides, Aratus, Menander, and uses more than thirty figures of Greek rhetoric. Baur says Paul has "the true ring of Thucydides," and the German C. L. Bauer and the English Farrar and the French Sabatier agree. Koester and Kypke say he "was familiar with Demosthenes, the model of Greek popular eloquence." Lightfoot has a long line of expressions to show Paul knew Stoic philosophy; others show he knew Aristotle and Plato. As Moses was skilled in all wisdom of the Egyptians, so Paul was skilled in all the wisdom of the Greeks. Dionysius Longinus says: "The following men are the boast of all eloquence and of Grecian genius, *viz.*, Demosthenes, Lysias, Aeschines, Hyperides, Isaeus, Anarchusor, Crithinus, Isocrates, and Antiphon; to whom may be added Paul of Tarsus, who was the first, within my knowledge, that did not make use of demonstration."

*Graduation.* — At the end of his course Saul was graduated and took his degree. Having passed a satisfactory examination as to his moral and literary character, he took a raised seat. A writing-tablet was presented to him to signify that he should write down and not forget his learning. Next he was given a key, to signify he might now open the treasures of knowledge. The following step was the laying on of hands. After this he received a certain authority, probably to be exercised over his own disciples. Finally he was saluted with the title of "Rabbi," or Master.

Paul learned the wisdom of the Rabbis, as, later, Luther learned the wisdom of the scholastics; both learned to know to overthrow.

The Pharisees would be righteous before God by keeping the written Law of Moses and also the unwritten law of the scribes, the traditions of the elders, a vast mass of restrictions and regulations. Rabbi Chanina challenged the Angel of Death: "Bring hither the Book of the Law and see whether there be aught written in it which I have not observed." On the other hand, Rabbi Johanan, called by his disciples the Light of Israel and Strong Rock, wailed in the face of death: "There are two roads before me, one leading to paradise, the other to hell, and I know not by which of these I go — should I not weep?"

*After Graduation.* — It was natural for Paul to return to Tarsus and set up teaching as a Rabbi and earn his bread by working at his craft of tent-making. It was natural for Paul at the age of eighteen to marry, a sacred obligation. "Whosoever doth not apply himself to begetting and multiplying is even as a homicide. It is as though he lessened the image of God." It was natural for Paul to go to Jerusalem for the Passover and to hear of Christ and to attend the synagog of the Cilicians.

## CHAPTER II.

## SAUL'S CONVERSION.

*Acts 9, 1—22.*

JANUARY 25, 32.

JOHN THE BAPTIST thundered repentance in the wilderness and baptized Jesus in Jordan and was beheaded in the prison of Machaerus by Herod Antipas. Christ went about doing good and preaching the Gospel and rose from the dead and, sending His disciples to preach, ascended into heaven.

Did Paul meet Christ? We do not know.

Peter preached at Pentecost and turned three thousand to Christ. Joseph of Cyprus was a Levite, who sold his land and laid the price at the feet of the apostles, who named him Barnabas, or Son of Exhortation, or Consolation. Ananias and Sapphira lied and died dreadfully. Acts 4, 36.

The apostles were put in the common prison, and the Council took counsel to slay them, when Gamaliel counseled against it. Acts 5, 12. Later he made, or at least approved, this prayer against the Christians: "Let there be no hope to them who fall from the true religion; and let heretics, how many soever they be, all perish as in a moment. And let the kingdom of pride be speedily rooted out and broken in our day. Blessed art Thou, O Lord, our God, who destroyest the wicked and bringest down the proud!"

The disciples grew in numbers and elected seven "deacons" to assist the apostles in the care of the poor, as well as in the money and business affairs.

A great company of priests also joined the Church.

Stephen, one of the "deacons," full of faith and the Holy Ghost, preached the Gospel in the synagogs, of which there were 480 in Jerusalem for the people from the various parts of the world. There was one of the Libertini, Jews who had been sold as slaves and later, by a decree of the emperor, made free; another, where the Jews from Alexandria in Egypt would congregate; another for the Jews from Cyrene, in North Africa; another for the ones from the Roman province called Asia, with Ephesus as capital; another for the people from Cilicia, where Paul would naturally go.

The Jews disputed with Stephen in these synagogs, and they were not able to resist the wisdom and the spirit by which he spake. Was Paul one of these disputers against Stephen?

THE STONING OF STEPHEN. ACTS 7, 58. 59.   C. G. PFANNSCHMIDT.

Stephen disputed with his opponents as did Luther with Eck at Leipzig in 1519.

Stephen was brought before the Sanhedrin, or Supreme Court of Seventy Judges, and false witnesses swore to lies against him, "while his face shone as the face of an angel." Then said the high priest, "Are these things so?" Guilty or not guilty? Despite the speech of Stephen they voted to stone him. They cast him out of the city, gave their clothes into the care of Saul, and stoned Stephen, who prayed, "Lord Jesus, receive my spirit!" And he kneeled down and cried with a loud voice, "Lord, lay not this sin to their charge!" And when he had said this, he fell asleep.

> Foremost and nearest to His throne,
> By perfect robes of triumph known,
> And likest Him in look and tone —
> The holy Stephen kneels. — *Keble.*

> With such a Friend and Witness near,
> No form of death could make him fear;
> Calm amid showers of stones he kneels
> And only for his murderers feels. — *Newton.*

> He heeded not reviling tones
> Nor sold his heart to idle moans,
> Though cursed and scorned and bruised with stones;
> But, looking upward, full of grace,
> He prayed, and from a happy place
> God's glory smote him on the face.
> *Tennyson, The Two Voices.*

He received what he was called; he was called Stephen, a crown, and he received the crown of victory.

"And Saul was consenting unto his death." — From this "consenting" some think he was a member of the Sanhedrin and therefore at least thirty and married.

"And Saul was consenting unto his death." Oh, the pity of it! Such a man voting to kill such a man! What thoughts rushed through his brain as he watched the death of Stephen?

"And Saul was consenting unto his death." How calm and cool and cruel! And these words were written by Luke, the beloved friend of Paul! Yes, the Bible is truthful.

The eastern entrance to Jerusalem is called St. Stephen's Gate because it is thought by some that hereabouts the "deacon" was martyred. An older tradition points north of the Damascus Gate to the place of a skull, where Jesus was crucified, which the Jews call the Hill of Stoning. Here they have dug up a very ancient church, which has been called the Church of St. Stephen, where many deacons were buried, according to the writing on the tombs.

Having tasted blood, the tiger thirsts for more gore. As a wild boar roots up a lovely garden, so "Saul made havoc of the Church, entering every house, and, haling men and women, committed them to prison."

# SAUL'S CONVERSION. 29

Acts 8, 3; 22, 4. "I verily thought with myself that I ought to do many things contrary to the name of Jesus of Nazareth. Which thing I also did in Jerusalem, and many of the saints did I shut up in prison, having received authority from the chief priests; and when they were put to death, I gave my voice against them. And I punished them oft in every synagog and compelled them to blaspheme; and being exceedingly mad against them, I persecuted them even unto strange cities."

Saul tried to compel the Christians to blaspheme, just as the heathen proconsul asked Polycarp years later, "Take the oath, and I shall release you; revile the Christ." Polycarp replied: "Eighty and six years have I been His servant, and He has done me no wrong; and how can I blaspheme my King, who saved me?" Rom. 8, 35—39.

The persecution of the Christians turned out for good. Christ had commanded the apostles to preach the Gospel to all nations, and yet they stayed at Jerusalem. The persecution scattered the sparks to light new fires.

ST. STEPHEN'S GATE, JERUSALEM.

Having scattered the church at Jerusalem, the zealous Saul sought more world to conquer. "Breathing threatenings and slaughter" against the disciples of Jesus, he asks the high priest — Theophilus — for letters to Damascus, about 150 miles away, for warrants to arrest Christians and bring them to Jerusalem to be punished. The Jews everywhere obeyed the high priest at Jerusalem much as the Romanists everywhere obey the Pope at Rome.

*Paul's Route.* — Saul leaves Jerusalem by the Damascus Gate, ascends a ridge with the tombs of the Judges to the left, and comes to Ramah of

VIEW FROM NEBY SAMWIL (MIZPAH).

SAUL'S CONVERSION. 31

TIBERIAS.

MOUNT GERIZIM. NABLUS, THE ANCIENT SHECHEM. MOUNT EBAL.

PAUL PREACHING AT ATHENS

Acts 17:22

CAESAREA PHILIPPI.

MOUNT HERMON.

Benjamin. 1 Kings 15, 17. To the left is Gibeah, 1 Sam. 10, 26, the birthplace of King Saul, whence Jonathan went to scatter the Philistines. To the right is Gibeon, Josh. 10, 12, where the sun stood still in the heavens till Joshua had gained his victory, and where the Tabernacle had been set up for many years under David and Saul. 1 Chron. 16, 39. On to Bethel, Gen. 28, where Jacob had rested his weary head on a pillow of stone and in his sleep had seen a ladder with the angels descending and ascending. At Shiloh Saul surely thought of aged Eli and young Samuel, 1 Sam. 1, 3; here he could see the heights of Jezreel, chap. 29, 11, where King Saul had

THE VALLEY BELOW MOUNT HERMON.
Traversed by St. Paul on his way from Jerusalem to Damascus.

been killed, and the mountains of Gilboa, where David lamented over Saul and Jonathan, 2 Sam. 1, 21. Across the hills of Ephraim into the valley between Ebal and Gerizim to Jacob's Well, where Jesus had given the water of life to the sinful Samaritan woman. John 4. At Shechem the Samaritans still have their high priest and observe their ancient ritual and still believe Mount Gerizim is the only place where the true God can be perfectly worshiped; they have dwindled to barely 170 souls. Not far away is Samaria with the ivory palace of Ahab and Jezebel, which American excavators have unearthed. To the east is Dothan, where Joseph was sold by his brothers into slavery in Egypt. Gen. 37. From Samaria into Galilee;

RIVERS OF DAMASCUS.

by "the Way of the Sea" he crosses the Jordan by the "bridge of Jacob's daughters," a few miles north of the lake.

On and on, a vast plain stretches for miles before him, and far in the distance, towering far up in the blue sky, is the brow of Mount Hermon, Deut. 3, 8, white with snow, as if hoary with age. On and on, over a vast desert.

> The midday sun, with fiercest glare,
> Broods o'er the hazy, twinkling air
>   Along the level sand.
> The palm-tree's shade unwavering lies,
> Just as thy towers, Damascus, rise
>   To greet yon wearied band. — *Keble*.

Damascus is the "Eye of the Desert," the "Pearl of the East," the oldest continuous city in the world. Abraham's trusted servant was Eliezer of Damascus. Gen. 15, 2. In order to rescue Lot, Abraham went as far as "Hobah, which is on the left hand of Damascus." David placed a garrison here, and Solomon was opposed by the city. Naaman of Damascus was cured by Elisha. 2 Kings 5. The Jewish population was so large that Nero could kill ten thousand. Our damson plums and damask silk and swords came from this celebrated city which Paul was nearing after a week's travel.

> Who yonder rides from Salem's gate,
> With scornful eye and brow elate,
>   As bent on distant prey?
> Horsemen and footmen in his train,
> He courses down to Jordan's plain,
>   And northward leads the way,
> By Bason's hill and Hauran's sand,
> To Trachan's wild and savage land.
>
> The noonday sun is towering high,
> No summer cloud obscures the sky,
>   The heavens are bright and clear.
> And yonder doth Damascus rise,
> Amid the wastes a paradise,
>   The pilgrim's heart to cheer.
> Up, Nazarene! Arise and fly!
> The desolater Saul is nigh!

Suddenly — what happened? Hear Saul's own account to Agrippa:

"At midday, O king, I saw in the way a light from heaven, above the brightness of the sun, shining about me and them which journeyed with me. And when we were all fallen to the earth, I heard a voice speaking to me and saying in the Hebrew tongue, 'Saul, Saul, why persecutest thou Me? It is hard for thee to kick against the pricks.' And I said, 'Who art Thou, Lord?' And He said, 'I am Jesus, whom thou persecutest.'" Acts 26, 13—18; 9, 1—20; 22, 1—16.

Like lightning it flashed into the soul of Saul: Jesus of Nazareth had been crucified and buried; Jesus of Nazareth is now speaking to me; Jesus of Nazareth rose from the dead and ascended into heaven; then Jesus of Nazareth is truly the Son of God and the Messiah; then I have been in deadly error, and I have been found fighting against God Almighty; yet God has not cast me off, but in His unspeakable grace He has appeared to me. Saul was not disobedient to the heavenly vision; he made a prompt and absolute surrender: "Lord, what wilt Thou have me to do?" Acts 9, 6.

*The Conversion.* — With his eyes Saul saw the heavenly vision; with his ears he heard the voice of Jesus; with his mind he understood the words; in his conscience he felt the truth and force of the warning; with his will

PAUL'S CONVERSION.     P. P. RUBENS.

he became obedient to the word of command. Christ gave clear instructions, which Saul could carry out, and Christ made a plain promise, which was literally fulfilled. It was one conscious person speaking intelligible words to another conscious person. It was a subjective experience, based on an objective appearance.

The revelation of Jesus wrought a revolution in Saul. The vision caused the decision. The antichristian Judaist became the anti-Judaistic Christian. The strong was overcome of the Stronger.

Dr. Porter, who lived long in Damascus, thinks the place of Saul's conversion is at a village ten miles south called Caucabe, "the place of a star." Certainly very fitting for the true Star of Bethlehem to shine upon Saul and never cease shining till he came to the perfect day. On January 25 the Christians of Damascus walk in procession to the scene of conversion and read the history of it from the Acts of the Apostles.

Returning from his father's house at Mansfeld to the University at Erfurt, Luther was overtaken by a thunderstorm; a bolt of lightning felled him to the ground. That was Luther's road to Damascus. He became

UNDERWOOD & UNDERWOOD.   NORTHWEST VIEW OF DAMASCUS.

a monk to get peace with God. The Briton Macduff and the Frenchman D'Aubigne quote Rubianus Crotus's letter to Luther: "Fire from heaven made thee, like another Paul, fall to the ground, near the city of Erfurt and, snatching thee from our society, drove thee to enter the sect of Augustine."

Next to the resurrection of our Savior the conversion of Paul is the most momentous event in the history of the human race. It is the most decisive victory of Jesus; it altered the course of all history and affected the entire world.

*Proof of Christ's Resurrection.* — Without the resurrection of Christ the conversion of such a one as Saul would have been impossible. The conversion of such a one as Saul is one of the strongest proofs of the resurrection of Jesus of Nazareth. As a mighty earthquake changes the whole course of a river, so the appearance of the risen Redeemer changed the whole life course of Saul of Tarsus. Saul of the Pharisees becomes Paul of the Nazarenes. The great persecutor of Christ becomes the great apostle of Christ. Christ "was seen of me also," the same as He was seen of the other apostles, and therefore Paul was not a whit behind the other apostles. 1 Cor. 15, 8; 9, 1. He could therefore testify from personal experience of the real resurrection of Christ and His glorified personal existence. As the resurrection of Christ made a tremendous change in the current of Paul's life, so the conversion of Paul made a tremendous change in the course of the world's life. Bishop Lee ranks it with Luther's reformation.

In order to write a book to destroy Christianity, the infidel Lord Lyttelton studied the history of Paul and was himself converted to Christianity and now wrote for Christianity his *Observations on the Conversion of St. Paul,* which Dr. Samuel Johnson called "a treatise to which infidelity has never been able to fabricate a specious answer."

Some say: "It makes no difference what a man believes as long as he is sincere." What folly and falsehood! Saul was sincere. He was putting Christians to death, thinking he was doing God service.

The first question was, "Who art Thou?" When that was rightly answered, the next question followed, "What wilt Thou have me to do?"

Browning is right in saying: "The acknowledgment of God in Christ solves for thee all questions in the earth and out of it."

| | |
|---|---|
| If Jesus Christ be a man | If Jesus Christ be God, |
| And only a man, I say, | And the only God, I swear, |
| Then of all mankind I cling to Him, | I will follow Him through heaven and hell, |
| And to Him will I cleave alway. | The earth, the sea, and the air. |

*Richard Watson Gilder.*

*Why Paul was Converted.* — Saul was converted, for one reason, to be "a pattern to them which should hereafter believe on Him to life everlasting." 1 Tim. 1, 16. In this pattern conversion we see clearly that Saul was not only "dead in trespasses and sins," Eph. 2, 1, but also, that his "carnal mind was enmity against God," Rom. 8, 7. It is clear that Saul did nothing, and could do nothing, toward his conversion. It is clear that Christ was the beginning, middle, and end of Saul's conversion; he did all he could against it, "he kicked against the pricks" — a common proverb, used by Aeschylus, Euripides, and Terence. Saul, proud Pharisee — a brute beast, a dull, driven ox, clumsily kicking against the will of his driver, and only foolishly drawing his own blood to his own hurt. Surely no glory for this man in his conversion, no cooperation on his part; all the glory

STREET OF THE PALACES, DAMASCUS.

of that glorious work belongs to the glorious Savior, and so Paul breaks out in the glorious doxology: "Now, unto the King eternal, immortal, invisible, the only wise God, be honor and glory forever and ever! Amen." 1 Tim. 1, 17.

*The Comfort for All Sinners.* — From this pattern conversion it is clear that no man need despair. Paul calls himself the chief of sinners because he had persecuted the Church of God; and yet he, even he, obtained mercy. Despair not like Judas and commit suicide. Say rather like Paul: "This is a faithful saying and worthy of all acceptation, that Christ Jesus came into the world to save sinners, of whom I am chief." 1 Tim. 1, 15.

> Chief of sinners though I be,
> Jesus shed His blood for me;
> Died that I might live on high;
> Lived that I might never die.
> As the branch is to the vine,
> I am His, and He is mine.

Charles Darwin thought it utterly useless to send missionaries to the savage and degraded Fuegians. After many years he saw the blessed results of the Gospel, owned up to his error, and sent $25 for the work to Admiral Sir James Sullivan. Ruskin reminds us the mud in the streets of the manufacturing city is made up of clay, sand, soot, and water: the clay can be transformed into a sapphire, the sand changed into an opal, the soot crystalized into a diamond, the water turned into a snowy star. So God touches the sinner and turns him into a saint.

From this pattern conversion it is clear a man is saved to serve. "Lord, what wilt Thou have me to do?" The Lord told him, and he did, always, till his death. John Newton prays: —

> Now, Lord, I would be Thine alone;
> Come, take possession of Thine own,
>   For Thou hast set me free.
> Released from Satan's hard command,
> See all my powers waiting stand
>   To be employed by Thee.

Paul said: "I was not disobedient to the heavenly vision." Acts 26, 19. He saw and he served. Isaiah saw the heavenly vision, and he heard the voice of the Lord, saying, "Whom shall I send, and who will go for Us?" "Then said I, Here am I; send me." Is. 6. He saw and he served. Luther saw the heavenly vision in Rom. 1, 16. 17. He saw and he served. When you see the gleam, —

> After it, follow it,
> Follow the gleam!

This pattern conversion shows it is not God who is angry with man, but man who is angry with God. "God is angry with me," moaned the poor monk Luther. "No," replied Staupitz, "you are angry with God."

From this pattern conversion we learn the union of Christ and His

Christians. Saul went to Damascus to persecute the *Christians.* Christ asked, "Saul, Saul, why persecutest thou *Me?*" Christ and the Christians are one; Christ is the Head, the Christians are the members of His body. What is done to the humblest Christian is done to the glorious Christ, be it good or evil. So Christ taught Saul two thousand years ago; so shall Christ teach us on Judgment Day: "Inasmuch as ye have done it unto one of the least of these My brethren, ye have done it unto Me."

> Know, though at God's right hand I live,
> I feel each wound ye reckless give
>    To the least saint below.
>
> I in your care My brethren left,
> Not willing ye should be bereft
>    Of waiting on your Lord.
>
> The meanest offering ye can make —
> A drop of water, for love's sake,
>    In heaven, be sure, is stored.
>
> He in the day of feeble flesh
>    Poured out His cries and tears
> And, though exalted, feels afresh
>    What every member bears.

"Lord, what wilt Thou have me to do?" Saul asked. The Lord said unto him: "Arise and go into the city, and it shall be told thee what thou must do." And Saul arose from the earth; and when his eyes were opened, he saw no man; but they led him by the hand and brought him into Damascus. "And he was three days without sight and neither did eat nor drink." He was in the house of one Judas in Straight Street, running straight one mile along from the eastern to the western gate, one hundred feet wide, divided into three avenues by Corinthian colonnades.

*Saul's Pastor.* — The Lord told a certain disciple of Damascus by the name of Ananias to go to Saul. But Ananias answered: "Lord, I have heard by many of this man, how much evil he hath done to Thy saints at Jerusalem; and here he hath authority from the chief priests to bind all that call on Thy name." But the Lord said unto him: "Go thy way; for he is a chosen vessel unto Me to bear My name before the Gentiles and kings and the children of Israel; for I will show him how great things he must suffer for My name's sake." And this is the chief reason for Saul's conversion.

This has been called Paul's ordination sermon. The Lord Himself preached it.

The hope of suffering great things for Christ fired the soul of Luther. On July 10, 1518, he wrote with holy humor to Wenzel Link at Nuernberg: "I hope I am a debtor to Jesus Christ, who perhaps says to me also: 'I will show him how great things he must suffer for My name's sake.' For if He does not say that, why has He placed me in the invincible office of this Word? Or why did He not teach me something else that I should say? This was His holy will. The more they threaten, the more I trust; my wife and my children are provided for; my fields, my house, my whole substance, are all disposed of; my glory and fame already vanished. One thing only remains — this weak and broken little body. If they destroy that, they will perhaps rob me of an hour or two of my life, but they will not take away the soul. I sing with John Reuchlin: 'He who is poor has naught to fear, for nothing can he lose; but he is joyful in hope, because he expects to gain!'" (Enders, *Luthers Briefwechsel*, I, p. 211.) Yes, the prospect of suffering great things in a great cause is an attraction for heroes. Emerson says: —

> The hero is not fed on sweets,
> Daily his own heart he eats;
> Chambers of the great are jails,
> And head-winds right for royal sails.

And Ananias went his way and entered into the house and, putting his hands on him, said: "Brother Saul, the Lord, even Jesus, that appeared unto thee in the way as thou camest, hath sent me that thou mightest receive thy sight and be filled with the Holy Ghost."

"Brother" Saul — the persecutor Saul must have felt this word in his wounded heart as a balm and benediction. Let us learn to greet and treat the returning and repenting sinner with love and kindness.

*Saul Received into the Church.* — "And immediately there fell from Saul's eyes as it had been scales; and he received sight forthwith and arose and was baptized." Here, too, the word of God came true: "I will bring the blind by a way that they know not; I will lead them in paths that they have not known; I will make darkness light before them and crooked things straight." Is. 42, 16.

> O blessed Paul, elect to grace,
>   Arise and wash away thy sin;
> Anoint thy head and wash thy face,
>   Thy gracious course begin.
> To start thee on thy outrunning race,
>   Christ shows the splendor of His face.
> What will that face of splendor be
>   When at the goal He welcomes thee?
>
> *Christina G. Rosetti.*

"And when he had received meat, he was strengthened. Then was Saul certain days with the disciples which were at Damascus."

*Saul Preaching.* — Paul straightway preached Christ in the synagogs, that He is the Son of God. But all that heard him were amazed and said: "Is not this he that destroyed them which called on this name in Jerusalem and came hither for that intent, that he might bring them bound unto the chief priests?"

After a trip into Arabia, Gal. 1, 17. 18, Saul returned to Damascus, increasing the more in strength. He confounded the Jews that dwelt at Damascus, proving that this is the very Christ. He did not simply cease to persecute the Christians, he began at once to prosecute the work of the Christians. Where he had worked against Christ, there he now worked for Christ. Where he had done wrong, he confessed the wrong and righted the wrong.

*The Persecutor Persecuted.* — After many days were fulfilled, the Jews took counsel to kill Saul; but their lying in wait was known of Saul. And they watched the gates day and night to kill him. In Damascus the governor, under Aretas IV, the King of Petra,

PAUL LET DOWN IN A BASKET.

"kept the city of the Damascenes with a garrison, desirous to apprehend me; and through a window in a basket was I let down by the wall and escaped his hands." 2 Cor. 11, 32. 33.

This Aretas was the father-in-law of Herod Antipas, who abandoned his wife in 29 and seduced the wife of his brother Philip, for which he was sternly rebuked by John the Baptist. Some think this happened about the year 37. Tiberius ordered Vitellius, proconsul of Syria, to take Aretas, dead or alive. This was prevented by the news of Tiberius's death, which reached Vitellius in Jerusalem in April, 37. The new emperor, Caius

WALL OF DAMASCUS.
Traditional Site of Paul's Escape.

# SAUL'S CONVERSION.

JERUSALEM, FROM SCOPUS.

Caligula, was friendly to Aretas, and in adjusting the Eastern frontier, presented Damascus to Aretas.

Saul went to Jerusalem "to interview Peter." Gal. 1, 18. Arriving there, he tried to join himself to the disciples; but they were all afraid of him and believed not that he was a disciple. Then Joseph, a Levite of Cyprus, who was called Barnabas, took Saul and brought him to the apostles and declared unto them how Saul had seen the Lord in the way, and that He had spoken to him, and how he had preached boldly at Damascus in the name of Jesus. Then Peter received Saul, who abode with Peter fifteen days. Saul also saw James, the Lord's brother. Gal. 1, 18. 19. And Saul was with them, coming in and going out at Jerusalem. And he spake boldly in the name of the Lord Jesus and disputed against the Grecians; but they went about to slay him. When the brethren knew that, they brought Saul to Caesarea and sent him forth to Tarsus. It seems Saul was not willing to leave until the Lord told him pointedly: "Make haste and get thee quickly out of Jerusalem. . . . Depart, for I will send thee far hence unto the Gentiles." Acts 22, 17—21.

*Preaching in His Home Town.* — Paul went from Caesarea to Tarsus, most likely by land, and of course preached on the way; for he told Agrippa he had preached throughout all the coasts of Judea and then to the Gentiles. Again, when Paul later landed at Tyre, he tarried there seven days with the disciples. Acts 21, 4. So when he came to Sidon, he was given leave by Julius to go to his friends. Acts 27, 3. "I came to the regions of Syria and Cilicia." He was there for about fourteen years. Gal. 1, 21; 2, 1. What did he do during all that time? Of course, he founded churches there; for he returned to them later to strengthen them. Acts 15, 41.

Perhaps it was during these years that Paul suffered some of the things he speaks of in 2 Cor. 11 and 12. And the churches of Judea glorified God in Paul when they heard that he which persecuted us in times past now preacheth the faith which once he destroyed. Gal. 1, 21—24.

> See me, see me, once a rebel,
>    Vanquished at His cross I lie;
> Cross to tame earth's proudest able!
>    Who was e'er so proud as I?
> He convinced me; He subdued me;
> He chastised me; He renewed me.
> The nails that nailed, the spear that slew Him,
> Transfixed my heart, and bound it to Him.
> See me, see me, once a rebel,
>    Vanquished at His cross I lie.

HAIFA, AT THE FOOT OF MOUNT CARMEL.

GORGE OF THE KADISHA, MOUNT LEBANON.

**THE FAMOUS LADDER OF TYRE,**
over which Paul likely traveled from Jerusalem to Tarsus.

When the Tarsians became Christians, they buried their idols, many of which have been dug up in our day. In 110 Dio Chrysostom praised the Tarsian women for their modesty — on the streets; they were heavily veiled. In 160 Abgarbarman placed the cross on the coins and forbade castration in honor of the vile goddess Cybele. Diodorus of Antioch became Bishop of Tarsus in 378 and teacher of Theodore of Mopsuestia and John Chrysostom, him of the golden mouth. Theodore of Tarsus became

ST. PAUL'S GATE, TARSUS.

Archbishop of Canterbury and organized the Church of England and founded schools and thus made possible the career of the Venerable Bede.

The Tarsians proudly point out a well and say Paul peered into its depths and drank from its waters. Why shouldn't it be true? They also show the gnarled and rugged "St. Paul's Tree" and say under its shady branches Saul rested. Who knows? A fine monument to the apostle is St. Paul's Collegiate Institute, founded by Colonel Elliot F. Shepherd, the Christian editor of New York, flourishing under the American Board. The foundations of one of the halls for boys are said to go down through six ancient cities of Tarsus, forty feet to a solid sea beach. "In the Institute of St. Paul," says Dr. Christie, "we have Armenians, Greeks, and Syrians. We have several students belonging to a strange race, called the Ansarieh, who are the descendants of the ancient Canaanites, driven by Joshua into the mountains. They come to us from Lebanon. Before they are converted, as from time to time some of them are, they are genuine pagans, worshiping the forces of nature, the buds on the trees, the foam of water, the stars of the heavens, and they have their high places where they worship once a year. In North Syria and in Cilicia there are at least 100,000 of these Ansarieh."

Tarsus has two churches, St. Peter's and St. Paul's.

## PAUL'S CALL TO THE CHURCH OF ANTIOCH.
*Acts 11 and 12.*

Sixteen miles up the broad historic Orontes River, Seleucus Nicator, 300 B. C., founded a city and named it for his father Antiochus. He built sixteen Antiochs, nine Seleucias in honor of himself, six Laodiceas in honor of his mother, and one Apamea for his wife. Seleucus Epiphanes enlarged the city and ringed it with the most remarkable walls on earth. In 65 B. C. Pompey brought it under the Roman yoke, but gave it home rule. Caesar built a basilica known as the Caesareum. Augustus added a suburb and a circus for 200,000. Tiberius restored the walls. Caius Caligula built baths and an aqueduct. Herod the Great paved the main street east and west for two and a half miles with blocks of white marble and erected on each side a magnificent colonnade in which one might walk under shelter in all weathers. Titus adorned the western gate with the colossal gilded cherubim from the Temple at Jerusalem.

Antioch was a city of 500,000, the third largest of the empire, and often styled the second Rome. It was the court of the Legate of Syria with his Roman garrison. The people of Antioch were famous for their culture, but all their culture could not keep them from becoming the easy dupes of a wretched quack named Debborius, who sold them charms to ward off earthquakes! Fortune-tellers found their easiest victims among the cultured classes of Antioch. In order to still the anger of the gods during a plague, Leius was ordered to carve the colossal crag of Mount Silpius on the south into the head of Charon, called the Charonium, of which the copper coins still give a good idea. Here was born and bred the poet Archias, in whose defense Cicero left us the classical *Defense of Poesy*. The orator Libanius praises his native city for the abundance and excellence of its water: "Every one has water within his doors. And this water is so clear that the pail appears empty, and so pleasant that it invites us to drink." It alone among ancient cities had its streets lighted up at night with public oil lamps, so that there was no difference between day and night, as Libanius boasts. Advertising does not seem to be

ANTIOCH.

UNDERWOOD & UNDERWOOD.

a modern discovery. Julian, the apostate Emperor, likened Antioch to Paris — a new part of Antioch was surrounded by two arms of the Orontes, just like the older part of Paris is surrounded by two arms of the Seine.

About five miles southwest of the city the unwilling Daphne fled from Apollo and was turned into a grove of bay-trees, where Seleucus founded a sanctuary in a beautiful park ten miles around. The statue of Apollo by Bryaxis was thought by Ammianus Marcellinus to equal that of Jupiter Olympus. Temples of Artemis and Isis and others were also built in this beauty-spot. Antiochus Epiphanes built a stadium, and the income of $150,000 was spent yearly on the public sports. Wealthy citizens offered prizes for a new form of luxury. At the Maiuma, the spring festival of Dionysius and Aphrodite, the prostitutes of Antioch exposed themselves in a crystal lake of Daphne to the gaze of the spectators. This grove of Daphne was a sanctuary for a perpetual festival of vice, so that "Daphnian morals" became a proverb, and even the pagan "soldier and philosopher wisely avoided the temptations of this sensual paradise, where pleasure [adultery], assuming the character of religion, imperceptibly dissolved the firmness of manly virtue," according to the infidel Gibbon. Avidius Cassius, the hardy general of Marcus Aurelius, made it a penal offense for a soldier to visit the place. All their commerce, architecture, literature, and philosophy could not keep them from the most degrading sensuality. Seneca speaks of Rome as a cesspool of iniquity, and Juvenal pictures her as a filthy sewer, but made still worse by the flood of vice pouring into the Tiber from the Syrian Orontes. Cicero tells us poets spent their younger days in Antioch. The great general Germanicus, the father of Caligula, died at Daphne, and many an emperor had visited or lived in this great city. Pompey loved to linger there.

After the stoning of Stephen the persecution drove some of the believers from Jerusalem as far as Phenicia and Cyprus, and some of them were men of Cyprus and Cyrene, and they came to Antioch, preaching the Lord Jesus to the Grecians. "And the hand of the Lord was with them, and a great number believed and turned to the Lord." Acts 11, 21. The first congregation of Gentiles!

Then tidings of these things came unto the ears of the Church which was in Jerusalem; and they sent forth Barnabas that he should go as far as Antioch — to make an investigation of these strange affairs. When he had come and seen the grace of God, he was glad and exhorted them all that with purpose of heart they would cleave unto the Lord. For he was a good man and full of the Holy Ghost and faith. And much people were added unto the Lord.

*Paul Called to Antioch.* — General advice was not enough, practical help was needed. Who was the man for the place? As God sent Moses out of exile, so Barnabas went to seek Saul in his solitude. Barnabas departed from Antioch to Tarsus for to seek Saul. When he had found him, he brought him unto Antioch, perhaps in 43. And it came to pass that a whole year they assembled themselves with the Church and taught much people. Perhaps in Singon Street, near the Pantheon and the Forum, in one of the most populous districts in the southwestern part of the city, called Epiphania, from the founder, Epiphanius. In the Syrian Sodom, Christ Crucified was preached. With what result? "The disciples were first called Christians at Antioch."

Yes, Christians can be made even in a Sodom. Yes, Christians can live Christian lives even in a Sodom and be so different from the heathen that they will note the difference. Real Christians are the best advertisements of Christ. Are you a Christian? Do your neighbors know you are a Christian? Is your Christianity a credit to Christ? Alexander the Great had in his army a coward, also named Alexander. The brave general said, "Either change your nature, or change your name." Scipio Africanus had a cowardly and dissolute son, who wore a ring with a lively picture of his father. The Senate forbade wearing the picture without imitating the virtue. Either be a Christian or do not call yourself a Christian. "Let every one that nameth the name of Christ depart from iniquity." 2 Tim. 2, 19.

When Agabus foretold a famine, the Christians of Antioch took up a collection for the poor brethren in Judea, every man according to his ability, and sent it to the elders by the hands of Barnabas and Saul.

Note first: Every man helped. Note secondly: Every man helped according to his ability. Note thirdly: They helped as soon as they heard the need was going to come and before the needy asked for help. It is thought the collection was delivered in 45, after King Herod Agrippa had slain James and imprisoned Peter. Suetonius refers to the famine prices under Claudius, while Tacitus and Dio Cassius speak of two famines in Rome. Josephus places the famine in the time of Cuspius Fadus and Tiberius Alexander, 44—48, both prefects under Claudius. He also tells us that the Syrian queen Helena of Adiabene, a Jewish proselyte, came to Jerusalem in 45 and imported corn from Alexandria and figs from Cyprus to feed the poor of Judea.

Barnabas and Saul returned from Jerusalem when they had fulfilled their ministry and took with them John, whose surname was Mark. This visit may be the one Paul refers to in Gal. 2, 1—10. Then he refused to have Titus circumcised. James, Cephas, and John gave to Paul and Barnabas the right hands of fellowship, that Paul should go to the heathen and they to the Jews, and that Paul should remember the poor at Jerusalem, which he was forward to do.

SYRIAN ANTIOCH, WHERE THE DISCIPLES WERE FIRST CALLED "CHRISTIANS."

## THE FIRST FOREIGN MISSION FESTIVAL.
### Acts 13, 1—3.

Now, there were in the Church at Antioch certain prophets and teachers, as Barnabas, and Simeon that was called Niger, or Black, and Lucius of Cyrene, in Northern Africa, and Manaen, who had been brought up with Herod Antipas, and Saul. Yes, Saul is also among the prophets. Another surprise. Among these prophets and teachers was Manaen, "brought up with," a foster-brother, a friend, of King Herod Antipas.

As they ministered to the Lord and fasted, the Holy Ghost said: "Separate Me Barnabas and Saul for the work whereunto I have called them." "In the sixteenth century the Holy Ghost said: 'Separate Me Martin Luther for the work whereunto I have called him,'" says the *Methodist Review,* 53, p. 569.

When they had fasted and prayed and laid their hands on them, they sent them away, bade them Godspeed. John Mark was their helper. Some think this was the great Fast of Atonement, on the tenth of Tishri, October. The Holy Spirit Himself directly inspired this mission-festival. The Church promptly obeyed, the men were eager to be sent.

*The First Foreign Missionary Society.* — The Church at Antioch thus has the proud distinction of being the first foreign missionary society, and the whole Church was the society. Barnabas and Saul were the first foreign missionaries sent out by the Church. This was something new in the history of the world. The blessings of Christ were now to be showered over the face of the earth among all nations. What an inspiration for us! Archbishop Whately said, "If a man has any religion, he must either give it away or give it up."

There were still heathen in Antioch, and yet the Holy Spirit told the preachers to go out. So must we not try to convert all the heathen at home before we go abroad. "Go ye and teach all nations" (Matt. 28, 19), is our Captain's marching order, and, as the Duke of Wellington said, Christians are simply to obey orders.

*The Harvest.* — Not many years after this, Antioch's famous bishop Ignatius was ordered to Rome by the Emperor Trajan and thrown to the lions. Antioch became the seat of a famous school of Christian theology, and ten synods were held there between 252 and 380. Chrysostom was born at Antioch in 347, and he tells us the city had 200,000 people, not counting slaves and children, and more than half were Christians. When Julian went there for the heathen festival, his was the only offering to the Daphnian Apollo save "a single goose, provided at the expense of a priest, the pale and solitary inhabitant of the decayed temple," as Gibbon gives it. In 362 lightning destroyed the temple and image of Apollo; Julian the Apostate promptly blamed the Christians for it and persecuted them.

The Bab-Boulus — Gate of Paul — still standing, reminds the traveler of the great Apostle.

## THE PREPARATION OF THE WORLD FOR THE GOSPEL.

Before we go with Paul upon his missionary journeys, it may be well to see somewhat how the world was prepared for the Gospel. After God had spoken through the prophets, He spoke at last through His Son Jesus Christ. Heb. 1, 1. And Christ told His disciples to "go and make disciples of all nations," to be His witnesses "unto the uttermost part of the earth." Acts 1, 8.

One preparation was the spreading of the Jews throughout the world. As early as 722 B. C. the Assyrian invaders carried 27,290 of the Northern Kingdom to the East. Not only did some of these Northern Israelites find an asylum in Egypt (Hos. 9, 6), but a century and a half later, when Jerusalem was destroyed by Nebuchadnezzar, their numbers were vastly increased by their Jewish kinsmen in the South who, especially after the murder of Gedaliah, likewise sought refuge in the land of the Nile, — carrying with them, against his will, the prophet Jeremiah. Subsequent to the conquests of Alexander when Greek had become the world language, the Old Testament Scriptures were translated into Greek for the benefit of the Greek-speaking Jews in Egypt. In 233 B. C. Antiochus the Great colonized the whole coast of Asia Minor with Jews from Babylon and Palestine. In 63 B. C. Pompey carried Jewish captives to Rome. The Jews furnished the funds with which Julius Caesar made himself the master of the world, and in return he, 47 B. C., decreed that "Hyrcanus and his children are to retain all the rights of high priest, whether established by law or accorded by courtesy. If hereafter any question arise touching the Jewish policy, I desire that the determination thereof be referred to him." Again: "Putting down all other assemblages, I permit these men only to meet together and comfort themselves according to the customs of their fathers and their own laws." So attached were the Jews to Caesar that at his death they wailed around his tomb for nights together. These favorable decrees of Caesar were confirmed after his death by the temporary republican Senate and also by Caesar Augustus. Jews from all over the world were at Jerusalem for the Pentecost. Acts 2, 9—11. The geographer Strabo says the Jews "had invaded every city, and it was not easy to find a place in the world which had not received that race and was not mastered by it." From Cicero's *Oration for Flaccus* it appears that many thousands of Jews were in the Roman province of Asia in the century before Christ.

JULIUS CAESAR.                AUGUSTUS.

In the second century before Christ the *Sibylline Books* said: "Every land and every sea is full of them." Agrippa wrote Caligula: "Jerusalem is the capital, not of Judea only, but of most countries." Philo says there were a million Jews in Egypt alone. In Paul's time Rome had about 6,000 Jews and many synagogs. During Nero's reign ten thousand Jews were massacred at Damascus.

*Jewish Power and Influence.* — And many of the Jews were wealthy. There were seventy golden seats in the principal synagog of Alexandria. The finest buildings in Alexandria and Antioch were the leading synagogs. Mithridates took 800 talents from the Jewish treasury of the island of

Cos. Flaccus, in the province of Asia, took large sums intended for the Temple of Jerusalem. The corn export trade of Egypt was largely in Jewish hands. And they were powerful and influential everywhere.

Ovid says the young Roman nobles attended the synagogs, where many of the most beautiful women were to be seen. Juvenal speaks of Romans who were circumcised and followed the Jewish religion handed down in the books of Moses. Dio Cassius noticed the vast spread of this religion in the empire. A Roman lady named Fulvia sent a costly offering of purple and gold to the Temple at Jerusalem, and Poppaea Sabina, Nero's wife, became a convert. Among men of high position who embraced the Jewish faith we know the treasurer of Candace of Ethiopia, King Asizus of Emesa, and King Polemo of Cilicia.

The cultivated classes hated the Jews. Cicero terms their religion "a barbarous superstition." Juvenal makes merry over their refusal to eat swine's flesh. Tacitus charges "the filthy race" with sloth for not working on the seventh day and in the seventh year. He accuses them of hatred of the rest of mankind. But Josephus says: "Among the masses there has long been much zeal for our religion; nor is there any city, Greek or barbarian, nor a single nation where the custom of our seventh day of rest from labor has not come into vogue." This is confirmed by Seneca, saying: "So far has the usage of the accursed race prevailed that it is now received throughout all lands; the conquered have given laws to the conquerors."

Thus, wherever the apostles came, they found prepared soil; for the Law is a schoolmaster to bring the people to the Christ who was foretold in the prophets. All the preacher had to do was to prove that Jesus was the promised Messiah.

*The conquest of Alexander the Great* was another preparation for the Gospel. His ambition was to weld the nations into one world, and he succeeded so well that Greek was the common speech all around the Mediterranean, in Egypt, in Jerusalem, in Rome. Plutarch did not learn Latin, yet he had no trouble in Rome when conducting political business and delivering philosophic lectures. Paul's great Epistle to the Romans was written in Greek, as indeed the entire New Testament. The graffiti chalked on the walls denouncing Nero's crime were in some cases Greek epigrams. Jerome says all the Orient spoke Greek. Thus the missionaries could speak Greek wherever they went and had no need of learning the language of the people.

*Caesar Augustus's statesmanship* was a third preparation for the Gospel. Under him the empire became the world. All roads led to Rome, and they were good roads and safe roads. The brigands and pirates had been put down with a strong hand, and the "Roman Peace" reigned in the world.

*The condition of the heathen religion* was a fourth preparation for the Gospel. The poems of Homer and Hesiod had been the sacred books.

THE PORT OF SELEUCIA.

Alexander the Great had Homer under his pillow. But as early as the sixth century Xenophanes had begun to ridicule the popular religion —

> All things unto the gods have Homer and Hesiod ascribed,
> Whatsoever of men reproaches and blame are accounted,
> Thieving and fornication and cozening one of another.

M. Terentius Varro, whom Augustine called "the acutest and most learned of mankind," said the mythic theology of the poets was a tissue of frequently immoral fables painting the gods as the basest of men. The physical theology of the philosophers traced all things to a natural origin.

The civil theology of the people was kept up by the state, which decreed what gods were to be worshiped and what sacrifices were to be performed. Religion was lost, only ritual remained. Gibbon gives it thus: "The various modes of worship which prevailed in the Roman world were all considered by the people as equally true, by the philosophers as equally false, and by the magistrate as equally useful." And yet, as Augustine says: "Thou hast made us for Thee, and our heart is restless till it rests in Thee." Many were groping for God. Though a native of Palestine, Justin Martyr was a pagan, who sought rest for his soul among the Stoics, then among the Peripatetics, then among the Pythagoreans, then among the Platonists, and then, at last, he found rest in Christ. It was custom to erect altars "to unknown gods." Here was the point of approach for the apostle to preach "the known God." The Christian religion was the world religion; Greek, the world language; Rome, the world empire. Paul came in the fulness of time. He was a Jewish Christian; he spoke the Greek language; he was a Roman citizen. He was God's chosen vessel to preach the world religion in the world language to the world empire.

## CHAPTER III.

# PAUL'S FIRST MISSIONARY JOURNEY.
### March, 46, to August, 48.

## THE FIRST STATION — THE ISLAND OF CYPRUS.
### Acts 13, 4—12.

> Men of a thousand shifts and wiles, look here!
> See one straightforward conscience put in pawn
> To win a world; see the obedient sphere
> By bravery's simple gravitation drawn.
>
> *James Russell Lowell.*

CONSECRATED for their service, the missionaries soon set out on their sacred journey for Seleucia by the sea, also founded by Seleucus Nicator and his place of burial. It is the port of Antioch, sixteen miles away, five miles north of the mouth of the Orontes, and the busiest harbor of all Syria. The piers of the outer harbor may still be seen under the water; some of the stones are twenty feet long, five feet deep, and six feet wide, fastened together with iron clamps.

From this historic harbor they sailed to the island of Cyprus, and "the second idyl of Christianity" began, Paul's Iliad and Odyssey, journeys greater by far than Xenophon's *Anabasis* and *Katabasis*.

From Cyprus we get the words cypress and copper. Augustus leased the copper mines to Herod the Great, and a large Jewish population grew up, so large that in 117 they rose under Artemio and massacred 240,000 natives. Hadrian suppressed them with great severity, and thenceforth no Jew might set foot on Cyprus on pain of death; if shipwrecked there, he was killed.

Because Teucer did not avenge the death of Ajax, Telamon, king of the famous Salamis, banished him, and he founded a city on the eastern shore of Cyprus and named it Salamis. It was a famous city in the time of Aeschylus, who founded his *Salaminai* on the fate of these heroes of Homer's Trojan war. Teucer introduced human sacrifices to Zeus, which were not ended till the time of Hadrian, in the second century, as Lactantius tells us.

PAUL IN THE SYNAGOGUE AT CORINTH

Acts 18:4

A swift sail from sunrise to sunset brought the missionaries the seventy miles from Seleucia to Salamis. Our Consul-General di Cesnola found the old sea-wall to measure 6,850 feet, and many relics he dug up may be seen in the Metropolitan Museum of Art in New York City.

After speaking to the Jews in one of the synagogs at Salamis, the preachers went west to Citium, known as Chittim in the Old Testament, where Zeno, the Stoic philosopher, was born, and Cimon, son of Miltiades, was buried. Near here was Amathus, famous for its copper mines. They came to New Paphos, about ten miles from the seat of the worship of

PAPHOS ON CYPRUS.

Astarte, Aphrodite, Venus, about a hundred miles from Salamis. Hesiod and Homer say here a drop of fecund blood fell from Uranus, the sky, into the Cyprian Sea and mightily stirred the waters, and from the pearly foam of the waves brought forth the fair Aphrodite, or Venus. Here stood one of her most splendid temples, with a hundred altars. Her sacred image was a white stone phallus, the symbol of generation. Mothers would bring their daughters to prostitute themselves to strangers, and a part of the hire of this holy harlotry was dedicated to the goddess, and the other part gave the girls a dowry for their wedding. The rich ladies went in splendid carriages, surrounded by servants, in order to avoid the poorer classes.

PAUL AND ELYMAS.

RAFFAEL.

The Noctuvigilia, as Plautus calls the feasts in honor of Venus, lasted three nights, with wine-drinking, wild prayers, and licentious singing and dancing to the song of the nightingale and by the light of the moon along the seashore, as Homer and Hesiod tell us. White slavery flourished here. Plautus paints the picture of a professional procurer unwilling to sacrifice the six lambs to Venus in order to make the sale, and he laments the greed of the goddess.

Aphrodite was the goddess of prostitutes; she was even called "Aphrodite the whore." Even in our day an abandoned woman is called a "Cyprian." Prostitution had become religion. Athanasius calls it "the deification of lust."

Pancaste, the mistress of Alexander the Great, posed for Apelles for a painting of this Venus Anadyomene.

On his way to the Jewish War, Titus, like other famous men, made a pilgrimage to the holy temple at Paphos.

*The First Missionary Victory.* — At Paphos the missionaries found a Jewish false prophet named Bar-jesus, known as Elymas, or "The Wise Man," who was with the Proconsul Sergius Paulus. Such quacks surrounded many high Romans. Augustus, Pompey, and Caesar consulted fortune-tellers, one of whom said to Caesar, "Beware the Ides of March!" Juvenal sneers at Tiberius seated on his rock at Capri amid his "herd of Chaldeans," sorcerers. Pliny tells us there were two schools of such quacks at Paphos, one Jewish, the other Cyprian.

Sergius Paulus is called a "prudent" man. Like many educated Romans of his time, he was dissatisfied with the pagan religion and philosophy and yearned for something to satisfy his heart and conscience. It seems Elymas could not satisfy him, and so, when he heard of Barnabas and Saul, he called for them and desired to hear the Word of God. He was not one who,

> Once wedded fast
> To some dear falsehood, hugs it to the last.

Fearing for his influence, Elymas withstood the preachers, seeking to turn the proconsul away from the faith.

Then Saul, who is called Paul, filled with the Holy Ghost, set his eyes on the sorcerer and said: "Oh, full of all subtilty and all mischief, thou child of the devil, thou enemy of all righteousness, wilt thou not cease to pervert the right ways of the Lord? And now, behold, the hand of the Lord is upon thee, and thou shalt be blind, not seeing the sun for a season." And immediately there fell on the sorcerer a mist and darkness; and he went about seeking some to lead him by the hand. Stalker recalls that Cajetan felt the "demonic" eyes of Luther, just as Elymas felt the eyes of Paul.

The kite does not rise with the wind, but against the wind. Opposition is to rouse us to greater efforts. Riding into battle, Marshall Turenne cried to his ailing body, "Aha, you tremble! But you would tremble far more if you knew whither I intend to take you to-day."

Then the proconsul, when he saw what was done, believed, being astonished at the doctrine of the Lord. Only one, but a lion! One soul is indeed as good as another, but a man of influence turned to the Lord can turn his influence to the good of the Lord. Paul's first battle was crowned with a glorious victory.

Christianity displaced the vicious Venus worship. We learn of a Christian church at Paphos in the fifth century, and Salamis became the chief seat of the bishop of Cyprus, and the Christian Church has existed to this day through all the changes of the centuries.

In 1913 Ramsay found the name Sergia Paula on an inscription at Pisidian Antioch and thinks she was a Christian daughter of our Sergius Paulus.

Strabo says Cyprus was governed by a propraetor, appointed by the Emperor, and so scholars promptly charged Luke with ignorance. But Dio Cassius says Augustus, 22 B. C., transferred Cyprus to the Senate, so that proconsul is the correct title. Our Consul-General di Cesnola discovered a Greek inscription at Soloi, in Northern Cyprus, dated "in the proconsulship of Paulus," and he thinks it refers to our Sergius Paulus. So Luke was right, and the critics are wrong. Likely this Sergius Paulus is the one that furnished the Cyprian material for the second and eighteenth books of Pliny's *Natural History*.

After serving in Cyprus, Sergius Paulus was appointed a Tiber commissioner under Claudius in 47, as appears from a cippus, or boundary stone, found on the Via Giulia thirteen yards from the river in August, 1887. The cippus also records the bounds laid down from the Trigarium, the chariot drive, to the bridge of Agrippa, the Ponte Sisto.

## THE SECOND STATION — PISIDIAN ANTIOCH.
### Acts 13, 14—50.

From Paphos the missionaries sailed about a hundred and seventy miles for the bay of Attalia, where the Athenian Cimon defeated the Persians on land and sea in 466 B. C., and where the united squadrons of the Romans and the Rhodians met the ships of Antiochus with the dreadful Hannibal on board, in 190 B. C.

**PISIDIAN ANTIOCH.**

For seven miles Paul sailed up the river Caestrus to Perga, the capital of Pamphylia, with the famous temple of Diana crowning the hill behind the city.

Here John Mark deserted and returned home to Jerusalem. Barnabas and Saul pressed on and toiled up through the wild mountains to the high table-land which forms the interior of Asia Minor. On the third or fourth day they would reach Adada, in a thick forest. Leaving by a wild pass, they would see Lake Karolis, with forty miles of blue mountain water and many islands and swarms of wild swans and storks. They went down the northern slope to Neapolis, where a paved Roman road brought them twenty miles to Pisidian Antioch, nearly 100 miles due north from the sea and 3,936 feet above.

Alexander the Great had found great difficulty making his way on this same road. Perhaps it was on this journey Paul met some of the difficulties and dangers mentioned in 2 Cor. 11, 23—27.

UNDERWOOD & UNDERWOOD.   A RECENT VIEW OF PISIDIAN ANTIOCH.

After the battle of Magnesia, in 190 B. C., which cost Antiochus the Great his rule north of the Taurus, the Romans made Antioch a free city. In 39 Mark Antony gave it to Amyntas, after whose death, in 25, it became a city of the vast Roman province of Galatia, and before the year 6 Augustus made it a colony and the center of the southern section of the province. The white marble ruins of temples, churches, a theater, and an aqueduct still attest the ancient splendor of the city, great in its trade in wool, oil, skins, goats' hair, etc. Men, the moon god, was worshiped with orgies so vile and vicious that even the heathen Romans had to stop the "worship" and banish the immoral priests and their slaves.

Among the ruins Ramsay, in 1912 and 1913, copied two inscriptions with the name of Quirinius and shows he was military legate of Cilicia and Syria about 10—8 B. C., when Augustus decreed the first census in the days of Herod the King. Which proves Luke 2, 1—3 first-class history despite the assaults of Schmiedel, Wilcken, and even Mommsen.

At Chai, not far from here, the army of Cyrus mutinied five days for an increase of pay. Near here, too, about a hundred years later, Seleucus I, founder of Antioch, defeated Antigonus, the one-eyed general of Cappadocia.

After their tiresome march through Phrygia the crusaders under Bohemund of Tarentum and Tancred will also find a welcome rest in Pisidian Antioch.

The missionaries likely first went to the "strangers' rooms," our modern hospice work, connected with the synagog, where they may have been helped to find lodgings and work in the "Ghetto."

On the first Sabbath they entered the synagog and were ushered to seats reserved for the "honorable" in front of the Ark containing the sacred rolls of the Law and the Prophets. They would thus face the congregation.

The famous Lutheran scholar Bengel thinks the pericopes, or lessons, read on that particular Sabbath were Deut. 1, 3—22, and Is. 1, 1—22, the lessons for the forty-fourth Sabbath, the latter part of July or the first part of August. The rulers of the synagog sent unto Barnabas and Saul, saying: "Ye men and brethren, if ye have any word of exhortation for the people, say on." Opportunity and obligation were one with Paul. He stood up and, beckoning with his hand, preached his first recorded sermon.

The congregation was made up of the "men of Israel," Jews by birth, and also Gentiles who had become Jews by circumcision, full members of the synagog. There were present also "ye that fear God," Gentiles interested in the Jewish religion, but who had not yet formally joined the Church by the rite of circumcision. After the courteous salutation, "Ye men of Israel, and ye that fear God," Paul promptly begins his sermon.

1. *The Historical Portion.* — a. God chose Israel. The choice was made in the eternal counsels of the Godhead. The choice was carried out when Israel was formed a nation in the bondage of Egypt and then

delivered by the mighty arm of God through Moses. The chosen people were educated during the forty years in the wilderness, during the conquest of Canaan, during the rule of judges, prophets, and kings, during the preaching of John the Baptist. God chose and educated Israel for no other purpose than to prepare the whole world for the coming of Jesus. Vv. 16—25.

b. Jesus was crucified, dead, buried, raised again from the dead according to the promise of the prophets, and so He is the promised Messiah, the Savior. Vv. 26—37.

2. *The Doctrinal Part.* Vv. 38—41. Paul's great Gospel of salvation the forgiveness of sins, or justification. How is a sinner justified before God?

a. Ye could not be justified by the Law of Moses. All have broken God's Law, and so there is no justification for us by our works of the Law.

b. By Christ, in Christ, all that believe are justified from all things.

This one short sentence is the full Gospel, and Paul's letters to the Galatians and Romans are only a fuller statement of this one sentence. Christ was put to death for our offenses. He sacrificed Himself for our sins, in our stead, as our Substitute. He was raised again for our justification that we might be declared righteous before God. Christ took upon Himself our sinfulness and put upon us His holiness. Thus did God make Jesus be our own Righteousness.

>Jesus' blood and righteousness      With my Savior's garments on,
>My beauty are and glorious dress.     I am holy as the Holy One.

c. All that believe this receive this. It is a perfect work of Christ, and it is a free gift; it cannot be bought or earned, it can only be received as a gift by faith.

d. This justification by faith is preached to you. It is not hung upon you, not flung upon you, not poured into you, not grafted upon you,— it is preached to you. With your mind you understand the message, and with your heart you receive it and rejoice in it. Justified by faith, we have peace with God.

e. Only the believer in Christ is justified; and so the apostle closes with an earnest warning: "Beware, therefore, lest that come upon you which is spoken of in the prophets, 'Behold, ye despisers, and wonder and perish; for I work a work in your days, a work which ye shall in no wise believe though a man declare it unto you.'" Is. 29, 14; Hab. 1, 5.

Where this doctrine of justification is preached, the Church stands; where this is not preached, the Church falls; and so Luther calls this "the article of the standing and the falling Church."

It is worthy of note that a most stupendous revolutionary truth is brought into Paul's sermon in a very simple, quiet way. No difference is made between Jew and Gentile; both are placed on the same level.

*Cordial Reception by Many.* — It seems the Jews at first did not take in the full meaning of Paul's words; for we read: "As they went out, they besought that these words might be spoken to them the next Sabbath."

"Now, when the congregation was broken up, many of the Jews and religious proselytes followed Paul and Barnabas, who, speaking to them, persuaded them to continue in the grace of God. And the next Sabbath-day came almost the whole city together to hear the Word of God."

*Bitter Rejection by Others.* "But when the Jews saw the multitudes, they were filled with envy and spake against those things which were spoken by Paul, contradicting and blaspheming." "Contradicting and blaspheming," denouncing and ridiculing;

MARK AND PAUL.   DUERER.

no reason, no arguments. As then, so since then; as there, so everywhere. At the Reformation the Protestants were met with the Inquisition. To-day the missionaries are met with persecution. To-day the Gospel is met with hateful ridicule in our own cities. No sun, no shadow; no success, no envy. Rejoice over the enemy's envy; it is a sincere compliment to your success, and envy at last destroys the envious. A wrestler was so envious of Theogenes, the prince of wrestlers, that he even wrestled with his statue, until one night he threw it, and it fell on him and crushed him to death.

Then Paul and Barnabas waxed bold and said: "It was necessary that the Word of God should first have been spoken to you; but seeing ye put it from you and judge yourselves unworthy of everlasting life, lo, we turn to the Gentiles. For so hath the Lord commanded us, saying: 'I have set Thee to be a Light to the Gentiles that Thou shouldest be for salvation unto the ends of the earth.'" Is. 42, 6; 49, 6; 45, 22. "And when the Gentiles heard this, they were glad and glorified the Word of the Lord; and as many as were ordained to eternal life believed. And the Word of the Lord was published throughout all the region." Converted themselves, they converted others. A live Christian is a missionary; are you a dead one?

Here was something new. Hitherto the Gentiles had been reached indirectly, through the synagog of the Jews; henceforth they were reached directly, without the vestibule of Judaism. Here God "had opened a door of faith to the Gentiles," as Paul reported. Acts 14, 27. This is the true turning-point at which Gentile Christianity begins. The Jews stirred up the devout and honorable women and the chief men of the city and raised a persecution against Paul and Barnabas and expelled them out of their coasts. Likely they were scourged by the rods of the lictors. 2 Cor. 11, 25. Strabo tells us the women of Asia Minor were leaders in religion and induced the men to take part in the religious feasts and ceremonies.

But the missionaries shook off the dust of their feet against them and came to Iconium.

*Paul's First Expulsion.* — Many more were to follow. Paul was to have many followers. Judson was driven from Calcutta; Milne was driven from Canton; Paton was driven from Tanna; in 1637 all missionaries were driven from Japan for two hundred years; in 1835 all missionaries were driven from Madagascar, etc., etc. But in every case Christianity came back all the stronger for its persecution.

Though the pure Gospel was preached by a Paul, some accepted it, and some rejected it. As then, so now. Some believe, and we are encouraged; some disbelieve, and we are not discouraged.

If a man is lost, it is because he chooses to be lost; he judges himself unworthy of eternal life. Men condemned are self-condemned. Man's undoing is his own doing. Sinners are suicides.

> O God of Truth, for whom we long,
> Thou who wilt hear our prayer,
> Do Thine own battle in our hearts
> And slay the falsehoods there. — *Thomas Hughes.*

*Still Not in Vain.* — About the year 300 we read of Eudoxius, bishop of this Antioch, and of Marcus, Alphius, and others being martyrs during the persecution under Diocletian. In 314 Sergianos was Antioch's delegate to the Council of Ancyra, and in 325 Antonius at Nicaea. We read of twenty-four bishoprics in the province of Pisidia.

Little Pisidia later had twenty-five bishops under the Metropolitan at Antioch and sent the Gospel to the neighboring Cappadocia, which brought forth a number of excellent men, standing head and shoulders above their fellows in the fourth century — Basil the Great, "The Theologian," his brother, Gregory of Nyssa, and Gregory of Nazianzus.

## THE THIRD STATION — ICONIUM.
### Acts 14, 1—5.

The missionaries traveled southeast for about sixty miles on a Roman military road, over bleak plains abounding in herds of sheep and wild asses, till they reached the green oasis, the most level plain in the world, according to Moltke, on which is Iconium, 3,368 feet above the sea. It is a place of some importance, lying on the great trade route between Ephesus and Tarsus. To the west rises a half-moon of snow-capped hills, to the east stretches a plain with a lake.

Luke places Iconium in Phrygia, for which he has been charged with ignorance by learned critics. But Ramsay's researches reveal the ignorance of the critics and the correctness of Luke, and he holds Acts "unsurpassed in respect of its trustworthiness, . . . written with such judgment, skill, art, and perception of truth as to be a model of historical statement. It is marvelously concise and yet marvelously lucid." (*Bearing of Recent Discoveries,* pp. 81. 85. 89.)

According to legend, Nannakos was king of Iconium when the great Flood came. Then Jupiter bade Prometheus make icons, or clay images of men, and then caused a wind to breathe them into life to replace the people drowned in the Flood, and from these icons comes the name Iconium. Others tell us it comes from the icon, or image, of Medusa brought there by Perseus. Ramsay thinks Iconium the world's oldest city.

When the beautiful young shepherd Adonis was killed, the lovely maiden Cybele called him back to life. These gods were worshiped every spring with wild, immoral dances by the priests to the blare of trumpets, the crashing of cymbals, the roaring of drums, and the shouting of the people that Adonis had come to life again. This went on for weeks with feasting and drinking and rejoicing and playing in the large temples.

In the year 51 B. C. Cicero spent August 21—31 at Iconium on his way from Ephesus to Tarsus to govern the province of Cilicia, and before

MODERN ICONIUM (KONICE).

him Xenophon with his Ten Thousand had been here 394 B. C., on his famous Anabasis, and hither came Paul in his much greater Anabasis.

*A Great Multitude Believed.* — Here Paul and Barnabas went into the synagog of the Jews and so spake that a great multitude both of Jews and also of Greeks believed. But the unbelieving Jews stirred up the Gentiles and made their minds evil affected against the brethren. Long time, therefore, abode they, speaking boldly in the Lord, who gave testimony unto the Word of His grace and granted signs and wonders to be done by their hands. But the multitude of the city was divided; part held with the Jews and part with the apostles.

And when there was an assault made both of the Gentiles and also of the Jews with their rulers to use them despitefully and to stone them, they were aware of it and fled.

AN OLDER VIEW OF ICONIUM.

*A Center of Christianity.* — It is said that the famous Thekla was converted by Paul at Iconium. *The Acts of Paul and Thekla*, based on a first-century document, describe Paul as "a man small in size, bald-headed, bow-legged, strongly built, with meeting eyebrows, and a rather large nose: full of grace, for at times he looked like a man, and at times he had the face of an angel." This place became one of the most influential centers of Christianity. We read of sixteen bishoprics in Lycaonia about the year 300. Hierax, a slave of Iconium and friend of Justin Martyr, was condemned as a Christian at Rome in 163. In 235 a council was held here, and in 371 Amphilochius was the vigorous bishop. Barbarossa passed here in 1190 on his crusade, and Godfrey of Bouillon laid siege to the city. When by his heroism old Barbarossa won a decisive battle and took Iconium, he ordered a thanksgiving service for all the crusaders and asked the Bishop of Mainz to preach on Acts 13, 51: "They shook off the dust of their feet against them and came unto Iconium."

Iconium is one of the few places of Asia Minor where the Christian religion has never been entirely suppressed. Here is "The Apostolic Institute," founded by Jenanyan, an Armenian Christian, where Armenian, Greek, and Turkish boys are educated. Here is also an American Christian hospital and dispensary.

The Seljukian Turks, the most virile and artistic of all, made Iconium the capital of the powerful empire of Roum. They made it so beautiful that the proverb arose, "See all the world: see Konia." Here is the tomb of Hazret Mevalana, who read about David's dancing before the Lord and then began to pray and dance and thus founded the Whirling or Howling Dervishes, the Holy Jumpers of that day. He is buried standing up, and his tomb is covered with a cloth of almost solid gold.

## THE FOURTH STATION — LYSTRA.
### Acts 14, 6—20.

Ovid says Lycaon disbelieved in the gods and therefore was turned into a wolf (Greek: *lykos*) and gave the name to the country, Lycaonia. Here Zeus and Hermes had come to earth and knocked in vain for hospitality at many a door. At last they were received into the humble hut of Philemon and Baucis. Their hovel was turned into a glorious temple and themselves into ministers. Finally he was turned into a hardy oak and she into a softer linden, while all the rest were drowned in the great Flood. (Ovid, *Met.*, 8, 626.)

> For in similitude of strangers oft
> The gods, who can with ease all shapes assume,
> Repair to populous cities, where they mark
> Th' outrageous and the righteous deeds of men.

So Homer tells us in Cowper's translation.

*Persistence.* — In spite of their experience, into this region came Barnabas and Saul when they fled from Iconium eighteen miles in a southerly direction, to Lystra. Since 6 B. C. it was a Roman colony,

## PAUL'S FIRST MISSIONARY JOURNEY.

UNDERWOOD & UNDERWOOD.

A RECENT VIEW OF LYSTRA.
Taurus Mountains in background.

AN OLDER VIEW OF LYSTRA.

4,034 feet above the sea, in a pleasant valley, bordered by gently sloping hills. In 1885 Professor Sterrett of Cornell found a Lystrian coin and an inscription and thus settled the site of the city, for which the explorers had been searching so long; about a mile from the modern village of Khatyn-Serai.

*Power.* — There sat a certain man at Lystra, impotent in his feet, being a cripple from birth, who never had walked. The same heard Paul speak, who, steadfastly beholding him and perceiving that he had faith to be healed, said with a loud voice, "Stand upright on thy feet!" And he leaped and walked.

*Popularity.* — When the people saw what Paul had done, they lifted up their voices, saying in the speech of Lycaonia: "The gods are come down to us in the likeness of men!" And they called Barnabas, Jupiter, and Paul, Mercurius, because he was the chief speaker. It was deemed beneath the dignity of the chief god to deign to talk much; that was left to a lesser god. In the summer of 1909 there was discovered, not far from here, a Greek inscription of a statue of Mercury dedicated to Jupiter. An inscription on a pillar shows the temple outside the gate was built in honor of Augustus.

Would the people risk the fate of Lycaon? Rather would they reap the reward of Philemon and Baucis. Then the priest of Jupiter, whose temple was before the city, brought oxen with garlands unto the gates and would have done sacrifice with the people, that is, worship Barnabas and Paul as gods.

*Preaching.* — When the apostles heard of this, they rent their clothes, to express their horror, and ran among the people, crying out and saying, "Sirs, why do ye these things? We also are men of like nature with you and preach unto you that ye should turn from these vain things to the living God, who made heaven and earth and the sea and all things that are therein; who in times past suffered all nations to walk in their own ways. Nevertheless, He left not Himself without witness in that He did good and gave us rain from heaven and fruitful seasons, filling our hearts with food and gladness." And with these sayings scarce restrained they the people from sacrificing to them.

"We are men of like nature with you" — the Christian does not pretend to be more than others. When Baron Cuvier was addressed by

PAUL AND BARNABAS AT LYSTRA. RAFFAEL.

a student as "Baron," the great scientist replied, "There is no baron here; there are two students seeking truth and bowing down only to her." The French ambassador found the illustrious Lord Bacon in his last illness with the curtains drawn around the bed and said, "You are like the angels of whom we hear and read much, but have not the pleasure of seeing them." The great Englishman replied, "If the complaisance of others compares me to an angel, my infirmities tell me I am a man." After the fall of Richmond the colored people kneeled before Lincoln. "Don't kneel to me; that is not right. You must kneel to God only and thank Him for the liberty you will hereafter enjoy. I am but God's humble instrument."

The Christian is a lover of nature and a natural philosopher; he looks through nature up to nature's God. He prays with Keble: —

>    Thou who hast given me eyes to see
>       And love this sight so fair,
>    Give me a heart to find out Thee
>       And read Thee everywhere.

To Addison the stars bring a message: —

>    Forever singing as they shine,
>    "The hand that made us is divine."

To the true God we will gladly sacrifice our thank-offerings of oxen and garlands.

*Persecution.* — No doubt, the people felt resentful against the preachers who had spoiled their holiday and banquet. And so, when certain Jews of Antioch and Iconium came and buzzed their venomous slanders into the ears of the rude barbarians, they easily persuaded them to stone these mysterious strangers. They drew Paul outside of the city, supposing that he was dead. Howbeit, as the disciples stood round about him, he rose up and came into the city.

Was it in the house of Eunice and Lois that Paul's bruises and wounds were bandaged? At any rate, this Jewess, married to a Greek now dead, was likely converted at this time, and also her son Timothy, whom Paul calls his "own son in the faith." 1 Tim. 1, 2. Likely also Timothy witnessed the stoning of Paul, for the apostle writes: "Thou hast fully known my persecutions, afflictions, which came upon me at Antioch, at Iconium, at Lystra; what persecutions I endured; but out of them all the Lord delivered me." 2 Tim. 3, 11.

Cicero camped around here for a few weeks and speaks of the people with the greatest contempt as a savage, fickle, and perfidious race, and Aristotle speaks of the untrustworthy character of the Lycaonians. When Jesus entered Jerusalem, He was greeted with "Hosannah!" A few days after, the people shouted, "Crucify!" Here the people would make a sacrifice to the preachers, next they would make a sacrifice of the preachers. As it was in those days, so now and here. When the pastor pleases the people, there comes a reception; when he displeases them, there comes

UNDERWOOD & UNDERWOOD. DERBE.

a rejection. Uninfluenced by popularity or unpopularity, we preach the Gospel, whether the people hear or forbear. The preacher, too, must through much tribulation enter into the kingdom of heaven.

Artemas, one of the Seventy, is said to have become bishop of Lystra. Zoilos of Lystra was martyred for his Christian faith. Eustochios visited relatives at Lystra and was condemned to death at Ancyra for leaving paganism and becoming a Christian. Tiberius was bishop of Lystra in 325. Paul of Lystra is named at the Council of Constantinople in 381. In 451 a bishop of Lystra was at the Council of Chalcedon.

## THE FIFTH STATION — DERBE.
### Acts 14, 20. 21.

The next day Paul left on the Via Sebaste, or Imperial Road, built about 8 B. C. by Publius Sulpicius Quirinius, the "Cyrenius" who was governor of Syria "in the days of Herod the King"; he was governor of Syria for the second time about the year 6 A. D. Paul made thirty miles southeast of Lystra and came to Derbe, an important frontier fortress and customs station, where the robber Antipater had entertained his friend Cicero. Here the missionaries made disciples of many; Gaius of Derbe was with Paul on his last visit to Jerusalem. Acts 20, 4. A monument to Paul, the martyr of Derbe, has been found.

## THE RETURN JOURNEY.
### Acts 14, 21—28.

The missionaries returned to Lystra and to Iconium and to Pisidian Antioch, confirming the souls of the disciples and exhorting them to continue in the faith, and that we must through much tribulation enter into the kingdom of God.

Much tribulation, much pressure, much trouble, no doubt of it! But what of it? We shall pass through it! Through it into the kingdom of God! It is the only way. Through the cross to the crown. A famous philosopher refused to receive Diogenes as a pupil; he insisted and persisted till the teacher finally raised his cane to strike. "Strike," said Diogenes; "you will not find a cane hard enough to break my will." Diogenes had his will. Let no blows be hard enough to drive us back from the kingdom of God.

When the apostles had ordained elders in every church and had prayed with fasting, they commended the people to the Lord, on whom they believed. After they had passed throughout Pisidia, they came to Pamphylia. And when they preached the Word in Perga, they went overland the sixteen miles to the flourishing seaport of Attalia, founded by Attalus Philadelphus, king of Pergamus, 159—138 B. C., at the mouth of the Katarrhaktes, which then found its way to the sea over a range of cliffs in floods of foaming waterfalls, which gave the name to the river.

From this port of Pamphylia they sailed for Seleucia, saw the steep cone of Mount Casius, climbed the slopes of Coryphaeus, traveled along the Orontes mid ilex and myrtle and arbutus, saw the grim head of Charon, crossed the bridge to the street Singon, to the Christians who had recommended them to the grace of God for the work they had fulfilled. And when they were come and had gathered the church together, they rehearsed all that God had done with them and how He had opened the door of faith unto the Gentiles.

Note what God had done with them and how He had opened the

**MOUNT CASIUS AT ANTIOCH.**
From Seleucia.

door of faith. "All glory be to God alone!" "Not unto us, O Lord, not unto us, but unto Thy name give glory!" Ps. 115, 1.

Thus ended the first foreign missionary journey of the Christian Church.

And there the apostles abode a long time with the disciples. They had covered 1,400 miles and needed a rest.

Here we may ask, Who were the people Paul had visited? In the fourth century before Christ the Gauls trekked across Europe, and some settled in Gaul, now France. Some, in 390, would have taken Rome itself but for the cackling of the geese. About 300 some were beaten back at Delphi. About 275 some twenty thousand crossed the Hellespont into Asia Minor. About 230 Attalus I of Pergamos made them settle on a high plateau in the interior. The capital of one of the Galatian tribes was Pessinus, so called from the falling down from heaven of the sacred image of Cybele, the Great Mother, removed to Rome to save the Eternal City from the terrible Hannibal in 204 B. C. The theater remains well preserved. Lutar had been the leader of this tribe, which is thought to have been German. Curious enough, the German Luther restored the teaching of Paul's letter to the Galatians.

PETER AND PAUL AT ANTIOCH.   RENI.

Midas found an anchor buried in the ground. He built a city over it and called it Ancyra, Anchor. The amount of electricity in the air at times makes a blanket seem a sheet of flame. The silky hair of the cats and dogs and goats of Angora is famous. When these animals are removed but thirty miles, their coats become like those of others. Ancyra was the capital of all Galatia, and to-day it is Angora, the capital of Turkey. Augustus was the first Caesar whom the Romans deified, and when that new religion was sprung upon the empire, the fickle Galatians were so swift and hot in their enthusiasm as to be recognized throughout Asia and by Augustus himself for its staunchest devotees. They built a splendid temple of white marble for the worship of the new god. As a distinguished mark of the imperial favor they were granted the right to inscribe upon its walls a copy of the will of Augustus from the bronze tablets in front of his mausoleum in the Campus Martius in Rome. The "Monumentum Ancyranum."

The capital of the third district was Tavium, noted for its sacred grove, probably a memorial of Druid worship, now changed to the service of Jove with his colossal bronze statue.

Julius Caesar found the Gauls of Europe "fickle in taking up plans, fond of innovating, and utterly untrustworthy." This unreliable fickleness was found in these Gauls of the East. To-day they fought for Pontus, to-morrow for Pergamos. They changed their allies as they changed their coats. They were mercenary *Landsknechte*, soldiers of fortune. Four hundred Galatian giants, armed with unequaled splendor, formed the body-guard of Cleopatra, until, with Gallic fickleness, they took a similar position under Herod, her bitter enemy. They still had the blue eyes and fair hair of the Kelts, and four hundred years after, when Jerome was in Galatia, he found their speech to resemble that of the Germanic people of Treves.

In 25 B. C. Augustus added to the country of the Galatians part of Pontus on the northeast, part of Phrygia on the southwest, and most of Lycaonia on the south, the whole known as the Roman province of Galatia. In the southern part of this Galatia we find Antioch, Iconium, Lystra, and Derbe. Formerly it was generally thought Paul's Galatians were in North Galatia; in our day most think they were in South Galatia. The question is quite interesting and quite unimportant.

## TROUBLE AT ANTIOCH.
### Acts 15, 1. 2; Gal. 2, 11—21.

Peter visited the brethren at Antioch and did eat with the Gentile Christians.

Now, certain men came down from Judea, from James, and kept on teaching the brethren: "Except ye be circumcised after the manner of Moses, ye cannot be saved." Then Peter withdrew and separated himself from the Gentile Christians, fearing them which were of the circumcision.

On this account Paul and Barnabas had no small dissension and disputation with the "false brethren unawares brought in, who came in privily to spy out our liberty which we have in Jesus Christ, that they might bring us into bondage; to whom we gave place by subjection, no, not for an hour, that the truth of the Gospel might continue with you."

The other Jews dissembled likewise with Peter, insomuch that Barnabas also was carried away with their dissimulation.

Here was the most serious situation; the whole liberty of the Gospel of Christ was at stake in this question. At this critical period Paul came to the rescue. "I withstood Peter to the face, because he was to be blamed. When I saw that they walked not uprightly according to the truth of the Gospel, I said unto Peter before them all: 'If thou, being a Jew, livest after the manner of Gentiles, and not as do the Jews, why compellest thou the Gentiles to live as do the Jews? We, who are Jews by nature and not sinners of the Gentiles, knowing that a man is not justified by the works of the Law, but by the faith of Jesus Christ, even we have believed in Jesus Christ that we might be justified by the faith of Christ and not by the works of the Law; for by the works of the Law shall no flesh be justified. But if, while we seek to be justified by Christ, we ourselves also are found sinners, is therefore Christ the minister of sin? God forbid! For if I build again the things which I destroyed, I make myself a transgressor. For I, through the Law, am dead to the Law that I might live unto God. I am crucified with Christ; nevertheless I live; yet not I, but Christ liveth in me; and the life which I now live in the flesh I live by the faith of the Son of God, who loved me. I do not frustrate the grace of God; for if righteousness come by the Law, then Christ is dead in vain.'"

Bengel calls this speech of Paul the very pith and marrow of Christianity.

## TROUBLE IN GALATIA.

"One woe doth tread another's heel, so fast they follow." The Judaizers told Paul's converts he was no apostle and his Gospel no gospel. They must not only believe in Christ, but also, in addition, be circumcised and keep all the rules of the Jews. Paul was stirred to his depths, and he dashed off his first and most famous letter. Renan calls these "the two most important pages for the study of nascent Christianity," and Ramsay says we have here "the most wonderful preface to the most remarkable letter that ever was written."

## THE EPISTLE TO THE GALATIANS.

### I. The Apostle of Liberty.

*Chaps. 1 and 2.*

1. "Paul, an apostle, — not of men, neither by man, but by Jesus Christ and God the Father."

The greeting trumpets the key-note of the whole letter. Do you hear the ring and feel the force of high authority in this formal declaration of his divine call? It is addressed "to the churches of Galatia." Do you note the absence of the endearing terms found in the other letters? Christ delivered us from this present evil world, — delivered us, mark you, not that we may backslide into it!

The thanksgiving — there is no thanksgiving here as in every other letter. Ominous omission. Instead of the usual thanksgiving an unusual complaint of their fickleness is shot as a bolt from the blue — "I am amazed that you are so quickly shifting from the grace of Christ into a different gospel, which is not another gospel," — it is no gospel at all, it is a perversion of the Gospel of Christ. 1, 6. 7.

Instead of the usual praise there flares forth a fierce curse: "But though we or an angel from heaven should preach any other gospel unto you than that which we preached unto you, let him be accursed!" And he repeats the curse. 1, 8. 9. Later Paul scourges the Galatians for their faults — fifteen! These Ramsay arranges in three groups: 1. five fostered under their heathen religion: fornication, impurity, wantonness, idolatry, and sorcery, or magic; 2. eight connected with the municipal life of the cities of Asia Minor: enmities, strife, rivalry, outbursts of wrath, caballings, factions, parties, jealousies; 3. two characteristic of the manners of the Greco-Asiatic cities: drinkings and revelings. 5, 19—21.

There is no let-up, the severity is sustained throughout.

2. Paul goes on to prove the independence of his authority by his divine revelation. "I certify you, brethren, that the Gospel which was preached of me is not after man; for I neither received it of man, neither was I taught it, but by the revelation of Jesus Christ." 1, 11. 12.

3. When it pleased God to reveal His Son in Paul that he might preach Him among the heathen, immediately he preached Christ, independently of the other apostles. Instead of going up to Jerusalem to see them, he went to Arabia and then returned to Damascus. It was all of three years before Paul saw any of the other apostles. 1, 13. 24.

4. The Church recognized the independence of Paul's mission. "When James, Cephas, and John, who seemed to be pillars, perceived the grace that was given unto me, they gave to me and Barnabas the right hands of fellowship, that we should go to the heathen and they unto the circumcision." 2, 1—10.

5. The independence of Paul's authority is proved by the fact that Paul withstood Peter to the face because he was to be blamed; and Paul did this before all the church in Antioch. He showed that if circumcision were necessary for salvation, then Christ had died in vain. 2, 11—21.

## II. The Gospel of Liberty.

Justification by faith; or, the contrast between Law and grace. Paul defends his teaching. Chaps. 3 and 4.

1. The Christian experience of the Galatians themselves proves the truth of Paul's Gospel. "O senseless Galatians! Who hath bewitched you, . . . before whose eyes Jesus Christ was so plainly painted as if He had been crucified right among you? This only would I learn from you, Received ye the Spirit by the works of the Law or by the hearing of faith?" You know you have become Christians through my Gospel; now, do you become better Christians by adding circumcision and so also becoming Jews? 3, 1—5.

2. History proves the truth of Paul's Gospel.

Your Jewish false teachers make much of Abraham. Very well, let us take the case of Abraham. How was Abraham justified?

"Abraham believed God, and it was counted to him for righteousness. . . . So, then, they which be of faith are blessed with faithful Abraham." 3, 6—9.

3. The Old Testament proves the truth of Paul's Gospel. Certainly, if a man keeps God's Law perfectly, he will be saved. Lev. 18, 5. But who can keep it perfectly? Then God says: "Cursed is every one that continueth not in all things which are written in the Book of the Law to do them!" 3, 10. Deut. 27, 26. "But that no man is justified by the Law in the sight of God, it is evident; for 'The just shall live by faith.'" 3, 10—12. Hab. 2, 4.

4. The very nature of the work of Christ proves the truth of Paul's Gospel. "Christ hath redeemed us from the curse of the Law, being made a curse for us; for it is written, 'Cursed is every one that hangeth on a tree'; that the blessing of Abraham might come on the Gentiles through Jesus Christ; that we might receive the promise of the Spirit through faith." 3, 13. 14. The whole work of Christ were useless could we save ourselves by our own good works.

Wherefore, then, serveth the Law? Is the Law against the promises of God? God forbid! The Law is not for salvation, but for illumination — to show us our total sinfulness and utter helplessness and thus bring us to Christ.

Two Illustrations.

1. An illustration for the Gentiles. A Roman boy was under a pedagog, a slave, who gave mental and moral training and even corporal punishment. Though an heir, he was treated as a slave till of age. So Israel under Moses, till Christ came and declared him of age. Likewise did the Gentiles become sons through faith in Christ. 3, 24; 4, 7. Do not fall back from sonship into the old bondage. 4, 8—20. You are of age; do not act like a minor.

2. An illustration for the Jews. The familiar story in Gen. 16 and 21 of Hagar and Ishmael and Sarah and Isaac is used to illustrate the Law and the Gospel, and the application is then made. 4, 21. 31. Be Israelites rather than Ishmaelites, freemen rather than bondmen!

### III. The Life of Liberty.

Its use and abuse. Chaps. 5 and 6.

For freedom did Christ set us free: stand fast, therefore, and be not entangled again in a yoke of bondage.

In Christ Jesus neither circumcision availeth anything nor uncircumcision, but faith working through love.

If you again rely on your good works and ceremonies, you really reject Christ's salvation and again fall under condemnation. Seeing this fearful ruin of his whole work, Paul fiercely cries out: "I wish those troubling you with circumcision would not only circumcise themselves, but also mutilate themselves!" "Luther-like in its force and its audacity," says Plumptre.

You have been called to liberty; abuse not that liberty, but by love be slaves one to another.

The duty of supporting the preacher is most earnestly urged. 6, 6. Paul ends with a personal reference: Henceforth let no man trouble me; for I bear branded on my body the marks of Jesus.

As the priests of heathen idols were branded with bodily marks, so Paul's body bore the stigmata to show he was the slave of the Lord Jesus Christ, a priest in His temple. The king's mark — *character regius* — was branded into the palm of the Roman soldier to keep him from deserting; so the marks of Christ were branded into Paul.

"It is not gold, precious stones, statues, that adorn a soldier, but a torn buckler, a cracked helmet, a blunt sword, a scarred face," said Pericles long ago.

The benediction: "The grace of our Lord Jesus Christ be with your spirit, brethren," — yes, brethren; though grievously erring and severely scourged and rebuked, they were brethren. Amen.

Galatians is a battlefield with the ring of sharp steel and resounding with the blows of a warrior fighting for God and God's people and shouting the battle-cry of freedom. It marches straight ahead like a battalion on parade; but the field lies covered with the slain among the foes. "It is not a sermon, it is not a treatise," says Gloel; "it is a sword-cut delivered in the hour of greatest anger by a combatant who is assaulted by determined foes." It is concise, compact, consistent, conclusive, conquering. Paul quelled the riot by hurling at white heat his thunderbolts of logic on fire.

The deeps were broken up, and a tidal wave rushed over the region. The outburst of indignant remonstrance rose from the quaking soul of Paul like a flood of fiery lava from Vesuvius and buried his opponents. "Give me liberty or give me death!" Paul would have no peace at the price of principle. "It is a unique and marvelous letter, which embraces in its six short chapters such a variety of vehement and intense emotion as could probably not be paralleled in any other work," writes Ramsay; and Godet says: "This epistle marks an epoch in the history of the race. It is the ever-precious document of man's spiritual emancipation." "Taking Galatians as his weapon, Luther plunged into the fearful conflict with the papistry and religious materialism of his time. This was the pebble from the brook with which, like another David, he went forth to meet the papal giant and smote him in the forehead."

In this epistle Luther found the secret of his own deliverance from the slavery of sin and Satan and his own sonship of God in Jesus Christ, and he says: "The Epistle to the Galatians is my epistle. I have betrothed myself to it. It is my wife." And on this book he wrote his immortal commentary, which has helped millions to spiritual liberty. John Bunyan says: "I prefer this book of Luther's on Galatians to all the books I have seen as being best suited to a wounded conscience." Spurgeon has a like estimate. James H. Brookes, of St. Louis, prized it next to his Bible.

Like the great oration of Demosthenes *On the Crown*, Galatians is at once a personal vindication and the presentation of a great cause.

Farrar says: "In vehemence, effectiveness, and depth of conviction this epistle is paralleled only by Luther's *Babylonian Captivity of the Church,* in which he realized his saying that his battle with the papacy required a tongue of which every word is a thunderbolt. What Luther did at Wittenberg and at Worms and at Wartburg, that, and more than that, Paul did when he wrote the Epistle to the Galatians. The words scrawled on those few sheets of papyrus were destined to wake echoes which have lived and shall live forever and forever. They were the Magna Carta of spiritual emancipation." Again, in his *St. Paul:* "As a Reformer, who altered the entire course of history, Luther alone resembles St. Paul. What the Reformer did when he nailed his theses to the door of the cathedral of Wittenberg, that St. Paul did when he wrote his Epistle to the Galatians. It was the manifesto of emancipation; it marked an epoch in history." Pfleiderer compares Paul to Luther in the boldness of his stand for Christ and its great results. Galatians was Luther's bugle-note in the Reformation.

Professor Moorehead of Xenia Theological Seminary writes: "What the Emancipation Act was to the slaves of our Southern States, what the Czar's edict was for the freedom of the serfs of Russia, the Epistle to the Galatians was to the primitive Church. It was the manifesto of the enfranchisement which Christ had won for all believers. It was by the study and the appropriation of the mighty truths of Galatians and Romans that Luther, the hero of the modern era, was enabled to strike off the fetters by which the Church of God had been so long bound."

Prof. B. W. Bacon holds without Galatians "the odds in the great battle of the Reformation would have been almost overwhelmingly against the right of private judgment; churchly authority might almost have crushed the attempt to vindicate the divine right of individual conscience."

Prof. G. G. Findlay writes: "Buried for a thousand years under the weight of the Catholic legalism, the teachings of the epistle came to life again in the rise of Protestantism. Martin Luther put it to his lips as a trumpet to blow the reveille of the Reformation. His famous *Commentary on the Galatians* summoned enslaved Christendom to recover 'the liberty wherewith Christ hath made us free.' Of all the great Reformer's writings this was the widest in its influence and the dearest to himself. For the spirit of Paul lived again in Luther as in no other since the Apostle's day. The Epistle to the Galatians is the charter of evangelical faith."

## THE FIRST CHURCH CONFERENCE AT JERUSALEM.

### Early in 50.
### Acts 15, 1—21.

At last the brethren at Antioch determined that Paul and Barnabas and certain other of them should go up to Jerusalem unto the apostles and elders about this question. And being escorted on their way by the church, they passed through Phenicia and Samaria, declaring the conversion of the Gentiles. And they caused great joy unto all the brethren — "like Luther on his way to the Diet of Worms," say Farrar and Peloubet.

There was a meeting of the Church and of the apostles and elders; and Paul and Barnabas declared all things that God had done with them. But there rose up certain of the sect of the Pharisees which believed, saying that it was needful to circumcise the believing Gentiles and to command them to keep the Law of Moses.

PAUL.    PETER.
From a medallion found in the cemetery of Domitilla, one of the Flavian family, related to Vespasian and Titus.

*1. Peter's Speech.* — And when there had been much disputing, Peter rose up and said to them: "Men and brethren, ye know that a good while ago [about six years, when the pagan Cornelius was received], God made choice among us that the Gentiles by my mouth should hear the word of the Gospel and believe. And God, which knoweth the hearts, bare them witness, giving them the Holy Ghost even as He did unto us; and made no distinction between them and us, purifying their hearts by faith. [Acts 10 and 11.] Now, therefore, why tempt ye God to put a yoke upon the neck of the Gentile disciples which neither our fathers nor we were able to bear? But we believe that through the grace of the Lord Jesus Christ we shall be saved even as they."

Peter recalls the words of Christ in Matt. 23, 4 about those pharisaical observances, and Paul's words could not be stronger. Gal. 5, 1.

This is the last of Peter in the New Testament. Peter did not preside, and he did not give the decision. He was no pope.

*2. The Report of the Missionaries.* — Then all the multitude kept

# PAUL'S FIRST MISSIONARY JOURNEY.

95

JERUSALEM, FROM THE MOUNT OF OLIVES.

silence and listened to Barnabas and Paul, declaring what miracles and wonders God had wrought among the Gentiles by them.

*3. The Speech of James.* — After they had held their peace, James, the brother of the Lord, from his holy life called "The Just," then proved from Amos 9, 11. 12 that Christianity is the fulfilment of Judaism and therefore decided "that we trouble not them which from among the Gentiles are turned to God." In other words, the Christians from among the Gentiles were not to be compelled to be circumcised. The Gentile Christians, out of love, were to avoid giving offense to the Jews scattered in so many places.

## THE REPORT SENT TO ANTIOCH.
### Acts 15, 22—35.

*4. The Committee.* — The speech of James pleased the apostles and elders, with the whole church, and they sent a committee to Antioch to notify the brethren there of the outcome of the meeting, namely, Judas, surnamed Barsabas, and Silas, chief men among the brethren at Jerusalem.

Not satisfied with an oral report, they also sent it written in a letter after this manner: —

*5. The Oldest Christian Church Document.* — "The Apostles and the Elders and the Brethren, to the Gentile Brethren in Antioch and Syria and Cilicia, Greeting.

"Whereas we have heard that certain men who went out from us have troubled you with words and unsettled your souls by telling you to circumcise yourselves and keep the Law, although we gave them no commission, it has been determined by us, having come to one accord, to choose some from amongst ourselves and send to you with our beloved Barnabas and Saul, men that have offered up their lives for the name of our Lord Jesus Christ. We have sent therefore Judas and Silas, who themselves also will tell you by word the same which we tell you by letter. For it has been determined by the Holy Spirit and by us to lay upon you no greater burden than these necessary things: that ye abstain from meats offered to idols, and from blood, and from things strangled, and from fornication. Wherefrom if you keep yourselves, it shall be well with you.

"Farewell."

*6. The Effect of the Letter.* — So, when they were dismissed, they

**PAUL AND THE ELDERS OF EPHESUS**

Acts 20:36

came to Antioch, and when they had gathered the multitude together, they delivered the epistle; and when the congregation had read it, they rejoiced for the consolation.

*The Work Strengthened at Antioch.* — Judas and Silas exhorted the brethren with many words and confirmed them. And after they had tarried in Antioch a space, they were let go in peace from the brethren unto the apostles in Jerusalem. Notwithstanding it pleased Silas to abide there still. Paul also and Barnabas continued in Antioch, teaching and preaching the Word of the Lord, with many others.

*Paul's Victory.* — This conference established Paul's position as an apostle independent of the others, called by Christ and not by man. The decision or decree is the Magna Carta of Christian Liberty.

a) The Liberty of Faith; saved by the faith in Jesus Christ, without the deeds of the Law of Moses. Chap. 15, 19. Gal. 2, 15—21.

b) Liberty of Love; faith worketh by love; not the liberty of libertinism. Faith in Christ leads to a life of holiness and purity. Chap. 15, 20. Gal. 5, 13—26.

It surprises us that the letter warns of fornication. However, in those days even the Rabbis were loose in their morals, and among some heathen, fornication was even a part of the religious worship of their idols. Socrates does not censure it; Cicero in *Pro Caelio* says no pagan moralist prohibits it; Terence and Horace say the same; Cato Censor, model of stern Roman virtue, was guilty of it. That shows us clearly the blessed influence of the pure Gospel of Christ.

c) Liberty of Charity, of fine fraternal feeling, of considerateness. In matters of indifference this liberty will give no offense, and it will take no offense. Chap. 15, 20. Gal. 6, 2.

This battle of Jerusalem was the crisis of Christianity. Had Paul given in to the false teachers, Christianity would have become a narrow Jewish sect and perished from the face of the earth. Here Christianity came out of its Jewish chrysalis and became the world religion. Adapting a famous couplet, we say: —

> Our Savior's teaching had not stood
> If Paul His foes had not withstood.

**Nietzsche admits Paul saved Christianity.** Baur says Paul set free the principle of universality in the Gospel of Christ; but it was there from the first in the person of Jesus, writes Orr. Renan thinks to disparage Paul by calling him a Protestant, the forerunner and author of Protestantism. Havet writes: "I do not say, This is the theology of Paul; I say, This is the theology."

Like unto Paul's battle at Jerusalem was the battle of Worms, where Luther alone stood out for the truth of Christ against the Emperor and the Pope.

> The councils called by rulers of the earth
>    Are fleeting shadows; for the mightiest state,
> Like to a bubble, has no sooner birth
>    Than it is scattered by the blast of fate.
> Not so where saints with holy zeal debate
>    Of truths eternal, and the living way
> That leads direct to the celestial gate.
>    Their high resolves will be the Christian's stay
> When time shall be no more and worlds have rolled away.

CHAPTER IV.

# PAUL'S SECOND MISSIONARY JOURNEY.

### After the Passover in the Year 50.
### Acts 15, 36—18, 22.

Two pilgrims issue forth in poor array —
No scrip, no purse, with only staff in hand.
Amongst the heathen folk they wend their way,
And as they journey on from strand to strand,
Aloud they herald forth their Lord's command;
"Awake, ye nations! Lo! the day doth break,
And dawns the light on your benighted land;
Your idols dumb and orgies foul forsake
And turn to Israel's God. Ye men of sin, awake!" — *Anon.*

She heard it, the victorious West,
In crown and sword arrayed!
She felt the void which mined her breast,
She shivered and obeyed.
She veiled her eagles, snapped her sword,
And laid her scepter down;
Her stately purple she abhorred
And her imperial crown. — *Arnold.*

"LET us go again and visit our brethren in every city where we have preached the Word of the Lord and see how they do," said Paul. Barnabas agreed and determined to take with them his nephew, or cousin, John Mark, who had returned to them. But Paul thought not good to take him with them who had left them at Pamphylia and not gone with them to the work. Acts 13, 13.

The paroxysm, or contention, was so sharp between them that they departed asunder one from the other. So Barnabas took Mark and sailed unto Cyprus. This is the last we hear of Barnabas in the New Testament. Legend has it that the Jews burned him at the stake under Nero at Salamis, where a church and a cave bear his name.

Mark had left them in the lurch on the first journey, and Paul would not run the risk of wrecking the second journey by an unreliable companion. It was a question of judgment between Paul and Barnabas as to method of work, not a question of doctrine or a personal matter.

Barnabas's encouragement and Paul's sharp tonic made a man of Mark, and later we find him helping Paul. Col. 4, 10; Philemon 24;

2 Tim. 4, 11. Peter also mentions him as a faithful worker. 1 Pet. 5, 13. Later the Holy Spirit led him to write the Gospel according to St. Mark.

*Paul chose Silas* and departed, being recommended by the brethren unto the grace of God. Leaving Antioch, they crossed the plain where Zenobia, Queen of Palmyra, will lose her crown in a battle and then grace the triumph of Aurelian in 273. Beyond is the Syrian Gate, where Darius would halt Alexander. Beyond this famous pass lies the Cilician Plain

THE ENTRANCE TO THE CILICIAN GATES.

where the decisive battle of Issus was fought, which made the young Macedonian the master of the East, 333 B. C. They likely visited along the coasts of Syria and in the Orontes Valley. Going north, they went through the famous Syrian Gates, which cross the Amanus Mountains, 3,000 feet high. Xenophon describes these gates, or pass, as two walls: "Between the two runs a river, called Carsus, a plethrum, or 101 feet in breadth. The whole space between the walls was three stadia, or 1,800 feet; and it was impossible to pass it by force; for the passage was very narrow, the walls reached down to the sea, and above were inaccessible rocks."

Alexander the Great passed here after the battle of Issus, in which he defeated the Persian King Darius Codomanus in 333 and paved his victorious march to the East. From the East came Paul on his vastly greater march to conquer the West.

Paul came to the Gulf of Issus, now called the Gulf of Alexander, Iskander in Arabic, shortened into Scanderoon. He touched Aegae, passed Mopsuestia, the hearth of Mopsus, where the famous Theodore was bishop for thirty-six years and died in 428. Thirty miles more to Adana, thirty more to Tarsus, 129 miles west of Antioch, 515 northwest of Jerusalem. They came to Mopsukrene, the Fountain of Mopsus, the first resting-place, and then pressed on through the Cilician Gates to the region beyond.

*Paul Takes Timothy.* — Timothy had been brought up from a child in the Old Testament by his mother Eunice and his grandmother Lois. 2 Tim. 1, 5. He was well reported of by the brethren that were at Lystra and Iconium. Acts 16, 1. His father was a Gentile Greek, and his religious education was left to his godly mother. They had heard Paul preach and witnessed his persecutions reported in chap. 14; 2 Tim. 3; 11, 15. "From a child" Timothy served the Lord. Of course, "better late than never"; but it did not seem right to the blunt dying soldier "to serve the devil in youth and then fling the fag-end of one's life in the face of the Almighty." When should a child's education begin? "Twenty years before his birth, by educating his mother," was the wise and witty answer.

Paul circumcised Timothy because of the Jews who were in those quarters, laid his hands upon him, and imparted to him the gift of the Holy Ghost and had him ordained to the church-work "with the laying on of the hands of the presbytery," or elders. 2 Tim. 1, 6.

Paul's "own son in the faith" had now arrived "at the estate of perfect manhood, in the fulness of the Christ," aiding him in the preaching of the Gospel as a child waits on his father. "I have no one who is so at one with me in heart and soul as he." 1 Tim. 1, 2; Eph. 4, 13; Phil. 2, 20. 22.

*Paul Publishes the Decrees.* — As the missionaries went through the cities, they delivered them the decrees for to keep that were agreed on at Jerusalem. And so were the churches established in the faith and increased in number daily.

"When they had gone throughout Phrygia and the region of Galatia, they were forbidden of the Holy Ghost to preach the Word in [the Roman province of] Asia. After they were come to Mysia, they assayed to go

THE CILICIAN PASS THROUGH THE TAURUS MOUNTAINS.

into Bithynia; but the Spirit suffered them not. Why not? Weiss thinks because Peter was preaching there. 1 Pet. 1, 1. Bigg thinks there may be much to that. There may be; who knows? Epiphanius says Peter superintended there. But Epiphanius died in 403, and so his word has no historical value.

The Gospel was preached there with great success. The younger Pliny was governor of Bithynia and Pontus in 112 and wrote from Amisos

ARCHES IN ALEXANDRIA-TROAS.

of the Black Sea letters 96 and 97 to the Emperor Trajan that Christianity had spread all over and the temples were almost deserted and the sacrifice interrupted. Surely man proposes, but God disposes. If men labor aright for God, they may thank Him for what they are not allowed to do, as well as for what they are enabled to do.

Then they passed by Mysia, went through without preaching, and came down to Troas, an important port and a Roman colony. The plain is still watered by the Simois and Scamander. Here the heroes of Homer fought the famous Trojan War. Here the "pious" Aeneas leaves burning

Troy and fares forth to found a new world empire at Rome, as Vergil's Aeneid tells us in polished numbers. Here Xerxes on his golden throne reviewed his millions on his way to conquer Greece. Here Alexander the Great kindled his enthusiasm at the tomb of Achilles and set out to conquer the East. Here Julius Caesar was after the battle of Pharsalia and thought of making it the capital of the world. Here Herod Atticus brought water from Mount Ida, and the piers of his great aqueduct are still standing. Here Heinrich Schliemann poured out his American money to dig long-buried Troy out of its grave.

## FIRST STATION — PHILIPPI.
*Acts 16, 8—15.*

Troy! What visions the name conjures up! Did Paul have a vision of this glorious past? We know not. We know here at Troas "a vision appeared to Paul in the night; there stood a man of Macedonia and prayed him, saying, 'Come over into Macedonia and help us!'"

*Vision and Decision.* — After he had seen the vision, immediately we endeavored to go. Note the *he* and *we;* it is thought Luke, the beloved physician, joined Paul at Troas. We endeavored to go into Macedonia, assuredly gathering that the Lord had called us for to go to preach the Gospel unto them. The die was cast; Paul crossed his Rubicon — to plant the republic of God. Sir Wm. M. Ramsay calls Acts 16, 6—10 "the most remarkable, the most emotional, the most instructive paragraph in Acts."

Greece had everything but Christ and so had nothing. Paul had nothing but Christ and so had everything. The need of Macedonia is the Macedonian cry for rescue. Our desperate distress was the Macedonian cry that pierced the ear and heart of God to send His Son over to rescue us. "I said unto thee when thou wast in thine blood, 'Live!'" Ezek. 16, 6. Wherever we see need, we see the Macedonian vision and hear the Macedonian cry. To know the need should prompt the deed. And what is our response?

> Shall we, whose souls are lighted
>   With wisdom from on high,
> Shall we to men benighted
>   The lamp of life deny?
> Salvation! O salvation!
>   The joyful sound proclaim
> Till earth's remotest nation
>   Has heard Messiah's name!

Granting the charter of Massachusetts, Charles I said the preaching of Christ "is the principal end of this plantation," and the first seal of the State has an Indian saying, "Come over and help us!" The Society for the Propagation of the Gospel was founded under William III and in 1701 prepared a symbolical seal, representing a ship in full sail, with a gigantic clergyman, half-mast high, standing by the bowsprit, with an open Bible in his hands, while small Negroes on a hilly beach cry out, "Come over and help us!"

> Through midnight gloom from Macedon
> The cry of myriads as of one,
> The voiceful silence of despair,
> Is eloquent in awful prayer:
> The soul's exceeding bitter cry,
> "Come o'er and help us, or we die!"
>
> How mournfully it echoes on,
> For half the world is Macedon!
> These brethren to their brethren call,
> And by the Love which loved them all,
> And by the whole world's Life they cry,
> "O ye that live, behold, we die!"
>
> By other sounds our ears are won
> Than that which wails from Macedon;
> The roar of gain is round us rolled,
> Or we unto ourselves are sold
> And cannot list the alien cry,
> "O hear and help us lest we die!"
>
> Yet with that cry from Macedon
> The very car of Christ rolls on!
> "I come; who would abide My day
> In yonder wilds prepare My way;
> My voice is crying in their cry,
> Help ye the dying lest *ye* die!"

*Paul Sails for Europe.* — The south breeze was strong enough to overcome the rapid current sweeping down through the Dardanelles, — named for Dardanus, father of the Trojans, — and they sailed past the Hellespont, sea of Helle, swum by Leander for his Hero and later by Lord Byron. Under the deep waters between Tenedos and Imbros was the cave of Neptune, the god of the ocean. To the left is Lemnos, where landed Vulcan, the artist blacksmith, when thrown out of heaven by his angry father, Zeus. Here is the cave of Morpheus, god of sleep, half-brother of

Death. Here Jason with his Argonauts repeopled the island. They came to the calm waters, sheltered behind the mountains of Samothrace, sixty miles away, from which Jupiter watched the Trojan battles.

> The lofty peaks of woody Samothrace
> The eye can then in shadowy distance trace,
> The plain where Simois and Scamander flow,
> And Priam's town and Ida's beetling brow.

Here many were initiated into the Mysteries of the Kabiri, *i. e.*, the mighty ones, originally Phenician deities, to insure against shipwreck.

Early next morning they set all sail and scudded before the wind past the mouth of the famous Strymon, north of Thasos, home of Polygnotus, first Greek painter of transparent draperies. They gazed on the crags of Pangaeus, saw a rock promontory crowned with a temple of Diana, anchored, and set foot on European soil at Neapolis, or New Town, in Thrace, the port of Philippi in Macedonia, seventy-five miles away.

As William the Norman crossed the channel and became William the

NEAPOLIS.

Conqueror of England, so Paul crossed over and became the conqueror of Europe. When Paul came, there came the sunrise of the Gospel.

> And we glode fast o'er a pellucid plain
> Of waters, azure with the noontide ray.
> Ethereal mountains shone around; a fane
> Stood in the midst, beyond green isles which lay
> On the blue, sunny deep, resplendent far away. — *Shelley.*

They made the journey in two days; five were needed to return. Acts 20, 6. Ruins of the aqueduct and the paved military road may still be seen at Neapolis. Leaving by the western gate, the missionaries took the great Via Egnatia, which begins here, and going north reached the ridge of the Pangaeus and beheld the Plain of Philippi. Right below them is a little river in which the pole of Pluto's chariot broke when he carried off Proserpine, and so the river is called Zygactes, or Pole-break.

*Paul Comes to Philippi.* — There stands the sacred mountain of Dionysius, the Greek Bacchus, whose priestesses, wild-eyed and loose-haired,

UNDERWOOD & UNDERWOOD.   CATHEDRAL RUINS AT SITE OF PHILIPPI.
RUINS OF THE MARKET.

danced to and fro in riotous orgies and formed one of the most diabolic features of paganism. The mountain was rich in gold and silver, and Philip took from it $15,000,000 a year to build up his Macedonian Phalanx, wherewith Alexander conquered the world. At the foot of the mountains were the Krenides, the Springs, from which the town was called, which Philip changed to Philippi.

"Thou shalt meet me at Philippi," said the spirit of Caesar to Brutus

SITE OF PHILIPPI.

at Sardis, according to Plutarch and Shakespeare, and to Philippi Brutus went and with Cassius gave battle to Octavius and Antony, the battle that ended the Roman Republic and began the Roman Empire under Caesar Augustus, 42 B. C.

"We must fly!" cried some one.

"Yes, but not with our feet, with our hands," said Brutus, and the "noblest Roman of them all," who took 48 per cent. interest, threw himself upon a sword held by his friend Strato, and his wife ended her life by swallowing live coals. Cassius had already done away with himself on the summit of the hill, and a great number of the nobles followed the example of their leaders.

To celebrate his greatest victory, Augustus built a triumphal arch on the banks of the Gangites outside the city and made this a Roman colony. It was a part of Rome flung out into the vast empire, but still a part of Rome itself. The names of the colonists were still enrolled in one of the Roman tribes, with the right to vote, the insignia of Rome were present, the law of Rome held sway, the Latin language was spoken and appeared on the coins, and the laws of the XII Tables were inscribed on bronze tablets in the market-place.

In those days but few cities enjoyed the great honor of being a Roman colony — "a small effigy and miniature duplicate of the Roman people," as Aulus Gellius puts it. The Emperor Claudius built a magnificent arch where one enters the main street from the east by the Neapolitan gate.

Another battle was fought about ninety years after these stirring days, and another world was won, with the sword of the Spirit, which is the Word of God. At the place where Brutus had uttered his dying curse, "May the gods avenge upon the enemies of Rome these multiplied misfortunes!" there Paul preached the Gospel that teaches men to pray for their enemies and to live for their country and their God, and there Paul made his first convert in Europe.

> Who hath not heard how erst by lavish gold,
> Dug from these hills by artful Macedon,
> Was freedom-loving Greece betrayed and sold,
> And flashed across the earth great Philip's son?
>
> Upon Philippi's field the laurels won
> (Torn from a Roman brow in civil fray)
> Lifted young Caesar to a prouder throne.
> Empires like these were meteors of a day.
> Heaven opens and descends, a realm that stands for aye.

### 1. PAUL AND LYDIA.

*Acts 16, 13—15.*

On the Sabbath we went out of the city by the side of the river Gangites, where prayer was wont to be made, in a *proseucha,* a light building, often without a roof. Where there was no synagog, the Jews generally worshiped by the waterside to make easy their washings.

And we sat down and spake unto the women who resorted thither.

And a certain woman named Lydia, a seller of purple, of the city of Thyatira, who worshiped God, heard us; whose heart the Lord opened that she attended to the things which were spoken of Paul.

The great scientist Ampere from childhood was short-sighted, but unconscious of the defect and always thought people strangely deluded when enthusiastic about the beauties of nature. When eighteen, he accidentally looked through the glasses of a fellow-traveler and burst out in tears at the beauty of the landscape — his eyes had been opened. So Lydia's heart was opened to see the beauty of the Savior.

And when she was baptized and her household, she besought us, saying, "If ye have judged me to be faithful to the Lord, come into my house and abide there." And she constrained us.

The province of Lydia, wherein is Thyatira, was famous for its dyes even in the time of Homer.

And so by Lydian or by Carian maid
The purple dye is on the ivory laid.
*Iliad, 4, 141.*

It seems to have been a paying business, for the Greek Anthology says: —

Our dyer was poor, but by dint of his art
He has dipped all his rags and dyed himself smart.

THE PLACE OF PRAYER BY THE RIVERSIDE AT PHILIPPI.

Saved by Paul, Lydia would now serve Paul. Service was a favor and pleasure and privilege. When Paul accepted her hospitality, he bestowed a favor on her. She had an open ear, an open mind, an open heart, an open mouth, an open hand, an open house.

If we have sown unto you spiritual things, is it a great thing if we shall reap your carnal things? 1 Cor. 9, 11; Rom. 15, 27. Let him that is taught in the Word communicate unto him that teacheth in all good things. Gal. 6, 6.

## 2. PAUL AND THE FORTUNE-TELLER.
*Acts 16, 16—25.*

It came to pass, as we went to the place of prayer, a certain damsel possessed with a Python-spirit met us, who brought her masters much money by fortune-telling, possibly ventriloquism. Python in Greek mythology is the serpent which guarded Delphi, the famous oracle on Mount Parnassus, killed by Apollo. In the *Aeneid,* Vergil describes the Cumaean Sybil Deiphobe as follows: —

>Unearthly peals her deep-toned cry.
>. . . . . . . .
>Her color changed, her face was not the same;
>Her hair stood up, convulsive rage possessed
>Her trembling limbs and heaved her laboring breast, . . .
>Her staring eyes with sparkling furor roll,
>When all the gods came rushing on her soul.
>Swiftly she turned, and foaming as she spoke.

Even great and educated heathen were often, as in our day, very superstitious and resorted for all kinds of advice to these oracles and fortune-tellers and paid roundly. The Phocians at one time plundered Delphi and carried off $11,000,000 in silver and gold.

The damsel followed Paul and us and cried, saying, "These men are the servants of the most high God, who show to us the way of salvation!" She acted as the herald of important visitors, proclaiming their coming and mission. And this she did many days. But Paul got tired of that and said to the spirit, "I command thee in the name of Jesus Christ to come out of her!" And he came out the same hour.

As Christ refused the homage of the Father of Lies, even when he spoke the truth, Mark 1, 25, so Paul here also destroyed the works of the devil, even when he spoke the truth. So must we refuse the aid of the devil in our work of the Gospel.

>No more shalt thou, by oracling, abuse
>The Gentiles; henceforth oracles are ceased,
>And thou no more with pomp and sacrifice
>Shalt be inquired at Delphos or elsewhere;
>At least in vain, for they shall find thee mute.
>God has now sent His living Oracle
>Into the world to teach His final will,
>And sends His Spirit of Truth, henceforth to dwell
>In pious hearts; an inward oracle
>To all truth requisite for man to know.
>
>Milton, *Par. Reg.*, B. I.

When her masters saw that the hope of their gains was gone, they caught Paul and Silas and drew them into the market-place to the ruler and brought them to the magistrates, saying: "These men, being Jews, do exceedingly trouble our city and teach customs which are not lawful for us to receive neither to observe, being Romans."

This is the first purely Gentile persecution of Paul. The love of lucre, not the love of the Roman religion, prompted the accusation. Touch

RUINS OF THE MARKET-PLACE, WHERE PAUL WAS SCOURGED.

a man's pocket, and you often touch the only sensitive spot about him. As long as they made easy money out of the girl, her owners cared not what became of her body or soul. Just so to-day men exploit human beings for money, not caring what becomes of their victims. What is cheaper than a human soul?

Knowing the court would not allow a suit to recover damages, these men shrewdly accused the missionaries of making converts to a new religion. By the Roman law Judaism was permitted to the Jews, but Romans were forbidden under penalties to receive circumcision, as Livy tells us.

"They are Jews," was craftily put in to remind the Roman judges that the Emperor Claudius had just banished the whole pestiferous race from Rome and that therefore they had no claim on clemency. The colony of Rome would surely imitate the city of Rome.

The Gentiles hated the Christians as Jews, the Jews hated the Christians as worse than Gentiles; surely the Christians were between the upper and the nether millstone.

And the multitude rose up against them; and the Praetors gave the order: "Go, lictors; strip off their garments; let them be scourged." And when they had laid many stripes on them, they cast them into prison, charging the jailer to keep them safely; who, having received such a charge, thrust them into the inner prison and made their feet fast in the stocks — punishment painful and shameful.

The ruins of the forum where this took place may still be seen.

Why did Paul not save himself from the disgrace of scourging by claiming his Roman citizenship? Perhaps he knew it would do him no good there. In the forum of Messana the victim of Verres in vain shrieked above the hisses of the lash, "I am a Roman citizen!"

*Singing in Prison.* — "Rejoice and be exceeding glad when men shall persecute you for My sake," said Christ. Matt. 5, 11. Can it be done? The pagan philosopher Epictetus said: "Show me some one person formed according to the principles he professes; show me one who is sick and happy, disgraced and happy!" While this challenge was flung to the world, Peter showed it could be done by doing it. The apostles were put in prison and beaten, and they departed "rejoicing that they were counted worthy to suffer shame for His name." Acts 5, 41. Paul showed it could be done. "At midnight Paul and Silas prayed, singing unto God; and the prisoners listened to them."

Songs in prison — a violent contrast! Again something new under the sun. It is a historical fact that Christianity is the only religion that inspires men to sing. "Mohammedanism has no hymnal, nor has Hinduism, nor Buddhism. No glorious outburst of sacred song from the hearts and lips of the people ever awoke the echoes of any heathen or Mohammedan temple." It is "God, my Maker, who giveth songs in the night." Job 35, 10. When pressed, the grapes give up their wine; when pressed, the Lutheran Church gave forth her choicest hymns. At Sebastopol a shot from the enemy opened a spring which refreshed those it was intended to kill; so Satan often tries to kill the Christian and only opens the springs of song. Flung into the filthy Bradford jail for preaching, John Nelson said, "My soul was so filled with the love of God that it was a paradise to me. I wished my enemies were as happy in their houses as I was in the dungeon." John Bunyan turned his Bedford jail into a sanctuary and sang his immortal *Pilgrim's Progress*. Savonarola wrote commentaries on Psalms 31 and 51 during his month's imprisonment before his execution. Francis Baker wrote his version of "Jerusalem, My Happy Home," in the Tower of London. Confined in York Castle, James Montgomery wrote "Spirit, Leave Thy House of Clay." Madam Guyon was placed in prison in the Castle of Vincennes in 1695 and sang and wrote songs of praise to God: —

> A little bird I am,
> Shut from the fields of air;
> And in my songs I sit and sing
> To Him who placed me there,
> Well pleased a prisoner thus to be
> Because, my God, it pleaseth Thee.
>
> My cage confines me round,
> Abroad I cannot fly;
> But though my wing is closely bound,
> My heart's at liberty.
> My prison-walls cannot control
> The flight, the freedom, of the soul.

What shall we sing? Perhaps this —

> Jesus, I my cross have taken
>   All to leave and follow Thee;
> Destitute, despised, forsaken,
>   Thou from hence my All shalt be.
> Perish every fond ambition,
>   All I've sought or hoped or known;
> Yet how rich is my condition!
>   God and heaven are still my own.

### 3. PAUL AND THE JAILER.

*Acts 16, 26—40.*

*An Earthquake.* — Suddenly there was a great earthquake, so that the foundations of the prison were shaken. And immediately all the doors were opened, and every one's bands were loosed. And the keeper of the prison awaking out of sleep and seeing the prison-doors open, he drew out his sword and would have killed himself, supposing that the prisoners had been fled — he had to answer for them with his life.

*The Jailer Converted.* — But Paul cried with a loud voice, "Do thyself no harm, for we are all here." Then he called for lights and sprang in, came trembling, and fell down before Paul and Silas and brought them out and said, "Sirs, what must I do to be saved?" They said, "Believe on the Lord Jesus Christ, and thou shalt be saved and thy house." And they spake unto him the Word of the Lord and to all that were in the house. And he took them the same hour of the night and washed their stripes; and was baptized, he and all his, straightway. "His children" are expressly mentioned in some manuscripts. When he had brought them into his house, he set meat before them and rejoiced, believing in God with all his house.

THE PHILIPPIAN JAILER BEFORE PAUL AND SILAS.

He washed their stripes with water, they washed his soul with the water of Holy Baptism. He asked for lights, they gave him the true Light; he loosed the chains of their bodies, they loosed the chains of his soul; he called them lords, they taught him the true Lord; he fed their bodies, they fed his soul.

"What must I do to be saved?" is the most important question — have you asked it?

"Believe on the Lord Jesus," is the most important answer — have you learned it?

"Christ died for our sins, the Just for the unjust, that He might bring us to God."

Saved by Jesus, the jailer at once served the servants of Jesus — have you? The jailer believed in Christ, though the preachers were jailed as criminals — have you such heroic faith?

## 4. PAUL AND THE MAGISTRATES.

*Paul's Protest.* — When it was day, the Duumviri sent the lictors, saying, "Let those men go." The keeper of the prison told this saying to Paul: "The magistrates have sent to let you go; now, therefore, depart and go in peace."

But Paul said unto them: "They have beaten us publicly uncondemned, being Romans, and have cast us into prison; and now do they thrust us out privily? Nay, verily; but let them come themselves and fetch us out." Words of true manly dignity.

The lictors reported these words to the Duumviri, and they feared when they heard the prisoners were Romans. And well might they fear. "It is a dreadful deed to bind a Roman citizen. It is a crime to scourge him," says Cicero, who prosecuted Verres for the like offense. The Lex Valeria, 509 B. C. and the Lex Porcia, 248 B. C., forbade this crime, and the punishment might be loss of office and property, and even life.

*The Officials Apologize.* — With trembling the Duumviri besought their victims and brought them out and desired them to depart out of the city. The apostles would not leave as fugitives from justice; they insisted on a public acquittal and apology. Christians may not fight evil with evil, but they may resent evil and resist evil with manly protest. They do this for the sake of the cause and for the good of others.

*Paul's Honorable Discharge.* — They went out of the prison and entered into the house of Lydia; and when they had seen the brethren, they comforted them and departed.

Paul left Timothy with the Philippians for a few months and Luke for a longer time; only after five years do we again find Luke in the company.

Other spoils of this Holy War were Evodia and Syntyche, "those women which labored with me in the Gospel"; also Epaphroditus, "my brother and companion in labor and fellow-soldier"; also Clement, and others as well, "my fellow-laborers, whose names are in the book of life." Phil. 2, 25; 4, 2. 3.

In 115 Ignatius of Antioch visited Philippi, and Polycarp of Smyrna wrote the congregation there a letter.

## SECOND STATION — THESSALONICA.

*Acts 17, 1—10.*

Leaving Philippi, Paul took the Via Egnatia, which was here paved with marble blocks, and walked thirty-three miles to where the Strymon River winds and almost encircles Amphipolis and thus gives it the name "The City between Two Rivers." It was a great business place, nine roads meeting there, and the old name was "Nine Ways." In reference to this, Xerxes here buried alive nine youths and nine maidens. Here were the

THE RUINS OF AMPHIPOLIS.

pine forests where the Athenians got the masts for their ships. In 422 the Athenian Cleon was sent to retake Amphipolis, but he was defeated and killed by the Spartan Brasidas, whose burial mound is also here. Thucydides was exiled for failing in his campaign against the city. In one of his great orations against Philip of Macedon, Demosthenes speaks of Amphipolis as of great importance in the struggle. After the defeat of Perseus at Pydna, L. Aemilius Paulus here proclaimed freedom to Macedonia; the true freedom was proclaimed by another Paulus.

Next morning Paul came through the wooded pass of Aulon and the Vale of Arethusa with the tomb of Euripides and could make out Stagira, the birthplace of the great philosopher Aristotle, the teacher of Alexander the Great; after a march of thirty miles he reached Apollonia.

The next day they crossed the neck of the promontory of Chalcidice, left Olynthus and Potidaea to the south, and went on for thirty-seven miles to Thessalonica. Originally called Therma, or Hot Springs, it was rebuilt by Cassander in 315 B. C. and renamed Thessalonica, in honor of his wife, daughter of Philip of Macedon, who named her so for a victory over Thessaly on the day he had news of her birth. It was the first European fortress taken by Xerxes. Here stood another arch to celebrate the victory of Augustus at Philippi. Here was the residence of the Roman Proconsul since 44 A. D.

In clear view of the city rises the "snow-capped, manifolded Olympus," 9,000 feet above the sea.

>The gate of heaven, where the Hours kept ward,
>The guardians of Olympus and high heaven,
>To draw the veiling clouds or roll them back.

Here Jove had gathered the gods of Greece in council before his throne; here the silver-footed Thetis had found him and clasped his knee with her left hand and his chin with her right. That was long ago; now it was a current jest here that none who

>. . . rose from the waves of Therma's sea
>Scaled in the misty dawn heaven and Olympus
>And found almighty Zeus sitting apart
>On the highest crag of many-peaked Olympus.

Cicero spent seven months, in 58 B. C., with Plancius, the quaestor, in this "lap of the Roman Empire" in melancholy exile and saw no helping gods, saw nothing but snow and ice. Hopeless heathenism!

Dense woods at the mountain's base hid the Pierian Spring, beside which the Muses were born and Orpheus first saw the light. Close to the southeast of Olympus stands Mount Ossa; the gorge between was called Tempe, "The Cut," made by a single stroke of Neptune's trident, — the most famous valley in the world. Here Orpheus practised the melodies which drew the enraptured trees to follow him and opened gates of death before him; here Apollo atoned for slaying the Python and plucked the branch which, planted beside the Castalian Spring, grew into the sacred laurel of Delphi.

*Some Receive Him.* — Hiring lodgings of Jason, the Jew, Paul worked at his trade of weaving to earn his own living and owe nothing to any man. 1 Thess. 2, 9; 2 Thess. 3, 8. At this time a famine raged and raised the price of wheat to six times its usual rate. Paul here gratefully accepted the gifts sent from Philippi. Phil. 4, 16.

As his manner was, Paul went into the synagog of the Jews, and three Sabbath-days or weeks reasoned with them out of the Scriptures, opening and quoting passages that the Christ must needs have suffered and risen from the dead, and that this Jesus whom I preach unto you is the Christ. And some of them believed and threw in their lot with Paul and Silas; and of the devout Greeks a great multitude and of the wives of the chief men not a few.

*Some Reject Him.* — But the Jews which believed not, moved with anger, took unto them certain market loafers, and gathered a company, and set all the city in an uproar, and assaulted the house of Jason, and sought to bring the preachers out to the people. When they found them not, they drew Jason and certain brethren unto the Politarchs, the rulers of the city.

The mob cried to the Politarchs: "These that have turned the world upside down are come hither also; whom Jason hath received; and these all do contrary to the decrees of Caesar, saying that there is another king [or emperor], one Jesus."

The Emperor Claudius was near to death, and the throne would fall a prey to scheming women, and men whispered: "To whom does the Empire belong?" Paul preached: "Your true King is Jesus." This was twisted into a dangerous weapon by his unscrupulous enemies; they made him appear a traitor to the realm. The Emperor had banished the Jews from Rome. It would be the fashionable thing for these provincials to follow suit and banish these Jews from Thessalonica.

And they troubled the people and the rulers of the city when they heard these things. And when they had taken bail of Jason and of the others, they let them go. Paul says that the Jews "please not God and are contrary to all men, forbidding us to speak to the Gentiles that they might be saved." 1 Thess. 2, 15. 16. The Jews started the riot, and now they accuse Paul of starting the riot. The Jews hated the Gentiles and the Roman oppressors, and here they appear to be friends of Caesar against the rebel Paul, the Roman citizen. When the Jews could not find Paul

**TRIUMPHAL ARCH, THESSALONICA.**
Across the main street of Thessalonica is the triumphal arch erected in honor of the victory of Octavius and Antony over Brutus and Cassius at Philippi.

in the house of Jason, they persecuted the friends of Paul. The brethren immediately sent away Paul and Silas by night unto Berea.

The word "Politarchs" is not found in all classical Greek literature, and so infidel scholars have charged Luke with ignorance. But on a Roman triumphal arch at Thessalonica, erected probably in the first century, the word "Politarchs" was engraved in large letters. The Turks destroyed this arch in 1876, but the stone with the word "Politarchs" was rescued and is now in the British Museum. So Luke is quite accurate, and it is the

THESSALONICA.

infidel scholars who are ignorant. Colonel Leake tells us the magistrates are still styled Politarchs at Thessalonica.

*The Success of Paul at Thessalonica.* — Only a few months later he could write: "From your midst the Word of the Lord has resounded, not only throughout Macedonia and Achaia, but in all places." 1 Thess. 1, 8. Having received the Gospel, they trumpeted out the Gospel, trumpeted it out in all places. Do we?

"He turned the world upside down," was the accusation of Paul's enemies. That clearly shows his great success. By sin the wrong is up, and the right is down; the Gospel turns the world upside down, the right up, the wrong down; yes, the Gospel is revolutionary, it brings a revival or a riot. Said Sir Bartle Frere, governor of Bombay: "I speak simply as to matter of experience and observation, just as a Roman prefect might have reported to Trajan; and I assure you that the teachings of Christianity among one hundred and sixty millions of civilized, industrious Hindus and Mohammedans in India are effecting changes, moral, social, and political, which, for extent and rapidity of effect, are far more extraordinary than anything you or your fathers have witnessed in modern Europe."

The Emperor Antoninus Pius wrote the people of Thessalonica to take no new steps against the Christians, as we see from Melito's *Apology*. Tertullian couples Thessalonica with Philippi as a church where Paul's letters were read in the original. In 303 a common soldier named Demetrius, stripped of his arms, stood naked in the arena of the amphitheater. He is ringed by soldiers, each pointing a spear at his heart. He is asked, "Will you curse Jesus Christ?" The reply rings out, "Christ is Lord!" The multitude gnash their teeth. The spears pierce the martyr's heart. Demetrius becomes the patron saint of Thessalonica, and on the site of the synagog in which Paul preached rose the splendid Church of St. Demetrius. In 324 the battle of Scutari made the first Christian emperor Constantine sole master of the world, and he banished his defeated rival and brother-in-law Licinius to Thessalonica. Here the Emperor Theodosius was baptized in 370. Here the same Emperor, in cruel revenge for a riot, massacred for more than three hours the crowds in the theater. The Emperor was excommunicated and compelled to do eight months' penance. Stripped of every emblem of power, he lay all night upon the stones before the altar of the Milan Cathedral before Ambrose would receive him to the Sacrament. Aetius was the bishop of Thessalonica at the Council of Sardica in 343.

From Thessalonica the Gospel was carried to the Bulgars and Slavs in the ninth century. In the tenth century Cameniata calls it "the orthodox city," and for centuries it was the bulwark of the Greek empire against the northern invaders. Here the learned Bishop Eustathius wrote his famous commentary on the poems of Homer and in 1185 prevailed on the Norman William II of Sicily to accept a ransom and stop the massacre in the captured city.

Strabo and Lucian call Thessalonica the most populous of Macedonian cities, and Meletius said: "So long as nature does not change, Thessalonica will remain wealthy and fortunate." It almost became the capital of the world in the place of Constantinople.

The charge of treason first brought against the Christians at Thessalonica troubled them for a long time. As Herod the Great feared for his throne on hearing of the birth of Jesus, the King of the Jews, so Domitian. He issued an imperial decree ordering the death of all the descendants of King David. A number of peaceful peasants, who were honored as the grandsons of Judas, called the Lord's brother, were cited before the Emperor. When he saw their horny hands and heard the kingdom of Christ was "not a worldly or earthly kingdom, but a heavenly and angelic," he felt easy, dismissed them, and revoked the edict.

## THIRD STATION — BEREA.
### Acts 17, 10—15.

Piso, Prefect of Macedonia, fled for safety and left Thessalonica by night and "stole secretly into the retired town of Berea," Cicero says. Just like Paul. In 355 Pope Liberius was banished to Berea. It was named for its founder Pheres, 50 miles southwest of Thessalonica, on both sides of the Astraeus River, at the foot of Mount Bermius, a part of the Olympian range. After the battle of Pydna, in 168 B. C., Berea was the first city to give in to Rome. Pompey went into winter quarters here, 50 B. C.

On coming to Berea, Paul and Silas at once went into the synagog of the Jews. These were more noble than those in Thessalonica, and they received the Word with all readiness of mind. Many people reject Christ without knowing anything about Him; they ridicule the Bible without reading it. These Bereans were not prejudiced, they were open-minded, open to conviction, fair-minded, willing to hear both sides, willing to judge according to the evidence.

As then, so now. As they, so we. Let us honestly and sincerely hear what the preacher has to say. Let us be noble. "A Christian is the highest style of man," says Young, and Hare has it, "A Christian is God Almighty's gentleman"; the good old Lutheran Bengel puts it, "They are the truly noble souls who lean to the things of God"; even the heathen Roman poet Ovid knew, "It is not wealth nor ancestry, but honorable conduct and a noble disposition that make men great."

*The Bereans Searched the Scriptures.* — These Bereans were not

BEREA.

shallow and giddy, eagerly swallowing every story any tramp preacher might tell them. After hearing Paul's preaching with open minds, they went home and searched the Scriptures daily whether those things were so. They did not settle the question by dispute and debate. They did not take a vote and settle the question by majorities. They searched the Scriptures. The Scripture was the supreme authority to decide the question. And why the Scripture? Because the Scripture is the inspired Word of God, the infallible rule of faith and practise.

As then, so now; as they, so we. Let us hear what the preacher has to say and then search the Scripture to see whether these things are so. "Prove all things; hold fast that which is good." 1 Thess. 5, 21; Rom. 12, 2. Prove all things by the Scripture, "Thus saith the Lord."

*The Bereans Believed the Scriptures.* — Therefore many of them believed; also of honorable women which were Greeks, and of men (husbands), not a few. Sopater was one.

"Therefore" — because they searched the Scripture — "therefore many of them believed." As then, so now; as they, so we. Let us attend, accept, appropriate, abide. Christ says: "If any man will do His will, he shall know of the doctrine whether it be of God." John 7, 17. John Ruskin says: "If you choose to obey your Bibles, you will never care who attacks them. . . . It is just because you don't care to obey its whole words that you are so particular about the letters of them." By a careful and prayerful study of the Bible we get a divine conviction of the truth of the Bible as God's Word and the only rule of our faith and practise. Charles Dickens wrote his boy in Australia: "I put a New Testament among your books because it is the best Book that ever was or ever will be known in the world, and because it teaches you the best lessons by which any human creature who tries to be faithful and truthful to duty can possibly be guided." John Quincy Adams, the sixth President, wrote: "The first and almost the only book deserving of universal attention is the Bible. The Bible is the Book above all others to be read at all ages and in all conditions of human life; not to be read through once or twice and then laid aside, but to be read in small portions of one or two chapters every day and never to be intermitted except by some overruling necessity. I speak as a man of the world to men of the world, and I say to you, 'Search the Scriptures.'" When King Suma of Uganda, Africa, died, 2,000 men were killed to escort him into the other world; when his son and successor Mtesa died, not a single life was sacrificed. What had wrought the revolution? Henry M. Stanley writes: "As I was turning away from his country, his messenger came and cried, 'The Book! Mtesa wants the Book.' The Bible was given to him. To-day the Christians number many thousands in Uganda. They have proved their faith at the stake, under the knobstick, and under torture, till death."

But when the Jews of Thessalonica had knowledge that the Word of God was preached of Paul at Berea, they came thither also and stirred up the people. Then immediately the brethren sent away Paul to go to the sea; but Silas and Timotheus abode there still.

Berea is now called Veria, and it is famous for its "hidden churches." When Turkish persecution was bitter many years ago, the Greek people hid their churches in places where there was no outward sign of a church. There are more than seventy such, and there is a little park with a modern speaker's stand called "St. Paul's Pulpit."

Some of his Berean friends took Paul likely to Dium, seventeen miles away, the nearest port, and sailed for Athens, 251 miles away, or three days and nights. Gliding by the Thessalian shore, they saw the storied mountains of Olympus, and Ossa, and Pelion. At the entrance of the Euboean Strait is Thermopylae, the famous pass where Leonidas with one thousand Greeks fell against the vast hordes of Xerxes in 480 B. C.; here, too, Brennus, with his Gauls, forced his way into Greece in 279 B. C.; here, too, the Roman Glabrio defeated the Syrian Antiochus the Great. Near by lie the fields of Marathon, where Miltiades gained a glorious victory over the Persians in September, 490 B. C. Then come the silvermines of Laurium, from which Themistocles had built the Athenian fleet. Doubling the cape of Sunium with its coronet of white columns of the temple of Minerva, the pilot makes the Bay of Aegina and the port of Salamis, where Themistocles, on September 20, 480 B. C., defeated the Persians in a most glorious naval battle. The journey ends at the Piraeus, the port of Athens, with the great harbor works destroyed by Sulla. Here is the tomb of Themistocles and a temple of Zeus, famous for its paintings by Arkesilaos.

Having brought the apostles through the five miles of the ruined Long Walls of Themistocles to the Piraic gate in safety to Athens, the Bereans left for home with word from Paul to Silas and Timothy to come with all speed.

## FOURTH STATION — ATHENS.
### Acts 17, 14—21.

Behold the Apostle of the Cross sublime,
    The warned of heaven, the eloquent, the bold!
Who spake to Athens in her hour of prime,
    Braving the thunders of Olympus old
And spreading forth the Gospel's snowy fold
    Where heathen altars poured a crimson tide
And stern tribunals their decrees unrolled.
    How does his zeal our ingrate coldness chide!

*Seeing the Sights.* — Paul went through the city and beheld the objects of devotion, the altars and temples and statues of gods and goddesses. Let us, with Pausanias, the old Baedeker, in our hands, look at some of the sights Paul may have seen. Just before entering the city through the Piraic gate, we see the building with the vestments for the yearly processions in honor of Minerva; and close by is Neptune on horse, hurling his trident, and a temple of Ceres with statues by Praxiteles. On passing the gate, we front a temple of Bacchus, surrounded by statues of many gods. We are on a long street with a splendid colonnade, and on either side are shops full of costly wares under the porticoes. There is the house of Polytion, where Alcibiades and his dissolute companions mocked the Eleusinian Mysteries. To the right the Pnyx, where Demosthenes hurled his fierce Philippics against King Philip of Macedon, and Solon and Pericles often addressed "ye men of Athens" in mass meetings. At the end of our street a triumphal gate with the sculptured victory of the Athenians over the cavalry of Cassander, and the fine bronze Hermes Agoraeus. To the left the broad and imposing Ceramicus, with the tombs of great Athenians, and there the Theseum, built 500 years before Christ and still standing. Beyond the Dipylum gate the Sacred Way to Eleusis. To the right is the Royal Porch, mounted by Theseus throwing Sciron into the sea, and Aurora carrying off Cephalus, and fronted by Conon and his son Timotheus.

*The Stoics.* — Solon, the founder of the Athenian constitution, stands among other celebrities in front of the Painted Porch, where we see the battle between Athens and Sparta at Oenoe, the battle of Theseus and the Amazons, the capture of Troy, the battle of Marathon, with Miltiades and Callimachus and Cynegirus, and Aeschylus and the faithful dog. In this Stoa, Zeno founded his Stoic school of austere philosophy which, besides insisting on virtue for its own sake, nevertheless sanctioned suicide; Zeno and Cleanthes and Cato and Seneca were suicides.

*The Epicureans.* — Near by is the garden where Epicurus founded his "School of the Garden" and taught the philosophy of pleasure, enjoyment as the object of life. His followers, perverting their master's teaching, were given to gross sensualism.

*The Academy.* — When blind King Oedipus was come to Athens,

THE PIRAEUS, PORT OF ATHENS.

Sophocles, in a charming chorus, praised to him the song of the nightingale on the wooded banks of the rushing Cephisus. In this olive grove Plato founded his school of dualistic philosophy, known as the Academy, and teaching an invisible and a visible world.

*Socrates.* — We come to a Doric portico of four columns built by Julius and Augustus to Minerva Archegetis. Near by is the famous Clock Tower, or Temple of the Winds, built by Andronicus Cyrrhestes, still standing, where Socrates, whom the oracle had called "wisest of men," taught the Athenian youth.

THE ARREST OF PAUL

Acts 21:33

*The Lyceum.* — Farther east, near the base of Mount Lycabettus, on the banks of the Ilissus, is the Lyceum, the grove so named from a statue of Apollo Lycicus, where another pupil of Socrates, the mighty Stagirite Aristotle, the teacher of Alexander the Great, walked up and down while teaching and so was called the Peripatetic.

In Mercury Street a statue of Mercury stands before every house,

THE STREET OF TOMBS AT ATHENS.

and Tripod Street is lined on both sides with three-legged tables, with bowls holding the prizes won by the athletes in the great public games.

*The Acropolis.* — A ragged rock rises three hundred feet, the upper city, the Acropolis, the center of Athens, of Attica, of Greece, of the world, in the opinion of the patriotic Aristides. Formerly a fort, it is now a museum of art, of history, of religion. Up the sixty steep steps on the western front and through the Propylaea, built by Pericles at a cost of $2,300,000 when ten cents equaled a dollar. On our right the temple of the Wingless Victory recalls the glories of Salamis and Marathon and the days of supremacy over the world. On our left the gallery of painting, where stood statues of Augustus and Agrippa and a temple of Rome and the Emperor. Here was Theseus battling the Minotaur; Hercules strangling the serpents; Earth imploring rain from Jupiter; Minerva causing the olive to sprout; Neptune raising the waves; Anacreon drunk and singing; Olympiodorus always cheerful when all others were cast down; a statue that turned around from east to west and spit blood; the silver-footed chair in which Xerxes watched the battle of Salamis not far away. Here the graceful Erechtheum encloses the Minerva Polias, the olive-wood statue fallen from heaven, and the olive which had sprouted from the rock at the behest of the goddess. Here stands the classic Parthenon, the house of the virgin Pallas Athene. Within this incomparable casket is the gold-ivory jewel chiseled by the magic hand of Phidias as the martial maiden sprang full-armed from the head of Zeus. This temple cost $4,600,000 when money was worth ten times as much as now. Between these two temples stood a third statue of the goddess, the Minerva Promachus, formed from the brazen spoils of the battle of Marathon, rising in giant proportions above all the buildings on the Acropolis, the gleaming helmet and lance striking the eye of the traveler on rounding the Cape of Sunium. At the southern base is the theater of Bacchus, where the Athenians crowded to hear the words of their great tragedians.

The Acropolis, planned by Ictinus, is counted the purest thing ever conceived by the religious genius of Greece and the most perfect work of art ever reared upon our earth. At the base it was two miles around, at the top 1,000 feet. Here stands a statue of Pericles, to whom the glory of the Acropolis was due.

Mardonius, the general of Xerxes, burned some of the fairest monuments; the Roman Sulla plundered the city and slew the citizens till the streets streamed with blood; the Roman Verres plundered the place; the Venetian Morosini tried to steal the "Victory" and spoiled it; on Friday, September 26, 1687, he threw a bomb into the Parthenon. Lord Elgin spent $800,000 to remove many marbles to London.

The *Stadium*, rebuilt by a Greek merchant, M. Averoff, was 680 feet long, holding 40,000 people; we can still see the tunnel through which the defeated escaped the hisses of the cultivated people, and the stairs up which

PAUL PREACHING IN ATHENS.

LA PORTA.

the victors went to the top of the hill to be crowned with laurel. Here the Emperor Hadrian saw 1,000 beasts slaughtered for one celebration of the refined Athenians. One of the largest and loftiest temples in the city must have interested Paul, coming from Antioch, for it was built by a ruler of Antioch, Antiochus Epiphanes, king of Syria.

*Mars Hill.* — To the north of the Agora, or Market, is a ridge about thirty feet high and sloping for about a quarter of a mile into the plain

PAUL IN ATHENS.   RAFFAEL.

in the west. On that hill the gods once met to judge Mars, which gave the name to the hill. Steps cut into the rock lead from the Agora to the top of the hill, where the City Council, or Areopagus, the pick of the Athenian citizens, — politicians, orators, and philosophers, — sat in judgment on all things human and divine and administered justice. In a deep cleft in the hill was, quite fitting, the sanctuary of the Furies, who pursued and punished the guilty. The Court sat at night to hide the faces of the judges and the lawyers, so that the cases might be tried according to cool and calm justice and not according to emotion and passion. From this hill the Persians easily and terribly assaulted the Acropolis.

*The Market.*— We go down from the Acropolis and turn a little southwest into the Agora, or Public Market, where everything but meat was sold for cash and without cheating, for the Agoranomi, or Market Masters, punished offenders severely. The Agora was also the center of social and political life; it had 360 societies for social conversation, and

Erechtheum.   Minerva-Promachus.                              Parthenon.

Propylaea.            Temple of Nike.
THE ACROPOLIS AT ATHENS.

the chief business of life was to ask, "What is the latest news?" Demosthenes had asked long ago, "Tell me, is it all you care for to go up and down the Market, asking each other: 'Is there any news?'" Demades sneered the crest of Athens ought to be a great tongue. Aristophanes calls Athens the city of gapers. Cleon said, "No men are better dupes, sooner deceived by novel notions, or slower to follow approved advice. You despise what is familiar, while you are worshipers of every new extravagance." Mahaffy writes: "Here was developed that critical idleness, that serious trifling, that earnest playing with great ideas, which is wont to gather round the real thinking of every great intellectual center." In the Agora were temples of Apollo, Mars, Vulcan, Venus, Mother of the Gods, Twelve Gods, etc., etc. Here Paul saw statues of Hercules, and Theseus, and Lycurgus, and Solon, and Conon, and Pindar, and Demosthenes, and the Cretan poet Epimenides, whom he quotes in Titus, and — and — could he believe his eyes? — a brass statue of Hyrcanus the Jew in his high-priestly robes! and also Bernice, the beautiful Jewish princess, before whom he would stand later, loaded with chains!

UNDERWOOD & UNDERWOOD.
THE ACROPOLIS, THE ANCIENT CITADEL OF ATHENS.

*The Altar.* — Epimenides ended a pestilence by ordering the Athenians to let go white and black sheep from the Areopagus and where each lay down to sacrifice them "to the Appropriate God," the unknown God who sent the pestilence. Diogenes Laertius adds: "Therefore there are at Athens anonymous or unnamed altars." In the dialog *Philopatris* one speaker swears "by the unknown God at Athens." Such an altar Paul saw, perhaps on that very hill. O the tragedy! Athens was

      The shining city,
      Full of all knowledge and a God unknown.

Pliny tells us at this time Athens had over three thousand public statues, besides countless images in private houses. Every gateway and porch had its protecting God. Petronius sneers: "At Athens it is easier to find a god than a man." Xenophon said all Athens was one altar to the gods. Josephus terms the Athenians the devoutest of the Greeks. Pausanias says: "The Athenians, more than any other Greeks, have a zeal for religion." Sophocles, in his *Oedipus Coloneus,* declares Athens to be preeminently celebrated for its reverence of the gods. Plato's *Alcibiades* tells us the Athenians "served the gods with more pomp and splendor than all the Grecians besides."

The world's finest architecture filled the city; the finest paintings of Athenian victories adorned the public porticoes; the world's finest sculptures of men and gods crowded the streets and squares; the world's greatest eloquence and poetry had been heard there; the world's finest philosophy was taught there. There studied Cicero, Brutus, Antony, and Horace; Vergil visited there shortly before his death, also Ovid. When Julian studied here, he was smitten with the sickly, sentimental love for dying paganism. Propertius is pleased with the prospect of a visit to Athens —

> With Plato's lore my mind I'll there improve
> Or in sage Epicurus' gardens rove;
> Learn rhetoric, rapier of Demosthenes,
> The while Menander's Attic salt shall please
> Or many a picture fair enchain the eye
> Or statues wrought in bronze or ivory.

*Morals.* — These gods and goddesses lie, cheat, murder, get drunk, commit fornication, rape, adultery, incest. All the vices are turned into gods — "worse than the worst of men," says Plutarch. Well might the dying Emperor Vespasian wail, "Woe is me, for I am about to become a god!" And these deified vices were worshiped! They had temples, priests, sacrifices, and festivals. The hymns of Homer telling all this vice were the "Bible" taught the boys and girls of Greece! What was the effect? Seneca says: "No other effect could possibly be produced but that all shame on account of sin must be taken away from men if they believe in such gods." Lucretius asserts: "Religion often has given birth to crimes and impious acts." Pythagoras, Plato, and Cicero say the same. "The most salacious" Zeus, father of gods and men, kept the beautiful boy Ganymede for the unnatural vice of pederasty. His example was followed by the Emperor Hadrian; when his boy concubine Antinous died, he was made a god and worshiped. By appealing to the example of the gods, Meleager and Martial and Athenaeus justify their pederasty, their unnatural vice with boys. Ovid's Byblis would commit incest with her own brother Caunus and justifies herself by the example of the gods; and the same poet advises a girl not to enter the temple, for there Jupiter had often made maids

GATE OF THE AGORA, OR MARKET, NORTH OF THE ACROPOLIS.
Here St. Paul disputed with the philosophers.

mothers. In Menander and Terence a boy and girl are encouraged to fornication by the example of Jupiter and Danae — "I rejoice to see a god had already done what I was about to do." Antisthenes, the friend of Socrates, said, "If I could only get hold of Aphrodite, I'd run her through with a sword; so many virtuous and excellent women has she seduced among us." In this "mother of arts and eloquence," as Milton calls Athens, nameless and shameless vices were sapping the very life of the city, and they were the subject of jests by even the best of the citizens. Science, art, poetry, culture, could not save Athens nor any other nation on the face of the earth in the history of the world — "The world by wisdom knows not God." And they were not happy. "Happiest he who never was born, next happiest who dies soonest after birth," said Theognis of Megara about 544 B. C. And this current saying was deeply felt by the best of men, Mommsen tells us. Martineau says: "The pagan worship of beauty . . . had ennobled art and corrupted nature; extracted wonders from the quarries of Pentelicus and horrors from the populace of Rome and Corinth; perfected the marbles of the temple and degraded the humanity of the worshiper. Heathenism had wrought into monstrous combination physical beauty and moral deformity." Heathenism, too, was "like unto whited sepulchers, which indeed appear beautiful outward, but are within full of dead men's bones and of all uncleanness." Matt. 23, 27.

Paul saw the statues, and his spirit was stirred within him when he saw the city full of idols. "They are the idols of the ancients," and sturdy Pope Hadrian VI turned away from the statues of the Belvedere on the Vatican.

Paul went into the synagogs and conversed with the Jews and with the devout persons — Greeks interested in the Jewish religion. As Socrates had conversed there with the Athenians, so Paul conversed in the Agora daily with them that met with him. Then certain philosophers of the Epicureans and of the Stoics encountered him. And some said, "What will this seed-picker say?" It seems they sneered at him, as Shakespeare in *Love's Labor's Lost* —

> This fellow picks up wit as pigeons pease
> And utters it again when Jove doth please.
> He is wit's pedler and retails his wares
> At wakes and wassails, meetings, markets, fairs.

Others said: "He seemeth to be a setter forth of strange gods" — because he preached to them Jesus and the resurrection. And they took him and brought him up the sixteen steps cut in the rock of Areopagus and placed him on the "Stone of Impudence," from which the defendants were wont to plead their cause. Here Anaxagoras, Diagoras, Protagoras, and Socrates had been tried and condemned on similar accusations of setting forth strange gods. Where the ugly Socrates, the noblest of all Greeks, had stood, there the "ugly little Jew," the noblest of all Jews, now stood. In this sacred spot the greatest Apostle brought the Gospel of Jesus Christ face to face with human culture at its highest. Curtius holds this meeting was not on the hill, but in the Stoa Basileos, the King's Hall, in the Market.

They said to Paul: "May we know what this new doctrine whereof thou speakest, is? For thou bringest certain strange things to our ears; we would know therefore what these things mean."

Paul begins as began all the great Athenian orators, "Ye men of Athens," and then tries to gain their good will by a tactful, yet truthful compliment: "I perceive that in all things ye are very religious. For as I passed by and beheld the objects of your devotions, I found an altar with this inscription —

"TO THE UNKNOWN GOD."

And this brings Paul so naturally and easily to his subject —

"That divine nature which ye unconsciously worship I set before you."

Sublime assurance! A poor preacher from Palestine, come to teach the teachers of the world! Carrying owls to Athens! Bringing knowledge to the fountain of knowledge! But so it was — the Athenians were ignorant. Paul knew. So it is, the world by wisdom knows not God; we do, and we mean to teach the wise men of this world.

>Listen that voice! Upon the hill of Mars,
>Rolling in bolder thunders than e'er pealed
>From lips that shook the Macedonian throne;
>Behold his dauntless outstretched arm, his face
>Illumed of heaven.

No wonder, for his Savior was

>Inspiring him with words,
>Burning, majestic, lofty as his theme —
>The Resurrection and the Life to come.

After introducing his theme, Paul comes to his

PART I: OF GOD. — "God, that made the world and all things therein" — and therein Paul contradicts their Epicurean philosophers, who held the world an accidental bunch of atoms. And so we teach God created the world, against the infidel evolutionists, who teach senseless cell-atoms evolved our universe.

An infidel friend visited the great astronomer Kirchner and asked who had made the very beautiful celestial globe he saw in a corner of the room. "It is not mine, and I do not think anybody made it. It must have come there by chance and of its own accord."

"Nonsense! Why such a reply?"

"Why, you cannot believe that this little, imperfect piece of workmanship sprang into existence of itself; how, then, can you imagine that the glorious heavens, which this merely represents, could have sprung into being of their own accord?"

PALLAS ATHENA IN THE PARTHENON.
The gold-ivory masterpiece of Phidias.

The infidel became a servant of God.

Anselm says: "The idea of God in the mind of man is the one unanswerable evidence of the existence of God."

"Seeing that He is Lord of heaven and earth, He dwelleth not in temples made with hands; neither is served with men's hands, as if He needed anything, seeing He giveth to all life and breath and all things."

Even your own Epicureans teach the owner of all things is not in need of ours. (Lucretius, II, 650.) And Euripides, in *Hercules Furens*, says: "God, if He is indeed rightly God, is in need of nothing; these are the wretched tales of poets." And Lactantius quotes Seneca: "Temples are not to be built to God of stones piled on high; He must be consecrated in each man's heart."

Part II: Of Man. — 1. "And hath made of one blood all nations of men for to dwell on all the face of the earth and hath determined the times before appointed and the bounds of their habitation."

Here Paul pricks the pride of the Athenians, who thought themselves sprung from their own soil and therefore much superior to all other nations, barbarians of common clay, or lesser breed, as Kipling has it.

"That they should seek the Lord if haply they might feel after Him and find Him, though in fact He is not far from every one of us; for [in the words of the *Minos* by Epimenides of Crete]: 'In Him we live and move and have our being'; as certain also of your own poets have said, 'For we are also His offspring!'"

Cleanthes sings in his *Hymn to Zeus:* —

> Most glorious of immortals, many-named,
> Almighty and forever, thee, O Zeus,
> Sovran o'er nature, guiding with thy hand
> All things that are, — we greet with praises thee,
> 'Tis meet that mortals call with one accord.
> For we thine offspring are, and we alone
> Of all that live and move upon this earth
> Receive the gift of imitative speech.

Aratus of Tarsus sings in his *Phenomena:* —

> From Zeus begin we; never let us leave
> His name unloved. With him, with Zeus, are filled
> All paths we tread and all the marts of men;
> Filled, too, the sea, and every creek and bay;
> And all in all things need we help of Zeus,
> For we, too, are his offspring.

a. Yes, we are the offspring of God, — let the fool spring from the ape.

b. God made us all of one blood, of Adam, the son of God. Luke 3, 38.

c. All nations are under the guidance of God; none in silly pride is to despise the other.

2. "Forasmuch, then, as we are the offspring of God, we ought not to think that the Godhead is like gold or silver or brass, graven by art and man's device."

With these words Paul's eyes doubtless swept the statues of the countless gods and goddesses surrounding him. He said the idol is naught. 1 Cor. 8, 4. He laid the ax to the root. What calm courage and sublime assurance!

PART III: THE ORDER OF SALVATION. — "And the times of this ignorance God overlooked, but now commandeth all men everywhere to repent, because He hath appointed a day in which He will judge the world in righteousness by that Man whom He hath ordained; whereof He hath given assurance unto all men in that He hath raised Him from the dead."

*1. Some Rejected It.* — a. "And when they heard of the resurrection of the dead, some mocked." Cato and Caesar confessed to the Roman Senate that the belief in a future life was fabulous, and so these Athenian wits thought the resurrection of the dead was ridiculous. They mocked. Where was the Athenian culture and politeness and refinement? Have we not seen similar cultivated boors mock at the Christian religion?

b. Others said, "We will hear thee again of this matter."

You will not! You may be there, Paul will not be there. When the five foolish virgins came back, the door was shut; shut, never to be opened again. It may be said to you, "Thou fool, this night shall thy soul be required of thee." Therefore, "To-day, if ye will hear His voice, harden not your heart." These wise Greeks rejected Paul and his Gospel of the Son of God, but soon after they erected a statue to Nero with the inscription: —

"THE COUNCIL OF THE AREOPAGUS AND THE COUNCIL OF THE SIX HUNDRED AND THE ATHENIAN PEOPLE TO EMPEROR GREATEST NERO CAESAR CLAUDIUS AUGUSTUS GERMANICUS, SON OF GOD."

Not Christ, but Nero, the son of God! Professing themselves to be wise, they became fools. Rom. 1, 22.

*2. Some Accepted It.* — "Howbeit certain men clave unto him and believed; among which was Dionysius the Areopagite," a member of the council, and so a man of distinction, "and a woman named Damaris, and others with them."

Thus ends what Ernst Curtius calls "one of the most important pages in the history of mankind." This "Sermon on the Rock" has been called by De Wette a "model of the apologetic style of discourse." Sabatier says: "The sermon is absolutely unique, and in the whole of Pauline literature there is nothing to compare with it. It is so exquisite in its rhetorical style and so admirable in the profundity of its thought that one can scarcely refuse to see the master's touch."

Of three things ardently desired by Augustine one was to hear Paul preach at Athens. We like Augustine for that human wish.

A church grew up in Athens — yes, even in Athens! And since then the greatest intellects have received the Savior. Dionysius the Areopagite became the first Bishop of Athens, according to Bishop Dionysius of Corinth, who lived about 150; and Nicephorus says he was martyred there under the Emperor Domitian. Legend sends him to Paris, where he was beheaded on Montmartre about 95, — which made St. Denys the patron saint of France; among the Irish his name is Dennis. His successor was Publius. When the Emperor Hadrian came to Athens in 125, Quadratus and Aristides presented to him the two earliest apologies in defense of Christianity. The church of Athens was represented at the Great Council of Nicaea in 325, and the two great Christian friends St. Basil and St. Gregory of Nazianzus were trained in its pagan schools. The Emperor Justinian closed the schools of philosophy in 529. The glorious gods of Greece fled for good. The Theseum was dedicated to St. George of Cappadocia, the Parthenon of the goddess who had fallen from heaven was dedicated to the Virgin Mother of Him who came from heaven. It is worthy of note that these very Greeks in time became such enemies of images that this fact was one cause of the split between the Eastern and the Western Church in the eighth century.

After his successful failure Paul departed from Athens and came to Corinth.

>They have mocked
>At Heaven's high messenger, and he departs
>From the mad circle. Athens! is it so?
>. . . . . . . . .
>Thou who didst smile to find the admiring world
>Crouch as a pupil to thee, wert thou blind?
>Blinder than he who, in his humble cot,
>With hardened hands, his daily labor done,
>Turneth the page of Jesus and doth read?
>Yet shall that poor wayfaring man lie down
>With such a hope as thou couldst never teach
>Thy kinglike sages.

## FIFTH STATION — CORINTH.

August, 51, to February, 53.

Acts 18.

Paul went from Athens to Corinth. By sea? A short sail would bring him to Cenchreae, the eastern port, where stood a statue of Neptune holding aloft a fish and a spear. From here it was a walk of eight miles to Corinth. Coming from Italy, Propertius sings: —

> Lechaeum next! The Ionian Sea safe past,
> In welcome port the sail sinks from the mast.
> Up, feet, 'tis your task now; up, carry me
> Where the slight isthmus sunders sea from sea.

Did Paul go overland? If so, he would leave Athens by the Dipylon gate, pass Kolonos Hippios on the Sacred Way to Eleusis, famous for its mysteries, so sacred that even the Emperor Nero durst not defile them by his presence, and come to Megara, where the robber Skiron kicked the captured travelers into the sea, according to legend. At Schoinos was the Diolkos, the Bridge of the Seas, a sort of wooden railroad to drag ships over the four-mile isthmus to save a sail around the Malea, or Cape Matapan; for the Greek wits said a man should make his will before sailing around that dangerous headland. Six hundred years B. C. a survey for a canal was made; Alexander and Caesar planned to build it; in 52 Nero began it by digging the first spadeful; Vespasian sent him 6,000 Jews from Palestine for the work; it was finished in 1893.

In a dense and well-kept pine grove was the shrine of Poseidon, in whose honor the famous Isthmian Games were held every three years under the management of "the two-sea'd Corinth," as Horace and Ovid call it. They included wrestling, jumping, racing, boxing, and throwing the discus. The contestants trained and dieted for ten months. Before the final thirty days of training under the eye of the president the sacrifices were offered, and each contestant swore he was a pure Greek and innocent of any crime and act of impiety. All Greece went to see the spectacle. The victor received a wreath of parsley or pine. They trained and strained for a perishable crown; we do the same thing, but for an imperishable crown in heaven. 1 Cor. 9, 25.

Jason, in the good ship *Argo,* set out from Corinth on the quest for the Golden Fleece and left his wife Medea and married Glauke, the daughter of King Creon of Corinth. Medea murdered her children, and his life ended in the sternest tragedy of Greek mythology. Here Tantalus stole gold and lied about it, thinking the treasure could satisfy his desires, but found it only worsened them. His punishment? He stands in a lake, but when he stoops to drink, the water runs away from his lips. Luscious fruits hang over him, but when he would pluck them, the boughs spring up beyond his reach. Polygnotus painted this so finely that the picture was placed at Delphi. Here Sisyphus cheated the merchants and rolled stones

THE ISTHMUS OF CORINTH.

on them from the citadel and then robbed them. His punishment? "Up the high hill he heaves a huge round stone." Almost at the top, it rolls down, and the weary man must begin his task again, and again, in all eternity. Here at the spring Peirene, Bellerophon put his golden bridle by night on Pegasus, the winged courser of Zeus, and rode him to the lair of the man-eating Chimaera. Hovering over it, he slew the monster with arrows shot from above. This was stamped on the coins to warn people to use their wealth aright. Here the first triremes, or war galleys, were built. Pindar praises the great inventions of the Corinthians. (*Ol.*, XIII.)

UNDERWOOD & UNDERWOOD.
THE CORINTHIAN CANAL ACROSS THE ISTHMUS OF CORINTH.

Callimachus designed the famous Corinthian column from the thistle. Here was a famous school of painters. Corinth was the first Greek city to introduce combats with wild beasts and gladiators. From Corinth come our "currants."

When Scipio destroyed Carthage in 146 B. C., "blessed Corinth," sung by Pindar and Homer and described by Thucydides and Livy, the head of the Achaean League, the light and glory of Greece, was destroyed by the Roman Consul Lucius Mummius, who carried off the treasures to Rome to adorn his triumph. The simple soldier, in his Roman innocence, gravely told the soldiers if they broke any works of art, they had to replace them with others at least as good! This was the beginning of the looting of the world to enrich Rome, to debauch Rome, to destroy Rome. The molten metal from the statues and public buildings flowed in the streets, and this famous Corinthian brass fetched a high price in the market. The "Beautiful Gate" of the Temple at Jerusalem was made of it. For a hundred years the city lay in ruins. Keenly alive to the beauty and importance of its position, Julius Caesar, in 47 B. C., rebuilt Corinth and made it a Roman colony. He owed it, he said, to Venus, his ancestress, whose favorite he had always been, and called it Colonia Laus Julia Corinthus. Like a Phoenix, Corinth rose from its ashes and renewed its youth. Being the key to the Peloponnesus and a very strong fortress and a great commercial center and the capital of the Roman province of Achaia, the city became very wealthy. It was a Chicago for quick growth and wickedness. South of the city the Acrocorinthus rises to a sheer height of 2,000 feet, and it takes a full hour to go up the winding way. From here Athens can be seen, some forty miles away. Here Apollo was mastered by Helios, who gave the sun-kissed height to Venus, whose famous temple crowned the walled summit. It had barracks for 400 soldiers and 50 fierce dogs. This temple had over 1,000 priestesses pandering to the passions of citizens and visitors as a matter of religion. Before entering himself for the Olympian games, Xenophon of Corinth vowed to consecrate a hundred courtezans to Venus if she gave him the victory. The thirteenth Olympiac of Pindar celebrates the victory, and the promise was promptly kept. In order to induce Venus to give success to Corinth, the city would first dedicate a number of courtezans to the goddess to pray to her for the city. Pindar Jesuitically justifies this custom with the words, "Necessity makes everything just." Strabo traces the wealth of Corinth in part to the money paid to the prostitutes of the temple of Venus. At the public festivals the prayers of these prostitutes to the goddess were held especially effective. To these prayers was ascribed the safety of Corinth against Xerxes, and the grateful city, at public expense, had portraits painted of these "holy maidens," and Simonides praised them in an epigram.

Under the cypresses of the cemetery outside the wall is the tomb of

Lais, Corinth's most notorious courtezan, who ruined so many wealthy men by the high price of her charms. The tomb? A stone lioness with a sheep in her claws! Yes, the experienced Corinthians knew a fit symbol of the terrible power of sensual sin and the sheepish folly of the sensual sinner.

At the gate was the statue of the cynic philosopher Diogenes, who had walked the streets with a lighted lantern in broad daylight looking for an honest man. Alexander asked him to ask a favor while basking in the

CORINTH.
On the top of the Acrocorinthus was the temple of Venus.

sun in his tun. "Please step out of my sunshine." "Were I not Alexander, I should like to be Diogenes."

The road from the sea led to the main market in the center of the city, where bargains were made before the Maid of Cyprus, as the red-capped sailors called Venus. Here, too, stood Poseidon on a hideous dolphin spouting a stream of clear water for man and beast.

The Corinthian banquet and the Corinthian drunkard became proverbial, and since Aristophanes to "Corinthianize" meant to indulge

THE FAMOUS FOUNTAIN OF PIRENE AT CORINTH.

in the most depraved debauchery; Shakespeare and Scott so use it. Chrysostom called it "a city the most licentious of all that are or ever have been." Renan says "the entire city was like a vast evil resort."

*Paul Boards with Aquila and Priscilla.* — Paul found a certain Jew named Aquila, born in Pontus, lately come from Italy, with his wife

Priscilla, because that Claudius had commanded all Jews to depart from Rome in 49, Orosius says. The Roman historian Suetonius writes: "The Jews, who were in constant tumult, Chrestus being their leader, he [the Emperor Claudius] banished from Rome." It is thought Chrestus stands for Christus, the cause of the tumult raised by the Jews against the Christians. Aquila's misfortune was his fortune; happy exile that made him acquainted with Paul! Of course, these people told Paul all about Rome, and he said, "I must also see Rome." Acts 19, 21. The worthy couple were a great help to Paul. "Salute for my sake Priscilla and Aquila, who have labored with me in the service of Jesus Christ, who have risked their lives to save me, and to whom not I alone am indebted, but also all the churches of the Gentiles." Rom. 16, 3; 2 Tim. 4, 19. None of his other helpers received such high praise from Paul's pen.

*Paul and Aquila Make Tents.* — Because Aquila was of the same craft, Paul abode with them, and wrought, for by their occupation they were tent-makers. Paul made tents as a side-line only, to meet expenses; his main business was to preach the Gospel. William Carey said: "My business is to preach the Gospel; I cobble shoes to make expenses." "Manual labor is dishonorable," Cicero said. Jesus sanctified toil, having Himself worked at the bench. Henry Van Dyke sings: —

> They who tread the path of labor follow where my feet have trod;
> They who work without complaining do the holy will of God.
> Where the weary toil together, there am I among my own;
> Where the tired workman sleepeth, there am I with him alone.
> This is the Gospel of Labor — sing it, ye bells of the Kirk,
> The Lord of Love came down from above to live with the men who work.

"It is a contemptible thing to luxuriate in idleness; it is a most royal thing to labor," said the royal Alexander the Great. And our own strenuous Theodore Roosevelt thinks: "Far and away the best prize that life offers is the chance to work hard at work worth doing."

> WORK!
> Thank God for the might of it,
> The ardor, the urge, the delight of it —
> Work that springs from the heart's desire,
> Setting the soul and the brain on fire.
> Oh, what is so good as the heat of it,
> And what is so glad as the beat of it,
> And what is so kind as the stern command,
> Challenging brain and heart and hand!
> ANGELA MORGAN, in *Outlook*, December 2, 1914.

*Paul in the Synagog.* — Paul reasoned in the synagog every Sabbath and persuaded the Jews and the Greeks. "Synagog of the Hebrews," cut in rough letters on a plain rock is to-day in the museum at Corinth, — likely the stone over the door of this very building in which Paul reasoned.

Silas and Timothy came from Macedonia with a contribution from the Philippian congregation, for which Paul was thankful. 2 Cor. 11, 9; Phil. 4, 10. Paul was emboldened and testified to the Jews that Jesus was the Christ, their promised Messiah. And when they opposed themselves and blasphemed, Paul shook out his raiment, — a symbolical act, not to curse them, but to warn them to flee from the wrath to come: "Your blood be upon your own heads! I am clean; from henceforth I will go unto the Gentiles."

*Paul in a Heathen House.* — Paul left the synagog and entered into a certain man's house, named Justus, one that worshiped God, whose house joined hard to the synagog. The Gospel of Jesus, the greatest Jew, was driven out of the synagog by the Jews and had to find shelter in the house of a friendly heathen!

Then spake the Lord to Paul in the night by a vision, "Be not afraid, but speak and hold not thy peace, for I am with thee, and no man shall set on thee to hurt thee; for I have much people in this city." Paul continued there a year and six months, teaching the Word of God among them.

*Paul's hearers* were Jews, Romans, Greeks, Asiatics, masters and slaves, men and women, rich and poor, educated and uneducated. The heathen had their magnificent temples, the Jews their sumptuous synagog, the Christians a hired hall. They meet on the first day of the week amid the noise of the city's traffic and revelry. The Jews sit out the whole service with their heads covered; the Greeks are bareheaded. Some women are veiled, others unveiled; some cover their heads, some uncover them; some are well fed and well clad, some are haggard and shabby; some faces are refined, some repulsive. To this motley assembly Paul preached Christ Crucified, unto the Jews a stumbling-block and unto the Greeks foolishness, but unto them which are called, both Jews and Greeks, Christ the Power of God and the Wisdom of God. 1 Cor. 1, 23.

How did Paul preach? "My speech and my preaching was not with enticing words of man's wisdom, but in demonstration of the Spirit and of power." 1 Cor. 2, 4. There was something doing at these services; people were converted. The worst became the best. "Fornicators, idolaters, adulterers, effeminate, abusers of themselves with men, thieves, covetous, drunkards, revilers, extortioners — such were some of you. But ye were washed, but ye were sanctified, but ye were justified in the name of the Lord Jesus Christ and in the Spirit of God." 1 Cor. 6, 9—11.

No wonder Bengel exults: "A church of God in the city of Corinth — a joyous and a great paradox." Verily, the Gospel of Christ is the power of God unto salvation. Crispus, the chief ruler of the synagog, believed on the Lord with all his house. Many of the Corinthians, hearing, believed and were baptized. Stephanas and his family dedicated themselves to the service of the saints. 1 Cor. 16, 15. 16. Gaius, too, was added, whose guest Paul was to be on his second visit to Corinth. And Erastus, the treasurer of the city; and Tertius, who wrote out the Epistle to the Romans; and Quartus, and Fortunatus, and Achaicus, and Chloe, mistress of a large household, and Phebe, who bore the Epistle to the Romans to Rome. Perhaps there were other men and women of means and position and education, but the majority of the church were poor and unlettered, some from the middle class and more from the slave population. 1 Cor. 1, 26—31.

*A Riot.* — Now, the Jews made insurrection with one accord against Paul and brought him to the judgment-seat of Gallio, the new proconsul, saying: "This fellow persuadeth men to worship God contrary to the Law."

When Paul was now about to open his mouth, Gallio said to the Jews: "If it were a matter of wrong and wicked lawlessness, O ye Jews, reason would that I should bear with you; but if it be a question of words and names and of your Law, look ye to it; for I shall be no judge of such matters." And he drove them from the judgment-seat.

This was the only right thing to do. This was a religious question, not a political question, and so the politician had no jurisdiction, and he dismissed the case.

*The Biter Bitten.* — Then all the Greeks took Sosthenes, the chief ruler of the synagog, and beat him before the judgment-seat. And Gallio cared for none of those things, — "he feigned not to see them," as an old text reads. He looked through his fingers and enjoyed the scene. From Cicero's oration *Pro Flacco* we see how troublesome and dangerous the Jews could be, even to the very highest persons, even at Rome, a hundred years before Gallio's day. Did Sosthenes, the persecutor of Paul, become Sosthenes, the brother of Paul? 1 Cor. 1, 1. We like to believe it. After this Paul tarried at Corinth yet a good while and then took his leave of the brethren.

*Gallio.* — Marcus Annaeus Novatus adopted the name Gallio when adopted by the rhetorician Lucius Junius Gallio. He was the uncle of Lucan, the poet of the *Pharsalia,* or, better, *The Civil War,* an elder brother of Seneca, the famous philosopher, who dedicated to him his works *On Anger* and *On the Happy Life* and speaks of him as a man of integrity and winning manners — "No one else is so agreeable to his most intimate friends as Gallio is to all. Even those who love my brother Gallio to the very utmost of their power yet do not love him enough." Gallio came to

CENCHREAE.

Corinth as Proconsul of Achaia in July, 52, according to an inscription at Delphi published by Bourguet. While in Achaia, Gallio traveled to get rid of a fever, and after his consulship he went to Egypt on account of phthisis. Later he was Nero's companion in debauchery, and Nero compelled him to commit suicide.

The great and glorious Gallio and the poor preacher Paul — what a contrast! And yet millions would never have heard of the proconsul had it not been for his one short meeting with the preacher; as a speck of dust he is visible only in the light of the mighty sun.

*Paul Goes to Cenchreae.* — Paul left Corinth and went to the port of Cenchreae, where the deaconess Phoebe showed him so much kindness that he gratefully remembered her all his life. Rom. 16, 1. Here Paul cut his hair short, for he had a vow — gratitude for this deliverance under Gallio? The Nazirite's vow was made by a pious Jew on deliverance from sickness or serious trial. He abstained from wine for thirty days and then shaved his head. If he chanced to be away from Jerusalem at the end of this period, he carefully kept the locks till he arrived there, then he purified himself for seven days, shaved his head, and burned all the hair in the fire of the sacrifice offered. Num. 6, 13—21. After the battle of Antietam, Lincoln said to his Cabinet: "I made a solemn vow before God that, if General Lee was driven back from Pennsylvania, I would crown the result by the declaration of freedom to the slaves." The Emancipation Proclamation made four million slaves free Americans.

*Paul Sails for Ephesus.* — From Cenchreae Paul sailed for Ephesus. With him went Aquila and Priscilla, likely to better themselves in business, for Ephesus was very renowned for its tents; Alcibiades did not think his outfit complete till he could boast of a tent from Ephesus. While waiting for a ship, Paul entered into the synagog and reasoned with the Jews. And when they desired him to tarry a longer time with them, he consented not, but bade them farewell, saying, "I must by all means keep this feast in Jerusalem; but I will return to you, if God will." And he sailed from Ephesus. As sailing did not begin until March, the feast Paul wished to attend was hardly the Passover, but likely Pentecost, May 12, 53.

On his arrival at Caesarea, Paul went to Jerusalem, March 22—29; saluted the brethren; left Silas with friends; and with Timothy returned to Antioch, ending his second missionary journey. Some think Paul went from Caesarea direct to Antioch without going to Jerusalem.

*Apollos.* — During Paul's absence there came to Ephesus a Jew named Apollos from Alexandria in Egypt, the home of Philo, the celebrated Jewish teacher of Old Testament religion and Greek philosophy. He was an eloquent man and mighty in the Scriptures, instructed in the way of the Lord. And being fervent in the spirit, he spake and taught diligently the things of the Lord, knowing only the baptism of John. And he began to speak boldly in the synagog. When Aquila and Priscilla heard him, they took him unto them and expounded unto him the way of God more perfectly. Aquila and Priscilla had been taught by Paul; now they were able to teach even an Apollos. And Apollos, with great good sense, took lessons from these plain people and received a clearer understanding of the Gospel. And now Apollo was in a better position to do still better work for the Lord.

The Western text reads: "Now certain Corinthian visitors in Ephesus heard him and besought him to cross over with them to their country." And when Apollo was disposed to go into Achaia, the brethren wrote, exhorting the disciples at Corinth to receive him. When he was come, he helped the Corinthians much who had believed through grace; for he mightily convinced the Jews, and that publicly, showing by the Scriptures that Jesus was the Christ.

"I have planted, Apollos watered; but God gave the increase." 1 Cor. 3, 6.

In 1851 Lewin found at Corinth barely fifty wretched hovels. Shaw says: "All traces of its former glory have been swept away. Wherever else one may find the famed Corinthian pillars, it is not in Corinth. Only a few massive Doric columns still stand like solemn monuments of the mighty past. Beyond these, and earth and sea and sky, there is nothing on which we can say the eyes of the Apostle rested."

>   Each rich Corinthian shrine
>   Grew dim and undivine,
>   Philippi heard the captor-captive's song.
>   Oh, ne'er from Grecian soul
>   Such golden streams did roll;
>   No Roman hand e'er smote, e'er built so strong.
>   Temples fell down where'er he trod,
>   And on from land to land stretched the one Church of God.

## THE FIRST EPISTLE TO THE THESSALONIANS.

While at Corinth, Paul had been repeatedly hindered from revisiting his Thessalonian converts, and he was anxious about their welfare.

Timothy had been sent there from Athens, and now he returned and reported the brethren there were still loyal, though persecuted, and desired a visit from Paul.

Some grieved because friends had died and missed the second coming of Christ. Others used this teaching as an excuse to be idle and disorderly. A few were tempted to fall back into their former heathen impure life, and a few others were minded to misuse spiritual gifts. The Jews were spreading slanders about Paul.

Paul dictated a letter to Timothy and sent it to the Thessalonians, hoping to follow it up with a visit in person.

## I. Introductory.

*1. The Greeting.* Chap. 1, 1.

"Paul and Silvanus, and Timothy, unto the church of the Thessalonians in God the Father and the Lord Jesus Christ: Grace to you and peace!"

The solemn Jew said, "Peace!" The lighter Greek said, "Joy!" Paul unites the two in "Grace and Peace!"

*2. The Thanksgiving.* Vv. 2—5.

"We remember without ceasing your works of faith and labor of love and patience of hope in our Lord Jesus Christ."

In 1 Cor. 13, 13 we have Paul's triad of faith, hope, and love; in Rev. 2, 2 we have John's triad of works, toil, and patience; here we have the two triads united. Faith is not dead, but works; love is lyrical and also laborious; hope is not peevish, but patient. Paul thanks God for this combination in the Christians of Thessalonica.

*3. The Testimony.* Vv. 6—10.

a. The Thessalonians were followers of Paul and of the Lord, having received the Gospel in much affliction, with joy of the Holy Ghost.

Joy amid affliction! That is a secret only the Holy Spirit can impart. Tribulation, consolation, coronation — as Christ, so the Christian; so — we?

b. The Thessalonians were ensamples to all believers in Macedonia and Achaia. Mark well, not examples for the godless heathen, but examples for all the other godly Christians. Such praise from Paul is praise indeed! Do we deserve it?

c. The Thessalonians' faith sounded like a trumpet blast throughout all regions. Does ours?

d. The Thessalonians' faith and life was a recommendation for Paul, which effectually disarmed all criticism of the Apostle. Are we a credit to our pastor?

## II. Personal Matters.

*1. The Self-Defense.* Chap. 2, 1—16.

Paul's letters are his autographs and spiritual photographs. His self-defense is a self-revelation.

a. Paul preached with boldness, which was only increased by conflict. Though shamefully treated in Philippi, he did not dream of quitting the work. Hard knocks only hardened him for harder work. Antagonism bred heroism.

b. Paul preached without deceit and guile. He preached the whole Gospel and hid nothing, he was perfectly frank with all, and no one was tricked into Christianity with false promises and vain hopes.

c. Paul preached without uncleanness. His motive was pure, his preaching was pure, his life was pure, and he called his hearers to be pure.

d. Paul's preaching was honest. God had entrusted him with the Gospel, and he tried to please God and not men. He did not flatter men into self-conceit, but flattened out their self-conceit. Paul was a manly man and not a cross between a man and a woman.

e. Paul's preaching was unselfish; it was not a cloak of covetousness. Paul was out for men, not money; for souls, not salary. He desired neither commendation nor compensation from them. He wished to be independent. As the apostle of Christ, Paul had the right to their support, but he labored night and day for self-support. All he wanted was a hearing for the Gospel of God.

f. Paul's preaching came from a loving heart — "We were gentle among you, even as a nurse cherisheth her children. We exhorted and comforted and charged every one of you as a father doth his children."

g. Paul's preaching was concrete; his practise was a picture of his preaching — "Ye are witnesses, and God also, how holily and justly and unblamably we behaved ourselves among you that believe." There was an agreement between preaching and practise, creed and conduct, doctrine and deed, word and work.

h. Paul's preaching was practical — "That ye would walk worthy of God, who hath called you unto His kingdom and glory."

i. Paul's preaching proved profitable — "For this cause also thank we God without ceasing, because when ye received from us the Word of God, ye accepted it not as the word of men, but, as it is in truth, the Word of God, which also worketh in you that believe. For ye, brethren, became imitators of the churches of God. . . . Ye are our glory and joy."

Here is an ordination or a pastoral sermon for you! As Paul, so all pastors; as the pastor, so all Christians. How about you?

2. *The Occasion for the Letter.*

This is explained in chap. 2, 17—3, 13.

### III. The Message of the Letter.

*1. Purity.* Chap. 4, 1—8.

The life of the Thessalonians had been fairly good; but they are to abound more and more.

For this is the will of God, even your sanctification, that ye abstain from fornication, that each one of you know how to possess himself of his own vessel — sexual organ — in sanctification and honor, not in the passion of lust, even as the Gentiles, who know not God; that no man transgress and wrong his brother in the matter; because the Lord is an Avenger in all these things, as also we forewarned you and testified. For God called us not for uncleanness, but in sanctification. Therefore he that rejecteth, rejecteth not man, but God, who giveth His Holy Spirit unto you.

With stainless delicacy, yet with absolute precision Paul lays his holy hand on the festering sore of the heathen world — the sin of unblushing unchastity. In fatherly and solemn tones he warns the Thessalonian Christians that this sin is a sin against God.

Epictetus, the noblest and purest teacher of heathendom, warns against impurity and then adds: "At the same time, do not be severe on those who do not abstain. You must not regard it as anything very serious."

That is the deep gulf between Christianity and heathenism — heathenism at its best.

*2. Brotherly Love.* Chap. 4, 9—12.

The Thessalonians exercised brotherly love — "But we exhort you, brethren, that ye abound more and more." And Paul fires their ambition.

a. "Be ambitious to be quiet." What a novel ambition! How soothing in our shrieking and strenuous age! Here is an energetic rest cure.

b. "Be ambitious to mind your own business." A businesslike ambition. The world's business would be a better business if carried on by men of this business.

c. "Be ambitious to work with your hands."

> For Satan hath some mischief still
> For idle hands to do.

To labor is to pray; Christian labor is religious worship. The Christian is more than a Knight of Labor, he is a Saint of Labor, a noble saint, a saintly noble.

Realize these three ambitions that ye may realize two results: —

1. That ye may walk becomingly toward them that are without;
2. That ye may have need of nothing.

*3. The Advent of Christ.* Chap. 4, 13—5, 11.

"We would not have you ignorant, brethren, concerning them which fall asleep, that ye sorrow not, even as the rest, who have no hope. For if we believe that Jesus died and rose again, even so them also that are fallen asleep in Jesus will God bring with Him" — when He comes to judge the quick and the dead.

"But concerning the times and the seasons, — the day of the Lord so cometh as a thief in the night. So, then, let us not sleep, as do the rest, but let us watch and be sober."

The key-note of the epistle is the second coming of Christ: He had come to save, He will come again to judge; He had come to be a sufferer, He will come again to be a sovereign.

He will come again — this glorious fact is to produce and strengthen faith in Him.

He will come again — this glorious fact is to produce the labor of love, to turn from idols to serve the true and living God.

He will come again — this glorious fact will produce the patience of hope. All wrongs will be righted. With patience, hope, comfort, confidence, and joy we watch and wait for the day of our death and the day of our resurrection from the dead. This is the Christian policy of "watchful waiting."

It is certainly worth while to note that each chapter ends with a reference to that "blessed hope" of the second coming of Christ. In the first chapter it is linked with salvation, v. 10; in the third with sanctification, v. 13; in the fourth with solace, vv. 13—18; in the fifth with sanctification in its completest expression, v. 23.

*4. Practical Applications.* Chap. 5, 12—22.

The preachers are laborers; they labor among you and are over you in the Lord and admonish you; therefore esteem them very highly in love for their work's sake. And be at peace among yourselves. Follows a series of short and sharp sentences of exhortation of wondrous force and freshness and sparkle, as jewels mounted by an artist.

### IV. The Benediction. Chap. 5, 23.

"The God of peace Himself sanctify you wholly; and may your spirit and soul and body be preserved entire, without blame at the coming of our Lord Jesus Christ! Faithful is He that calleth you, who will also do it."

### V. The Final Charge. Chap. 5, 27.

I charge you by the Lord that this epistle be read unto all the holy brethren.

### REMARKS.

This letter came fresh and warm from the tender and loving heart of the Apostle to comfort his Thessalonian friends in their affliction and to warn them against threatening dangers. It is an occasional letter, not a doctrinal treatise, and yet almost the whole Christian religion is seen in all its freshness, purity, and beauty as it appeared in the earliest days of Christianity, from the pen of a contemporary of our Savior, only about twenty years after His crucifixion.

We have the Holy Trinity, Father, Son, and Holy Spirit. 1, 1. 5; 3, 2.

The Jews killed Jesus; He died for our sins; He rose again; we shall rise with Him; He shall come again. 2, 15; 5, 10; 4, 14; 2, 19; 4, 15; 5, 2. 23.

His work brings holiness, resurrection, salvation. 4, 2; 5, 7.

The ministers are to preach this good news of Christ to men and are over them in the Lord and are to be esteemed highly in love for their work's sake. 2, 6. 13. 8; 3, 2; 5, 13.

This Gospel is not the word of men, but in truth the Word of God, and it is to be received as the Word of God. This God's truth is also God's power, His means of grace, which works effectually in them that believe. 2, 13.

This Gospel brings salvation, life after death with Christ in a world to come, 5, 9; but also a certain kind of life here and now, a life of faith, hope, and charity, 1, 3; 5, 8.

The Christian purity demanded in 4, 1—7 produces a holy wedlock, a new status of the wife, a new idea of the home and family.

The life of brotherly love is based on the love of Christ, and this life is something new in the world. 4, 9. 10.

This heavenly life is also very earthly; hard, honest work with the hands to gain an independent living is demanded. 4, 11.

At death the body falls asleep, but it shall be raised again, and the

Christian will be with Christ. The hopeless sorrow of the world is turned to hopeful joy for the Christian. 4, 13—15. This is the new life of the new community formed by the new Word of God in Christ Jesus. There is only one closing word: "The grace of our Lord Jesus Christ be with you."

## THE SECOND EPISTLE TO THE THESSALONIANS.

Sober and serious heathen historians like Tacitus, Suetonius, and Dio Cassius tell of wonderful signs, portents, and prodigies about this time, which made many hearts faint with fear of the end of the world. Naturally the panic spread to some of the Christians at Thessalonica. It was worsened by false teachers, by forged letters as from Paul, and by their misunderstanding parts of his first letter to them. Christian prophecy seemed to confirm pagan augury, and some of the weak brethren were shaken out of their wits and out of their work. If the Lord would come at once, what's the use of anything? So they fanatically quit work and in idle daydreaming gazed into the sky watching for the Lord's return and, when hungry, lived off the sweat of other men's brows.

Paul heard of this and at once tried to mend matters in his Second Letter to the Thessalonians.

### I.

In chapter one he greets them and thanks God for their love and faith and patience.

### II.

In chapter two he corrects their false notions as to Judgment Day.

While it is quite true that the Day of the Lord is near, it is not "just at hand." It will not come except the falling away come first and the man of sin be revealed, the son of perdition, he that opposeth and exalteth himself against all that is called God or that is worshiped, so that he sitteth in the temple of God, setting himself forth as God. There is one that restraineth now, until he be taken out of the way. And then shall be revealed the lawless one, whom the Lord Jesus shall slay with the breath of His mouth and bring to naught by the manifestation of His coming; even he whose coming is according to the working of Satan, with all power and signs and lying wonders and with all deceit of unrighteousness for them that perish, because they received not the love of the truth that they might be saved. And for this cause God sendeth them a working of error that they should believe a lie, that they all might be judged who believed not the truth, but had pleasure in unrighteousness.

PAUL BEFORE THE COUNCIL

Acts 23:6

What is it that "withholdeth" and "letteth," that hindered and restrained the man of sin?

The Roman Empire, according to such Church Fathers as Cyril, Jerome, Chrysostom, Lactantius, Theodoret, and others. Tertullian said: "We have also another and a greater need to pray for the emperors and, moreover, for the whole estate of the empire and the fortunes of Rome, knowing, as we do, that the mighty shock which hangeth over the whole world, and the end of time itself, threatening terrible and grievous things, is delayed because of the time allowed to the Roman Empire. We would not therefore experience these things, and while we pray that they may be put off, we favor the long continuance of Rome." — *Apology*, XXXII.

As the restraint of the Roman Empire slipped away, the Roman papacy slipped in. The papacy is the ghost of the Roman Empire sitting crowned upon its grave, is the way Hobbes puts it. The man of sin slipped into the temple of God, and he was revealed fully by the light of God from the Bible opened by Luther at the Reformation. As the Roman emperor was called "our lord and god," so the new Roman Pope is placed on an altar, and the cardinals kiss the feet of "our Lord God the Pope," as he was called in the *Corpus Juris Canonici* at the time of the Reformation.

Says Tholuck, that learned historian and pious theologian: "I have a real hatred for the Pope. I had never held him to be Antichrist, but when I saw him recently sitting on his throne in the Sistine Chapel, with the black senators to the right, on the steps of the throne; on the left the other dignitaries; on their low benches, in a wide circle, the blood-red cardinals, as one of them arose, his train-bearer carrying his train and, censer in hand, he kneeled before the Pope, swinging the incense toward him, while on either side the serving clerics held out the sides of his vestment, and all sang their hymns, — then I would have done like Samson, grasped the pillars of the house and dashed it on the heads of the Philistines. At such a time something from 2 Thess. 2, 4 concerning the Antichrist flashes into one's mind."

The Catholic emancipation in England in 1829 was made possible by the declaration of the Irish bishops, with the assent of the papal legate, that papal infallibility was not a part of the doctrine of the Catholic Church.

On July 18, 1870, the Pope was declared to be infallible. The great Catholic scholar Doellinger, on the eve of the Council, had pointed out that before the doctrine could succeed, all libraries would have to be burned and that civilized nations would have to become strangers to their own past. In spite of that the Pope was declared to be infallible, and Cardinal Manning boasted, "Dogma has conquered history." Bishop Hefele, the learned historian of the Councils, was one of the opposition minority at the Vatican Council. In the same year he could still write: "I can as little hide from myself in Rottenburg as in Rome that the new dogma lacks a true, honest, Biblical, and traditional foundation and that it has caused incalculable injury to the Church, so that the Church has never suffered a more violent and deadly blow than on the 18th of July of this year." About a year later he conformed and proclaimed the doctrine because "the unity of the Church is of such value that it is allowable to bring great and costly personal sacrifices for its maintenance." The rest who had fought so valiantly against the violation of Scripture and the falsification of history did the same. The deception of papal infallibility brought with it the additional error, into which thousands of reluctant, but weak souls were plunged, of proclaiming as the truth what they did not believe in their own hearts. During the Vatican Council the Archbishop of Avignon, Dubrevil, preached at the Church of St. Andrea della Valle: "There are three incarnations of God: in the manger at Bethlehem, at the Mass on the altar, and in the Vatican."

In 1904 Arsene Pierre Milet dedicated his *De la Devotion au Pape* to Pius X and applies to the Pope: "Thou shalt love him with all thy mind, with all thy will, with all thy heart, and with all thy strength." Mark 12, 30. "Since the Pope represents God on earth, we ought to love him, although in a subordinate degree, as God Himself. When we fall at the Pope's feet to offer him the homage of our minds and to accept his teachings, it is, in a sense, Jesus Christ whom we adore in his Doctrinal Presence. If we truly love the Pope, nothing will be dearer to us than the Pope's will; and even when obedience to the Pope means sacrifices, we shall never hesitate to follow any direction whatsoever emanating from Rome." Cardinal Merry del Val, Papal Secretary of State, expressed to the author the Pope's satisfaction with the tract as a work of intelligent piety, worthy of a devout priest.

The Jesuit Father George Tyrrell, not long before his death, called attention to this Lamaism in the *Guardian* of December 16, 1908. Good Catholics themselves have called the Pope "The Antichrist."

## III.

Chapter three shows us the teaching of the Lord's coming is not to fanaticize nor to paralyze, but to energize us. It is not to throw us into a feverish delirium, but to sober, steady, stimulate, and strengthen us to do our daily duties. It is to consecrate us to useful work, and we are not to desecrate it into an excuse for sanctimonious babble and gabble, gadding and gabbing.

"Now we command you, brethren, in the name of our Lord Jesus Christ, that ye withdraw yourselves from every brother that walketh disorderly. If any will not work, neither let him eat. For we hear of some that walk among you disorderly, whose only business is to be busybodies. Now, them that are such we command and exhort in the Lord Jesus Christ that with quietness they work and eat their own bread.

"But ye, brethren, be not weary in well-doing."

Paul commanded work in the name of the Lord Jesus Christ. The Carpenter of Nazareth sanctified labor by the sweat of His brow. He said: "The Father worketh hitherto, and I work." And Paul, the weaver and tent-maker of Tarsus, preached work by precept and practise. No loaf to the loafer! Death to the drones, death by starvation! Kill or cure, and in either case the world will be better off. Eat sparingly, but work unsparingly, to have to give to worthy needs. Work and wait, wait and work!

The matter is so serious as to call for church discipline, the first case on record.

"And if any man obeyeth not our word by this epistle, note that man that ye have no company with him, to the end that he may be ashamed. And yet count him not as an enemy, but admonish him as a brother."

When the famous Dark Day came, some one in alarm moved to adjourn Congress since it seemed the Judgment Day had come. An old Puritan objected. "If this be indeed the Judgment Day, it cannot find us better employed in any respect than in quietly doing our duty. I move that the candles be lighted."

Asked what he would do if he knew this would be the Judgment Day, John Wesley answered he would do just as he had planned to do — "preach, sup, converse, say my prayers, go sound to sleep at ten, and wake up in glory."

What are you doing to-day? What would you do if you knew this would be the Judgment Day?

## CHAPTER V.

## PAUL'S THIRD MISSIONARY JOURNEY.

*Acts 19—21, 17.*

Summer 53—56.

EPHESUS on the Cayster with its famous white swans was in "the wide field of Asia," sung by Homer. Mountains framed the fertile valley except to the west, where the sea shimmered in the setting sun.

The patriotic Ephesians pointed with pride to the hill where Hermes announced the birth of Apollo and Diana, twins of Zeus and Leto, in the grove of Ortygia; the very olive-tree under which it took place was still shown in the days of Tacitus. Here the Curetes protected the infants from wild beasts and the jealous Juno; here Apollo hid from the wrath of his father Zeus after killing the Cyclops; here Diana slew Orion and Pirene; here Bacchus conquered and spared the Amazons.

1040 B. C. Androclus, son of King Codrus of Athens, made a Greek settlement here and was met by the armed virgins of the temple, which likely gave rise to the famous legend of the Amazons. In 560 B. C. Croesus took the city.

Xenophon and Plutarch tell us Ephesus had two ports, and Lysander built docks and an arsenal about 404 B. C., and the Panormus, the great harbor, made the city the most flourishing place in Asia, according to Strabo. It was the most magnificent of what Ovid calls "the magnificent cities of Asia"; the inscription on the Temple of Diana calls it "The first and greatest metropolis of Asia"; Pliny calls it "The Light of Asia."

The walls were ten feet thick, about thirty-six thousand feet in extent, strengthened every hundred feet by a tower forty feet square, enclosing about a thousand acres; the population reached beyond the walls.

In 133 B. C. Attalus III willed his kingdom to the Romans, who called it Asia. In 88 the Ephesians sided with King Mithridates of Pontus and slaughtered the resident Romans. For this Sulla ravaged the city four years later. In 51 Cicero visited the city, and in 48 Caesar reorganized the province. In 44 Brutus and Cassius were welcomed. Augustus improved the city.

ANCIENT EPHESUS.
The inner port, the market-place (Agora), and the amphitheater.

Here the weeping philosopher Heraclitus, the author of the Logos idea, meditated 500 B. C. and sneered at the superstition of the Ephesians and thought every one of them ought to be put to death. Here the virtue of Hermodorus was a silent rebuke to the vices of the city, and they banished him, bidding him, if he would surpass his fellows, to surpass them elsewhere. He went to Rome and explained the laws of Solon to the Decemvirs when they drew up their Twelve Tables, the foundation of Roman law,

THE TEMPLE OF DIANA AT EPHESUS.

and for his merits they honored him with a statue. Here Hipponax wrote his iambics, so cutting that he was expelled. Here Anacreon sang lightly in praise of love and wine. Here Mimnermos sang his elegies and Kallinos his war-songs. Here Apelles painted, and Zeuxis painted so as to deceive the very birds, but Parrhasius so as to deceive even Zeuxis. Here, later, Alexander was called "The Lamp" for his many-sided brilliance as an orator, a statesman, a historian, a poet, an astronomer, and a geographer.

The shepherd Pixodoros found a quarry, and from its fine stone

Phidias, Praxiteles, Polycletus, Scopas, Myron, and many others hewed their beautiful sculptures.

Here was the statue of the manly orator Artemidorus, who persuaded the Romans to restore to the temple the lakes of Selinus with their delicious fish. The geographer Artemidorus wrote a description of the earth, a third Artemidorus wrote a book on *The Interpretation of Dreams*. In Paul's day the physician Xenocrates wrote his work on *The Nourishment to be*

RUINS OF THE THEATER AT EPHESUS.

*Derived from Water,* and here Nero employed the Jewish astrologer Balbillus. Here Phormio lectured on military matters, and Hannibal said he had never heard a worse fool.

A broad, paved street, lined with libraries, lecture-halls, and smaller temples, ran a straight mile east from the harbor to the largest of Greek theaters, partly faced with white marble and holding 24,000 people; some say 56,700. It was 600 feet in diameter, 40 more than the length of the Roman Colosseum, which held 87,000. The stage and auditorium are still standing.

In front of the theater the street was crossed by another, and here was the market. Xenophon speaks of "our peaceful walks in the Agora." In this market-place orators would declaim and enchant their listeners. To the north is the Circus, or Stadium, holding 76,000 people. Here were foot-races, wrestling matches, prize-fights, and beast-fights. The *bestiarii*, or fighters with the wild beasts, were mostly condemned criminals, sent naked into the arena to be torn to pieces — the last number on the program. To these *bestiarii* Paul likens the champions of the Gospel — "God hath set forth us apostles last, as men doomed to death; for we have been made a spectacle unto the world and to angels and to men. . . . I have fought with beasts at Ephesus." These words Paul wrote from Ephesus. 1 Cor. 4, 9; 15, 32.

The sophist Damianus built a colonnade for rest and shade a stadium long on the Sacred Way to the temple northeast from the Coressian and Magnesian gates. The Persians hated idols and burned the temples in Asia Minor, but Xerxes spared this temple of Diana, or Artemis, the Artemision, it was so beautiful; Croesus had given columns and sculptures; Chersiphron was the builder in the sixth century B. C.

Herostratus thirsted for immortal renown; he got it by firing the Ephesian dome, October 13 and 14, 356. Hegesias of Magnesia sneered it was no wonder the temple burned up, for Artemis was away acting as midwife at the birth of Alexander the Great. A remark frigid enough to have put out the fire, remarks Plutarch.

After the battle of Granikos, in 334, Alexander offered to pay the whole enormous cost of the temple for the honor of having his name on it, but the proud and jealous Ephesians refused him with the flattering excuse: "It is not fit for one god to build a temple to another god." The conqueror contented himself with sacrificing to Artemis.

All Asia leaped up to rebuild the temple in still greater glory. The elder Pliny says it took 120 years to do it. Deinokrates was the architect. Vitruvius, the great Roman architect, tells us Ctesiphon admired greatly the symmetry of the Ionian order. Many women gave their jewelry, says Aristotle.

A flight of fourteen steps led on the four sides to the temple 323 by 151.6, of white marble, with 127 columns of Parian marble four feet in diameter and sixty feet high supporting the mammoth and magnificent roof of cedar. Thirty-six of the columns were sculptured, one by Scopas; many of them were contributed by kings. Eight of them have been built into St. Sophia at Constantinople. It is four times the size of the Parthenon in Athens, one and one half of the Cologne Cathedral. Here are Amazons by Cydon, and Phradmon, and Ctesilaus, and Phidias, and, best of all, Polyclitus. Here hangs the masterpiece of Calliphon the Samian — Patroclus donning the armor of Achilles; also the greatest painting of Apelles, prince of painters, a portrait of Alexander wielding a thunderbolt, — cost twenty gold talents, now about $200,000. Against the walls hang the votive offerings of the devout worshipers. In the center of the shrine is the altar with rich carvings of Praxiteles. Behind the purple embroidered veil stands the "Great Diana of the Ephesians," fallen from heaven, whom all the world worshipeth. Was it made of cedar or vine or ebony? Pliny says no one could tell.

The most sacred idol of classic heathendom was crowned with towers; the bust was crowded with paps, the symbol of reproduction, from the waist down she was swathed like a mummy, covered with magical inscriptions, the "Ephesian writings," repeated as charms.

ARTEMIS, THE DIANA OF EPHESUS.

Around her stood statues that shed tears. The air was moistened with perfumes. The walls multiplied the scene by concaved mirrors. "Fountains tossed in sheaves of light and fell in showers of diamonds."

Back of the shrine are heaped the treasures of kings and nations; for such is the sanctity of the temple that no safer bank can be found in all the world. Xenophon deposited money here after his successful retreat with his 10,000 Greeks. Aristides calls it the "common treasury of all Asia." Caesar twice saved the treasury from Scipio and from Ampius; but Nero robbed the temples of Greece and Asia Minor and spared not even this temple of Diana.

The high priest of Diana was the Megabyzos, a eunuch, in whose train swarms of priestesses with the lewd dances enticed men to the grossest and most degrading debauchery. These shameless orgies were the "divine worship of the goddess."

May was called Artemision, and the whole month was given over to festivals in honor of the goddess. People from all over Asia came for the dissipation of the religious orgies. By day and night Ephesus rang with revelry and drinking songs. The games were almost as famous as those of Corinth and Olympia.

Troubled souls from Spain and India came here on pilgrimage to atone for transgressions or sent for amulets to charm away their sorrow.

About forty years later a wealthy Roman named Gaius Bibius Salutarius presented gold and silver statues literally by dozens. The city voted them to Artemis and decreed that on the 25th of May, her birthday, they should be carried from the temple and placed on exhibition in the theater.

THE "EPHESIAN LETTERS," OR CHARMS.

This yearly parade was something like that of the Veiled Prophet at St. Louis.

First a band of damsels in fawn skins scattering flowers; then priests in leopard skins surrounding a float drawn by white mules bearing the gifts of Salutarius; follows a car drawn by stags bearing the golden image of Diana, gleaming with jewels, supported between two golden scepters fastened to the floor of the float. After the musicians follows a woman clad as the divine huntress with bow and quiver, with troops of dogs, deer, lions, and specimens of most beasts that hunt or are hunted.

At the Magnesian Gate the parade is met by young men in holiday attire and conducted to the theater, where the gifts of Salutarius are placed on exhibition. Each one of the enormous crowds wears a tiny gold or silver image of the temple to mark him as a devoted follower of the Great Diana of the Ephesians. These models of the temple were the "shrines" made by Demetrius and his guild.

After the speeches praising the gift of Salutarius the crowd rushes from the theater to the temple to see the most accomplished female dancers in the world perform with clanging shields and flashing swords, the far-famed dance of the Amazons, which can be witnessed nowhere else. Kallimachos makes mention of these sword dances of the temple women.

There were temples to about twenty other gods, so that Ephesus was the pantheon, the high seat of all gods, Grecian and Roman, Eastern and Egyptian.

Democritus tells us the Ephesians were very effeminate; their undergarments were of violet or purple or scarlet stuffs, interwoven with diamond-shaped figures. Their overgarments were decorated with figures of animals. They wore also a light yellow robe going down to the ankles. They took four or five hot baths a day, many lay in them most of the time; authors wrote books while in them.

Athenaeus quotes from Anaxilas a description of an Ephesian gentleman: —

> The skin anointed with golden ointment,
> Effeminately dressed in soft robes
> And delicate slippers;
> Chewing onions, munching cheese,
> Eating raw eggs, sucking shell-fish,
> Quaffing goblets of rich Chian,
> And carrying in sewn leather bags
> The Ephesian letters of good omen.

The most famous of their charms ran "Aski Cataski Lix Tetrax Damnameneus Aision." Croesus, on his funeral pile, repeated these charms. Suidas says the Milesian wrestler could not throw the Ephesian at the Olympian games on account of the Ephesian letters bound to his heel; when these were removed, the Ephesian was thrown thirty times on the wrestling mat.

"Ephesian" was the name given to smutty love stories, just as we call them "French" novels.

Parrhasius, the painter, said the Ephesians admire virtue, but practise licentiousness. Antiochus the Great fled from Ephesus to flee fornication with the beautiful priestesses of Diana. Forty years before Christ Antony came to Ephesus and abandoned himself to licentiousness. He personified and called himself Bacchus, women danced before him as bacchantes, says Plutarch, and Strabo says he gave to one the taxes from four cities. When Cleopatra came and was carried through the Agora, Antony was enchanted by the eyes of the enchantress. In 31 they set out with 800 ships and $23,000,000 and provisions and tribes of players and musicians to battle with Augustus at Actium and meet with a disgraceful defeat.

In 37 A. D. Apollonius of Tyana found the city immersed in dissipation, the noise of debauchery resounded from every quarter; in the portico of the temple he rebuked the people for their licentiousness. Achilles Tatius, as late as 500, writes: "It was the festival of Artemis, and every place was full of drunken men, and all the market-place was full of a multitude of men the whole night." Pseudo-Heraclitus says the morals flourishing under the protection of this Diana were worse than those of beasts, her torch festivals and rituals the cloak for every abomination and crime. "No dog ever mutilated another dog as you have treated your goddess Megabyzus, because you are ashamed to let a man minister before her virginity. Should not the high priest rather curse the wooden image in whose honor he has been ill-treated? Is it not folly to impute unchastity to the goddess by the ordinance that only eunuchs shall approach her?"

So great was the wickedness of Ephesus that one of the Sibylline oracles foretells its destruction: —

> Hereafter, turned to dust,
> Diana's fane, reared high in Ephesus,
> Shall in the stress and shock of the whelming sea
> Sink like a ship sucked down by sea-waves,
> And fallen Ephesus wail upon the strand,
> Seeking her temple still, where none dwell more;
> For the sky-shaker, with his bolts of flame,
> In one vast ruin hurls the wicked down.

To this wealthy and wicked city came Paul with the Gospel.

## PAUL AT EPHESUS.

On his way back to Ephesus, Paul went over all the country of Galatia and Phrygia in order, strengthening all the disciples, and they took up a collection for the needy brethren at Jerusalem. 1 Cor. 10, 1. Gaius of Derbe was with Paul at Ephesus and likely at this time joined the apostle.

Pressing through Phrygia, Paul likely followed the Hermus River through Sardis, crossed a range, and followed the river Cayster to Ephesus, where he arrived in the fall of 53. He likely lodged with Aquila and Priscilla, as he had done in Corinth.

Paul found certain disciples and said to them, "Have ye received the Holy Ghost since ye believed?"

And they said to him, "We have not so much as heard whether there be any Holy Ghost."

And Paul said to them, "Unto what, then, were ye baptized?"

And they said, "Unto John's baptism."

Then said Paul, "John verily baptized with the baptism of repentance, saying unto the people that they should believe on Him who should come after him, that is, on Jesus Christ."

When they heard this, they were baptized in the name of the Lord Jesus. And when Paul had laid his hands on them, the Holy Ghost came upon them, and they spake with tongues and prophesied. And all the men were about twelve.

Weak in knowledge, these disciples were quite willing to be taught more; having been taught more, they were quite willing to obey.

Have we received the Holy Ghost? Are we willing to learn more and obey more? Unto what were we baptized? Do we live up to our baptismal vow?

*Paul's Main Work.* — 1. *Decision.* Paul went into the synagog and spake boldly for the space of three months, disputing and persuading the things concerning the kingdom of God.

2. *Collision.* Divers were hardened and believed not, but spake evil of that Way before the multitude.

3. *Division.* Paul departed from them and separated the disciples, disputing daily in the school of Tyrannus, likely in a rented lecture hall, from 11 A. M. to 4 P. M., when school and workshop were closed.

*4. The Result.* This work of Paul continued by the space of two years, so that all they who dwelt in Asia heard the Word of the Lord Jesus, both Jews and Greeks.

No doubt among these was "Epaenetus, my beloved, who is the firstfruits of Asia unto Christ." Rom. 16, 5.

*Special Miracles.* — And God wrought special miracles by the hands of Paul, so that from his body were brought to the sick handkerchiefs or aprons, and the disease departed from them, and evil spirits went out of them.

The common miracles are so common that we commonly pay no attention to them. But open your eyes and think! Look at all the hospitals, asylums, orphanages, schools, etc., in heathen lands. Are they not miracles of mercy which God in grace performs through His servants? Let us put ourselves in the hands of God that He may use us still more to perform these miracles of mercy to prove our own faith, to serve our neighbor, to glorify our Savior.

*Imitation Miracles.* — Then certain of the strolling Jews, exorcists, took upon them to call over them who had evil spirits the name of the Lord Jesus, saying: "We adjure you by Jesus whom Paul preacheth." And there were seven sons of one Sceva, a Jew, and chief of the priests, who did so. And the evil spirit answered and said: "Jesus I know, and Paul I know; but who are ye?" And the man in whom the evil spirit was leaped on them and overcame them and prevailed against them, so that they fled out of that house naked and wounded.

And this was known to all the Jews and Greeks also dwelling at Ephesus; and fear fell on them all, and the name of the Lord Jesus was magnified.

Imitation is the sincerest flattery. In the time of Nero the famous *Goes,* or wonder-worker, Apollonius of Tyana, had a school at Ephesus and was there honored with a statue. Later they made of him an imitation Jesus with an imitation gospel. It turned out a miserable failure and only served to magnify the Lord Jesus Christ. Paul refers to these Goetes in 2 Tim. 3, 13. In our own day the Buddhists are making frantic efforts to bolster up their tottering superstition by a close imitation of the Christian missionaries. This, too, please God, will serve to magnify the name of the Lord Jesus Christ.

BURNING THE BOOKS OF MAGIC IN EPHESUS.

*The Standing Miracle.* — And many that believed came and confessed and showed their deeds — misdeeds.

This is the standing miracle — a changed life. A true Christian is the best proof of the truth of the Christian religion. One fact is worth more than a ton of argument.

Many of them also who had used curious arts brought their books together and burned them before all men; and they counted the price of them and found it fifty thousand pieces of silver. So mightily grew the Word of God and prevailed. About $75,000 in our money went up in smoke!

After the searching sermons of Savonarola at Florence the people brought their vanities and burned them in the Piazza of St. Mark.

When George Borrow told the Spanish servant girl Geroncina that Volney, the author of *Ruins of Empires,* was "an enemy of Jesus Christ and the souls of mankind," she quietly burned the book and prayed the while it was burning. This was an auto da fe in the best sense of the word.

Have you any books and pictures and songs and statues that ought to be burned? Burn them! Have you a business or habit or pleasure that ought to be given up? Give it up! Have you an offending eye? Pluck it out! Have you an offending hand? Cut it off. Matt. 5, 29.

"Is not My word like as a fire? saith the Lord, and like a hammer that breaketh the rock in pieces?" Jer. 23, 29.

Lord Melbourne rushed out of church in a great rage and stormed, "Why, the preacher actually insisted upon applying religion to a man's private life!" Gladstone adds: "But that is the kind of preaching which I like best, the kind of preaching men need most, but it is also the kind of which they get the least."

In place of the wicked books the Ephesians received good books — Paul's Epistle to the Ephesians, John's gospel, his epistles, and Revelation.

After these things were ended, Paul purposed in the spirit, when he had passed through Macedonia and Achaia, to go to Jerusalem, saying: "After I have been there, I must also see Rome."

So he sent into Macedonia two of them that ministered unto him, Timotheus and Erastus; but he himself stayed in Asia for a season, perhaps for the feast of Pentecost on May 9.

## WHY DO THE HEATHEN RAGE?
### Acts 19, 23—40.
#### THE UPROAR.

*1. The Dishonest Origin.* — At the same time there arose no small stir about "that Way," the Christians. For a certain man named Demetrius, a silversmith, who made silver shrines for Diana, small models of the temple sold as souvenirs to visitors, brought no small gain unto the craftsmen, whom he called together with the workmen of like occupation and said: "Sirs, ye know that by this craft we have our wealth. Moreover, ye see and hear that not alone at Ephesus, but almost throughout all Asia this Paul hath persuaded and turned away much people, saying that they be no gods which are made with hands, so that not only this our craft is in danger to be put at naught, but also that the temple of the great goddess Diana should be despised and her magnificence should be destroyed, whom all Asia and the world worshipeth."

And when they heard these sayings, they were full of wrath and cried out, saying: "Great is Diana of the Ephesians!" the usual shout at their sacred processions.

"They wore these images as our pilgrims wear the images of the Holy Virgin of Loretto or place them in their homes," says the Roman Catholic Cornelius a Lapide. Such silver shrines of the Virgin of the Pillar are still sold in Saragossa, in Spain.

When the people of Ephesus became Christians, they no longer bought idols. When their business was hurt, the merchants persecuted the preacher. One reason why some hate the Church is because the Church hurts their business. The grafters are not fond of the reformers.

*2. The Absurd Process.* — When the members of the labor union left their meeting hall, they rushed into the street, and the whole city was filled with confusion. Unable to find Paul, they caught two of his disciples, Gaius and Aristarchus, men of Macedonia, and rushed with them to the theater — the usual place of popular gatherings.

And when Paul would have entered in unto the people, the disciples suffered him not. And certain of the Asiarchs who were Paul's friends sent unto him, desiring him he would not adventure himself into the theater.

The Asiarchs were the high priests of Asia, who supervised the worship of the Emperor and the games. Wealthy men were chosen for this honor, for they had to bear a large part of the expense of the games.

The mob in the theater cried some one thing and some another; and the more part knew not wherefore they were come together — dry humor.

And they drew Alexander out of the multitude, the Jews putting him forward. And Alexander beckoned with the hand and would have made his defense unto the people. But when they knew that he was a Jew, all with one voice, about the space of two hours, cried out, "Great is Diana of the Ephesians!" They howled him down. Perhaps this Alexander is the coppersmith who showed so much malice to Paul. 2 Tim. 4, 14.

"Great Artemis" was a common form of devotion and prayer, as is seen from several inscriptions. Like howling dervishes the people shouted this name for two hours and thought they were praying; Luke says they were merely howling. The Mohammedan monks of India still repeat the name of Allah so long till they drop exhausted. Some "Christians" still use vain repetitions, thinking they shall be heard for their much speaking. Matt. 6, 7.

*3. The Harmless End.* — And when the *Grammateus* had quieted the people, he said: "Ye men of Ephesus, what man is there that knoweth not how that the city of Ephesus is the *Neocoros*, the guardian of the great goddess Diana and of the image that fell down from the skies? Seeing, then, that these things cannot be spoken against, ye ought to be quiet and to do nothing rashly. For ye have brought hither these men, who are neither robbers of churches nor yet blasphemers of your goddess. Wherefore, if Demetrius and the craftsmen who are with him have a matter against any man, the law is open, and there are the proconsuls; let them sue one another. But if ye inquire anything concerning other matters, it shall be determined in a lawful assembly — three times a month.

"For we are in danger to be called in question for this day's uproar, there being no cause whereby we may give an account of this 'mob-meeting.'"

And when he had thus spoken, he dismissed the assembly.

The *Grammateus* was the most important official of the city. Ephesus was a free city; under Rome rule it had home rule during good behavior. But there was the death penalty on unlawful gatherings; this riot might at least cost the people their franchise. When the *Grammateus* sent this home, the people went home.

Luke writes the *Grammateus* referred the rioters to the proconsuls — plural! That is striking. It may mean the proconsul and his assessors. It may mean the two procurators, Publius Celer, a Roman knight, and Helius, an imperial freedman, who probably were vice-proconsuls, for a reward for murdering the Proconsul Junius Silenus, a descendant of Augustus, in the year 54, at the command of Agrippina, who would thus steady the throne of her darling Nero.

In verse 27 Artemis is called *he thea,* feminine; in verse 37, *he theos,* masculine, for which Luke has been needlessly criticized, since the terms appear side by side since Homer.

Luke's account of the riot is, "for vividness and humor, the best record of such an incident in literature."

After the uproar Paul called to him the disciples and embraced them and departed for to go into Macedonia.

## THE FIRST EPISTLE TO THE CORINTHIANS.

While Paul was still in Ephesus, Apollos returned from Corinth and brought bad news of the state of that church. Later on members of the household of Chloe — Stephanas, Fortunatus, and Achaicus — brought a letter asking the Apostle to clear up certain points in Christian teaching and practise. From this letter and from talks with these men Paul gathered a full view of the dark picture of the Corinthian conditions. He had labored there for eighteen long months, but had now been absent about four years.

Paul did not throw up his hands in utter despair; he did not write a fierce and crushing scolding. He recalled Timothy from his journey to Corinth overland; he sent Titus in place of Timothy to make the most pressing arrangements; he gave up for the present his intended visit to Corinth; he called Sosthenes and dictated to him his First Epistle to the Corinthians. "Out of much affliction and anguish of heart I wrote unto you with many tears; not that ye should be grieved, but that ye might know the love which I have more abundantly unto you." 2 Cor. 2, 4.

After the greeting and thanks to God for the good that was in them and praise for all he can honestly praise,

## I. Paul Corrects Abuses.

1. He severely scores the quarrels in the church at Corinth. There was a Paul party, a Peter party, an Apollos party, and a Christ party. Even in his greeting Paul had prepared for the remedy by "nailing them down," as Chrysostom puts it, to the name of Christ. "Is Christ divided? You are divided." That alone puts them in the wrong. Christ is the only foundation, and the Church is the only temple on this one foundation. Divisions destroy this temple of God. "If any man destroy the temple of God, him shall God destroy."

Their divisions were caused by their cleverness; let them become fools that they may become wise; let them imitate Paul and work in humility to build the temple of God and as ministers of Christ seek the glory of God. Party spirit melts away in loving labor for Christ. 1, 10—4, 21.

Ramsay calls these chapters "that masterpiece in all literature of graceful and delightful irony."

2. In the fifth chapter Paul disposes of a scandal in the church. "It is actually reported that there is fornication among you, and such fornication as is not even among the Gentiles, that one of you hath his father's wife. Put away the wicked man from among yourselves."

3. In the sixth chapter, 1—11, Paul scores their lawsuits. "Brother goeth to law with brother, and that before unbelievers! Already it is altogether a defect in you that ye have lawsuits one with another. Why not rather take wrong? If ye have to judge things pertaining to this life, cannot there be found among you one wise man who shall be able to decide between his brethren? Know ye not that the saints shall judge the world and angels? How much more the things that pertain to this life! The covetous shall not inherit the kingdom of God."

4. Corinth was the most licentious city, and some members were Antinomians and boasted of their Christian liberty — "all things are lawful for me."

Now Paul builds a bulwark against this sewer of sensuality. "The body is not for fornication, but for the Lord, and the Lord for the body. Know ye not that your bodies are members of Christ? Shall I, then, take away the members of Christ and make them members of a harlot? God forbid! Or know ye not that he that is joined to a harlot is one body? For 'the twain shall become one flesh,' saith the Lord. [Gen. 2, 24.] Flee fornication. Every sin that a man doeth is outside the body; but he that committeth fornication sinneth against his own body. Or know ye not that your body is a temple of the Holy Spirit which is in you, which ye have from God? And ye are not your own; for ye are bought with a price; glorify God, therefore, in your body."

### II. Paul Answers Questions.

Chapter 7 discusses, Is married life wrong? Is it better to be unmarried? Is it right to remarry? Are mixed marriages allowed?

Chapter 8 treats meats.

"They all had knowledge," knew that an idol was nothing; might they not with their superior "knowledge" freely go to heathen festivals, especially if they belonged to a trade-gild?

Knowledge puffeth up, charity buildeth up. Love limits liberty. Kindness is nobler than knowledge. The greatest liberty is to waive liberty in favor of love and never wound a weak soul.

Chapter 9 illustrates that truth by Paul's own example.

Chapter 10 gives more warnings against selfish abuse of liberty.

"The cup of blessing which we bless, is it not the communion of the blood of Christ? The bread which we break, is it not the communion of the body of Christ? For we many are one bread, one body; for we are all partakers of that one bread."

Therefore be at one, in union, as well as in communion.

"Ye cannot drink the cup of the Lord and the cup of devils; ye cannot be partakers of the Lord's Table and of the table of devils." Saints separate from the sin of idolatry.

Chapter 11 answers the question as to covered and uncovered heads, 1—16, and sternly rebukes even their Holy Communion celebrations, 17—34.

Chapter 12 answers questions as to spiritual gifts. There are diversities of gifts — all to work together for the good of the whole Church, just as the members of the body work together for the good of the whole body.

Chapter 13 sings the sublime Song of songs, the divinest love-song. Love sanctifies all gifts and makes them truly practical.

Chapter 14 tells speakers not to show off with their gift of tongues that no one understands, but to use "words easy to be understood," "that the Church may receive edifying."

Chapter 15 answers questions as to the resurrection. It is the glorious Resurrection Chapter, ending with the shout of victory: "Thanks be to God, which giveth us the victory through our Lord Jesus Christ!"

Chapter 16 answers the question how to take up collections for the poor at Jerusalem, 1—4; when he will be with them, 5—11; when Apollos will return to them, 12; gives personal messages, 13—18; greetings, 19—22; the benediction, 23. 24.

## THE GROWTH OF THE WORK IN EPHESUS.
### Acts 19.

"All they which dwelt in Asia heard the Word of the Lord Jesus." Acts 19, 10; 1 Cor. 16, 9. Likely at this time "the seven churches of Asia" and others were founded by Paul's helpers. Rev. 1, 4.

About ninety miles east of Ephesus the Meander receives the waters of the Lycus, and on the banks of this strange river, in the world's greatest fig region, stood three famous cities.

1. *Hierapolis,* the "Sacred City," had the great temple of Cybele, the mother of gods, who was worshiped by rites of cruelty and self-mutilation. Besides a holy city it was also a healing city, for it had a hot spring of 91 degrees Fahrenheit, whose vapors inspired priests, but poisoned laymen who ventured too near.

The merchant Flavius Zeuxis made seventy-two business trips to Italy! The union of purple dyers was to garland the grave of P. Aelius Glykon on every Jewish Easter and Pentecost. In 62 B. C. the Propraetor Flaccus confiscated twenty pounds of gold, the temple tax for Jerusalem; hence about 10,000 Jews lived there. Here was born Epictetus, the lame slave of Epaphroditus, an ex-slave of Nero, the famous teacher of the Stoic philosophy. Here lived Papias, the famous bishop in the second century. The city was destroyed by an earthquake soon after Paul had written his letters. The Church of St. Philip is still intact except the roof; even the frescoes may still be seen. Frederick Barbarossa fought a battle at the foot of the falls. About the beginning of this century there was discovered a curious tombstone of Abercius, bishop of Hierapolis, prepared by himself, showing a man who had traveled from the Tiber to the Tigris and who rejoiced he had found everywhere among the brethren no other faith than that of St. Paul.

2. *Laodicea.* Six miles south was Jove's Town, rebuilt about 250 years B. C. by Antiochus II, Theos, as a guardian of the great road from Smyrna and Ephesus to the uplands of Anatolia. He named it Laodicea in honor of his wife. Cicero held court here when governor of Cilicia.

Laodicea was famous throughout the world for its fine woolens, doctors, and drugs, especially for an eye-salve of great merit and an ointment for "strengthening the ears"; Galen mentions both. Rich and prosperous, the city became noted for its banks and millionaires.

Strabo tells us one of its citizens, Polemo, became a king and a father of kings; another, Hiero, left 2,000 talents to adorn the city. When destroyed by an earthquake in 60, the city proudly declined help from the state and unaided rebuilt itself from its ruins, rising like a Phoenix from the dust, as Tacitus tells us. It was the oldest and least faithful of the seven churches of John's Revelation. Though the Council of Laodicea in the fourth century forbade the worship of angels, in the Middle Ages the Archangel Michael was worshiped in this region.

3. *Colossae.* Ten miles southeast was Colossae, great and flourishing in the days of Herodotus and Xenophon, but in the time of Strabo and Paul a dwindling town, the least important to which any letter of Paul is addressed. It retained a fair amount of trade in Colossinus, a woolen of rich dye, made by a special process of the citizens. The city was on the great highway on which Xerxes had led his hosts against Greece, and which linked Rome with her eastern provinces.

Though near to Paul when he was in Ephesus for three years, the Colossians had never "seen his face in the flesh"; and yet he was indirectly the founder of the churches on the Lycus. For among Paul's hearers of Ephesus had been Philemon and Epaphras of Colossae and Nymphas of Laodicea, and they founded these churches on Paul's behalf. Col. 1, 6; 4, 13.

In 2 Cor. 1, 8—10; 11, 23 Paul speaks of his afflictions and imprisonments, and an early Christian tradition says Paul was in prison, and "The Prison of Paul" is one of the prominent ruins of Ephesus shown to this day.

Paul describes his hard work at Ephesus as fighting with wild beasts. He was "without daily bread, without assurance of a lodging-place, wretchedly clad, maltreated by the working people among whom he was trying to gain a livelihood; insults, slanders, blows — he was spared nothing; he was treated as the refuse of the earth, the offscourings of the world." 1 Cor. 4, 11—13. 15—32; 16, 9; 2 Cor. 1, 8; 11, 23; Rom. 16, 4. 7.

What was the effect of Paul's labors in and about Ephesus? Fifty

EPHESUS.

years later, when Pliny the Younger governed neighboring Bithynia, he finds to his dismay "the temples abandoned, religious festivals long since discontinued, while the priests have stopped selling the meats from the sacrifices, which no one will purchase any more. . . . Not the cities merely, but the villages and all the countryside as well" have become Christian. (*Epistolae*, 96, 9b.) In vain did Emperor Trajan present the temple with new bronze doors, in vain did Hadrian and Valerian support it by their imperial favor, — the tent-maker Paul with his Gospel was too powerful for them all. The temple stood without the town, on the slope of a mountain now known as Aia-Solouk. And what may be the meaning of Aia-Solouk? *Hagios Theologus,* Greek for the Holy Theologian, St. John, who lies buried on the slope of that same mountain. The Church of St. John Theologus here was built by Justinian, and it is surpassed only by the larger St. Sophia at Constantinople.

Here is the cave of the Seven Sleepers of Ephesus. Seven young Christian brothers hid during the persecution under Decius, fell asleep, and slept for two hundred years, is the tradition.

In this cave the young Julian was led by juggling priests to swear a great oath to restore the worship of the pagan gods or perish in the attempt; and he wasted a brilliant life in the vain attempt. Pierced with an arrow and falling from his horse, he is said to have cried out, "At last Thou hast conquered, O Galilean!"

The pagan temple was turned into a Christian church, and Diana was displaced by the Virgin Mary. Ephesus became the metropolis of a line of eminent Christian bishops. In 431 the great Ecumenical Council met in Ephesus and officially declared Mary to be the "mother of God," in order to vindicate the godhood of Christ, and also deposed Nestorius, the Patriarch of Constantinople, for his heresy. The mob shouted, "Anathema to Nestorius!"

In 449 the Emperor Theodosius II, for the second time, had to call a synod to Ephesus to consider the case of Eutyches, who taught only one nature in Christ and denied His body was like ours. A disgraceful riot resulted, and the meeting has been branded in history as the "Ephesian Robber Synod." This happened in the Ephesus to which Paul had written to "forbear one another in love."

J. T. Wood spent six years and $80,000 to find the temple, and he found it on the last day of December, 1869, about twenty-five feet under ground, at the place pointed out before by Guhl.

Paul left Ephesus for Troas to hear from Titus what effect his severe letter had on the Corinthians. While waiting, he preached with great success — "A door was opened unto me of the Lord."

And yet — "I had no rest in my spirit because I found not Titus, my brother; but taking my leave of them, I went from thence into Macedonia," escorted to the shore by the whole congregation gathered by his brief labor. 2, 12. 13.

"When we were come into Macedonia, our flesh had no rest, but we were troubled on every side; without were fightings, within were fears." 7, 5.

At last "God comforted us by the coming of Titus" and the good news he brought from the Corinthians; they had "refreshed the spirit of Titus," had received him well, obeyed him, "though with fear and trembling." 7, 6. 13—15.

They had received the severe letter of Paul in the right spirit; they repented of their sins, they disciplined the incestuous brother who lived with his father's wife, he repented, and they forgave him, and Paul also forgives him in the person of Christ. 7, 8—12; 2, 2—11. He now writes

## THE SECOND EPISTLE TO THE CORINTHIANS.

In First Corinthians we can best study the Church; in Second Corinthians we can best study the Church's great Apostle. Findlay tells us: "If we would measure Paul as a man amongst men, as a minister of Christ; if we would sound the depths of his heart and realize the force and fire of his nature, the ascendency of his genius, and the charm of his manner and disposition, we must thoroughly understand the second letter to the Corinthians."

According to Weizsaecker, "joy and happiness, anxiety and hope, trust and resentment, anger and love, follow one another, the one as intense as the other. Yet there is no touch of changeableness nor any contradiction. The circumstances dictate and justify it all, and he is master of it all, the same throughout, and always his whole self. An extraordinary susceptibility of feeling and impression, such as only an extraordinary character can hold in control," is set forth here.

Going from First to Second Corinthians, we pass from a park to a trackless forest. The former is Paul's best-ordered letter, the latter the least-ordered. Deissmann thinks "it is the most letter-like of all the letters of Paul. The great difficulty in the understanding of it is due to the very fact that it is so truly a letter, so full of allusions and familiar references, so pervaded with irony and with a depression which struggles against itself — matters of which only the writer and the readers of it understood the purport, but which we, for the most part, can ascertain only approximately." Godet says: "The language is all full of emotion, of outpourings of grief, anguish, and love, outbursts of indignation, quivering sarcasms, dashes like torrents of sorrow." Marvin R. Vincent sees that "ecstatic thanksgiving and cutting irony, self-assertion and self-abnegation, commendation, warning, and authority, paradox and apology will meet and cross and seethe, and yet out of the swirling eddies rise like rocks grand Christian principles and inspiring hopes." Alford finds "consolation and rebuke, gentleness and severity, earnestness and irony, succeeding one another at short intervals and without notice." And yet, following the trail blazed by Godet and Zahn, we may make out three sections — Past, Present, and Future.

### I. The Immediate Past with Its Misunderstandings and Explanations.
#### Chapters 1—7.

Paul at once gives hearty thanks to God for the good news and generously writes of his joy, 1, 3—7; 7, 1; and explains why he had not returned sooner, 1, 15—2, 4.

The Gospel triumphs against all enemies. 2, 14—3, 3.

The Gospel is most glorious, far more so than the legalism of the false teachers who oppose Paul's spiritual Gospel. 3, 4—18.

The Gospel is honest; it appeals to the conscience in the sight of God; it can be rejected only by those in whom the god of this world hath blinded the minds. 4, 1—6.

The Gospel brings suffering. 4, 8—15.

The Gospel supplies the needed strength and comfort. 4, 16—5, 8.

The Gospel gives the proper motive for preaching it. 5, 9—21.

The Gospel is not to be received in vain; it is to produce holiness. 6 and 7.

### II. The Present with Its Practical Problems.
#### Chapters 8 and 9.

Paul's sensitive nature must have shrunk from such an unpleasant task as collecting money; yet the work had to be done, and he gave much time and thought to the doing.

1. The Christians in Jerusalem were in dire need.

2. Paul had given his personal promise and pledge to remember the poor.

3. The Gentile Christians had received the Gospel from the Jews, and gratitude should prompt them to show their appreciation.

4. A generous contribution would surely help to meet the Jewish prejudice against the Gentile Christians.

5. Paul had harried the Jewish Christians out of their homes and even killed some; it was now his bounden duty to repair and repay as much as lay in his power.

While Paul, for certain reasons, would take no pay for his preaching, the congregations were not to be robbed of the joy and blessed privilege of

CHRISTIANS PRESSING THEIR GIFTS ON PAUL.

giving. Whenever people received the Gospel, Paul always urged them to collect money for the ever-needy brethren at Jerusalem. He had briefly urged this on the Corinthians in his first letter, and takes it up more fully in his second epistle.

1. Paul makes known to the Corinthians the remarkable truth that it was the grace of God bestowed on the churches of Macedonia that had made them so liberal. That is a truth worth pondering — liberality a result of God's grace!

Then Paul holds up the Macedonians as a shining example for the

Corinthians to follow. The Macedonians were in a great trial of affliction and in deep poverty; yet in the abundance of their joy they gave liberally to their power, yea, and beyond their power. And they needed no pounding and prodding; they were willing of themselves. Paul did not pray them to get the gift, they prayed Paul with much entreaty to receive the gift, as a favor to the Macedonians. They gave their money to the Lord, because they had first given themselves to the Lord. Since the poor Macedonians had done so well, surely the wealthy Corinthians would do still better. 8, 1—5.

2. Paul appeals to the sense of the fitness of things.

"As ye abound in everything, in faith and utterance and knowledge and in all diligence, therefore see that ye abound in this grace also." Your privileges are abundant; your appreciation ought to be abundant in proportion. Lack of liberality would be a gaping defect staring the beholder in the face and shrieking in his ears. The sense of symmetry and beauty of form demands a well-rounded character.

The pay envelope points out the size of the church envelope. Personal religion is "purse-and-all" religion. 1 Cor. 16, 1. 2; Acts 11, 29.

A man told Wesley, "I have the disposition, but not the means." Later he said, "I have the means, but not the disposition."

3. Paul appeals to the Corinthians' love of him. "You abound in your love to us; abound in the grace of giving, to prove the sincerity of your love." 8, 7. 8. Giving a proof of love! Giving a proof of sincerity! Giving a measure of sincerity and love! Yea, verily, "money talks."

4. Paul appeals to the example of Christ: "For ye know the grace of our Lord Jesus Christ, that, though He was rich, yet for your sakes He became poor that ye through His poverty might be rich." 8, 9.

5. Paul urges them to consider their professions; they had promised, now they were to perform. 8, 10. 11.

6. The offering would be appreciated not according to its size, but according to the fine spirit in which it would be given. 8, 12.

7. The care of the poor saints should not fall on a few, but it should be shouldered by all. 8, 13—15; Ex. 16, 15.

8. There would be no danger of money going astray; there would be witnesses, and an account would be rendered; everything would be honest in the sight of God and of business men. 8, 16—23; 1 Cor. 16, 3.

9. Paul appeals to their loyalty. His honor is at stake. He had

boasted to the Macedonians of the Corinthians, who had begun a year ago to collect, and this Corinthian zeal had started very many Macedonians to get busy and collect. Now you Corinthians get busy and finish the collecting begun a year ago, so that when the Macedonians arrive with me, you will not be found unprepared, and I will not appear to them as an idle boaster. Now, do not leave me in the lurch; live up to the good reputation I gave you to the Macedonians. 8, 24—9, 1—5.

10. Paul appeals to their prospects of reward — "He which soweth sparingly shall reap also sparingly; and he which soweth bountifully shall reap also bountifully. Every man according as he purposeth in his heart, so let him give; not grudgingly or of necessity; for God loveth a cheerful [hilarious] giver. And God is able to make all grace abound toward you, that ye, always having all sufficiency in all things, may abound to every good work, being enriched in everything to all bountifulness, which causeth through us thanksgiving to God." 9, 6—11.

11. Paul appeals to their sweet satisfaction. 9, 12—14.

a) Their gifts will certainly supply the wants of the saints at Jerusalem; there is solid satisfaction in that certain knowledge.

b) Their gifts will cause many thanksgivings to God for the help; there is solid satisfaction in that certain knowledge.

c) Their gifts will glorify God for the real Christianity of the Corinthians; there is solid satisfaction in that certain knowledge. A preacher said, "We will now praise God by having the collection."

d) Their gifts will cause prayers and love for the Corinthians; there is solid satisfaction in that certain knowledge.

12. Paul appeals to their love of God — "Thanks be unto God for His unspeakable Gift!" "God so loved . . . that He gave His only-begotten Son." "Christ loved me and gave Himself for me." John 3, 16; Gal. 2, 20; Eph. 5, 2. 25.

### III. The Future with Its Anxieties.

God was slandered in Eden by the serpent; Christ was slandered by His enemies; Luther is the best-slandered man in history. "They say! What do they say? Well, let them say!" This inscription over the gateway to Marischal College at Aberdeen may sometimes point our best policy. Sometimes we must defend ourselves by simply pointing to the facts of our lives, like the old Roman general — "My accuser says I have taken bribes from the enemy. I, M. Aemilius Scaurus, deny it. Which of the two do you believe, gentlemen?" Sometimes we must take Solomon's first advice: "Answer not a fool according to his folly, lest thou also be like him." Sometimes we must take Solomon's second advice: "Answer a fool according to his folly, lest he be wise in his own conceit." Prov. 26, 4. 5. For a long time Paul had followed the first advice, now he takes the second piece.

Paul's person and preaching had been slandered all along by the Judaizers, who dogged his every footstep. In all his epistles there had been mutterings of a storm; but now the storm breaks in fury; the thunder crashes, and the livid lightning strikes. Full of withering logic and scorching irony, it is the most splendid apology of which the world has knowledge — "the Great Invective."

*1. Paul's Personal Appearance.* — "They say . . . his bodily presence is weak" and he is abject or base in his bearing. 10, 10. 1. Paul retorts, Ye glory in outward appearance and not in heart. 5, 12; 10, 7. Character and conduct are more than apparel and appearance.

*2. Paul's Speech.* — They say Paul was rude and contemptible in speech. 10, 10; 11, 6. Cicero declares the Greeks cared not for what one said, but how one said it. These enemies of Paul attacked both his manner and his matter.

Paul replies, My speech and my preaching were not in persuasive words of wisdom, but in demonstration of the Spirit and of power. 1 Cor. 2, 1. 4; 2 Cor. 10, 4. 5. Not polish, but power; not rhetoric, but results. Bernhard Weiss says: "Paul refused to weaken the divine power of the Gospel by mixing it with human wisdom and rhetoric." The pagan Longinus places Paul among the greatest orators. A great American orator said: "The world has not seen Paul's equal as an orator, and the earth still vibrates with his speech."

*3. Paul's Authority.* — They said Paul was a nobody. He had never seen Christ in the flesh. 6, 16. He had no commendatory letters from the mother church at Jerusalem. 3, 1.

Paul said: "I am not meet to be called an apostle." 1 Cor. 15, 8. 9; 2 Cor. 12, 11. "But I reckon that I am not a whit behind the very chiefest apostles." 11, 5. 22—28; 12, 11. 12; 3, 1—3; 10, 8; Gal. 1, 1; Acts 9, 15.

4. *Paul's Teaching.* — Paul corrupts the Word of God, handles it deceitfully; he teaches a most obscure and hidden doctrine; he preaches no true Jesus. 4, 2. 3; 5, 11. 4.

Paul curtly denies all these charges. 4, 2. 5; 2, 17; 3, 18; 4, 3. 4.

5. *Paul's Character.*

a) They said Paul was fickle and unreliable, uncertain in his own mind, and insincere in his promises. 1, 15—17.

Paul replied he had good reasons for changing his plans for his visit. 1, 18—23.

b) They said Paul was a coward and did not dare come to Corinth. 10, 10. Paul says he will show them. 13, 1. 2; 10, 9. 11.

c) They said Paul was still walking according to the flesh. 10, 2.

Paul disproves this charge. 10, 3—6.

d) They said Paul was boastful. 10—15, 13. 10; 3, 1. 5—12.

Paul enters denial: "We do not commend ourselves; the Lord commends us." 10, 12—18.

e) They said, Paul is crafty; he will deceive you and catch you with guile. 12, 16.

Paul disproves the slander. 12, 16—18; 11, 31. 3; 4, 2.

f) They pretended to suspect him of embezzling money. 12, 16—19; 8, 20—23.

Paul shows up the absurdity. 8, 20; 11, 9; 12, 14. 16.

g) They said Paul's mind was affected. 5, 13; 11, 16—19; 12, 6. 11.

In the passage cited Paul ridicules the slander.

h) They said Paul was forsaken of God. 4, 7—17; 12, 7—10.

Paul replies. 4, 16; 12, 7; 4, 8. 9; 10, 7; 6, 4—10; Gal. 6, 17.

6. *Paul's Glory.*

a) *The Glory of Independence.* — True, I abased myself, but why? To exalt you. How much did you pay me? I worked freely, that is, gratis, for nothing. I robbed other churches, taking wages of them, to do you service. And when I was with you and in want, I was chargeable to no man; I have kept myself from being burdensome to you, and so will I keep myself. As the truth of Christ is in me, no man shall stop me of this boasting. 11, 7—21.

b) *The Glory of Race.* — Are they Hebrews, Israelites, seed of

**PAUL BEFORE FELIX**

Acts 24:2

Abraham? So am I; I can match every claim; I am their peer in every respect.

*c) The Glory of Service.* — Are they ministers of Christ? I speak as a fool, I am more. And then follows a combined Iliad and Odyssey of battles and adventures for Christ such as has never been equaled. 23—33.

*d) The Glory of Revelation.* — In some respects Paul was the peer of all; in some, superior to all; in this matter of revelations he was in a class by himself, absolutely unique. So great the glory that God Himself had to keep him from overweening pride by giving him a stake or thorn in the flesh, the messenger of Satan to buffet him. Three times Paul prayed for its removal; but the Lord said: "My grace is sufficient for thee; for My strength is made perfect in weakness." Chap. 12, 9.

We do not know what Paul's thorn or stake in the flesh was. Farrar thinks it was ophthalmia; Sir William Ramsay says it was malaria.

Paul sent this letter with Titus and two other brethren. 8, 16—24.

Leaving Philippi, Paul now went "over those parts and gave them much exhortation" in Thessalonica and Berea; and also "round about unto Illyricum he fully preached the Gospel of Christ." Rom. 15, 19.

Perhaps after about three months Paul proceeded to Corinth and during the winter of 56—57 fully restored order and strengthened the disciples; for Clement of Rome, not many years after, praises the virtues of the Corinthian Christians to the highest degree. Likely he spent most of this time at Corinth, guest of his convert and friend Gaius. Here he likely wrote the Epistle to the Romans.

## SOME ESTIMATES OF ROMANS.

When Paul had planted the Church in the East, he would first carry a collection for the poor to Jerusalem and then preach the Gospel as far west as Spain and on the way visit Rome. In order to prevent prejudice against his person and preaching, he dictated a letter to Tertius and sent it by "Phoebe, our sister, who is a servant of the church that is at Cenchreae [the western port of Corinth], who had been a helper of many and of mine own self."

As early as the second century an unknown writer calls Romans "the whole tenor of the Scriptures," and Luther says it is "the true masterpiece of the New Testament, the purest Gospel. It deserves not only to be known word for word by every Christian, but to be the subject of his meditation day by day, the daily bread of his soul; for it can never be too much or too well studied, and the more time one spends on it, the more precious it becomes, the better it appears. . . . This epistle is to my mind at the same time a commentary upon, and an epitome of, all the sacred Scripture and always its light and apocalypse" — revelation, explanation.

While hearing these words in Luther's Preface to the Epistle to the Romans from Peter Boehler in Aldersgate Street in London, John Wesley felt his "heart strangely warmed" and felt he did trust in Christ, Christ alone, for salvation. And so the Methodist Professor Hayes of Garrett says: "Paul was responsible for all Protestantism through Martin Luther and Luther's Preface to the Epistle to the Romans for all Methodism through the conversion of John Wesley."

Melanchthon called Romans a "compend of Christian doctrine" and based on it his famous *Loci Communes*, in 1521, the first systematic theology of the Protestant Reformation. He copied the epistle twice with his own hands. Chrysostom had it read to him twice a week.

PAUL WRITING THE EPISTLE TO THE ROMANS.

Matthew Henry writes: "If we compare Scripture, David's psalms and Paul's epistles are stars of the first magnitude, that differ from other stars in glory; but Romans is superlatively excellent, the largest and fullest of all." Coleridge calls it "the greatest effort made by the human intellect." Tholuck considers it "a Christian philosophy of universal history." Godet knows not "which to admire the more, the majesty of the whole or the finish of the details, and every look makes the discovery of some new perfection. . . . It is the cathedral of the Christian faith, . . . the greatest masterpiece which the human mind had ever conceived and realized, the first logical exposition of the work of God in Christ for the salvation of the world." Deissmann calls it "the Magna Carta of evangelical Protestantism" and goes on: "It was the religious power concealed in the epistle that made such a deep impression on Augustine and Luther; it is this which so deeply impresses still every evangelically disposed conscience. We stand upon volcanic soil in reading this epistle. Paul wrote it . . . with his heart's blood. . . . The deep understanding of human misery, the terrible shuddering before the power of sin, but at the same time the jubilant rejoicing of the redeemed child of God — this is what for all time assures to the Roman Epistle a victorious sway over the hearts of men who are sinful and who thirst for redemption. . . . It has a power not to be destroyed by any lapse or change of time."

### THE EPISTLE TO THE ROMANS.
#### INTRODUCTION.

1. The sublime salutation in a single sentence of marvelous matter in wondrous words and consummate compression, 1, 1—7, is followed by the

2. Thanksgiving for the faith of the Roman Christians and the hope of preaching to them, 1, 13—15, which at once brings Paul to his theme: —

#### THE GOSPEL OF CHRIST,
##### JUSTIFICATION BY FAITH, THE GIFT OF GOD'S RIGHTEOUSNESS. 1, 16. 17.

##### I. THE NEED OF THE GOSPEL.

1. The Gentiles, or heathen, cannot be saved by their good works, for they are utterly sinful, condemned by their own conscience. 1, 18—32.

The fiery indictment here hurled at heathendom by Paul requires no proof. The pagan poets, orators, satirists, and historians show the pagan world one huge open sore. Seneca says: "They are full of crimes and vices and no longer under cover." Dug-up Pompeii is a standing proof of Paul's terrible charges.

2. The Jews cannot be saved by their good works. They had the Law; they gloried in the Law; they broke the Law; they dishonored God. "By the works of the Law shall no flesh be justified in His sight; for through the Law cometh the knowledge of sin." 2—3, 20.

The Jews thought themselves certain of heaven because they were the circumcised sons of Abraham; yet that generation of Jews was so wicked that the Jewish historian Josephus thinks earthquake and lightning must have destroyed them had the Romans not done so under Titus in the year 70.

## II. The Nature of the Gospel.

If there is no distinction between Jew and Gentile, if all have sinned before God and therefore are unrighteous, how, then, may they be justified?

They are justified without price, by God's grace, through the redemption that is in Christ Jesus; whom God set forth to be a propitiation, through faith, in His blood, to show His righteousness, that He might Himself be just and the Justifier of him that hath faith in Jesus. 3, 21—31. This is the impregnable rock of the Christian faith.

How does the unrighteous become righteous? God presents His own righteousness to the sinner, who has no righteousness. Though we are sinners and deserve nothing but punishment, God so loved the world of sinners that He gave His only-begotten Son to live for us, to suffer and die in our stead, as our Surety and Representative and Substitute, and thus propitiate, or still, the wrath of God, and satisfy the demands of His justice, and thus save us. In the death of Christ God views our whole race as redeemed and pardons and acquits us. God condemns and pardons. In the Law God is just and condemns; in the Gospel God is just and pardons.

This universal salvation is applied and appropriated by faith. By faith we own it; by unfaith we disown it. By accepting it, we escape damnation; by rejecting it, we remain in damnation.

Luther wrote opposite 3, 25: "Mark this; this is the chief point and very central place of the epistle and of the whole Bible." Stolz says: "Whosoever understands it understands the apostle; whosoever misunderstands it runs the risk of misunderstanding the entire epistle." Vitringa calls this paragraph "the brief summary of divine wisdom." Calvin says: "There is probably no passage in the whole Bible that sets forth more profoundly the justifying righteousness of God." The poet Cowper found peace for his despairing heart in this twenty-fifth verse. The truth of the teaching is illustrated in Abraham and David. Chap. 4.

## III. The Effect of the Gospel.

1. Peace with God. 2. Joy in the hope of the glory of God. 3. Glory in tribulation. All this through the atonement of Christ. Chap. 5. 4. Holiness of life. Faith in Christ is not a dead formula of the head, repeated by rote from memory as a cold creed. Faith is a living leaven, leavening the whole lump. Faith is a living seed, growing in the heart and driving out sin and producing the glorious fruits of good works. Justification produces sanctification. Good works in no way produce the

Christian; the Christian in every way produces good works. Christ saves us *from* our sins, not *in* our sins. Chap. 6, 1—14.

This duty of holiness, of a full surrender to the service of God, is illustrated from slavery, chap. 6, 15—23, and from wedlock, chap. 7, 1—16.

If I cannot be saved by the Law, is the Law sin? God forbid! The Law is holy and righteous and good. It reveals to me my sins. Despairing of my own goodness, I flee to Christ, who gives me the victory over sin. Chap. 7, 7—25.

This victorious holiness is by the Holy Spirit. 1. He gives victory over sin and death. 8, 1—11. 2. He gives witness to our adoption as the sons of God. 8, 12—17. 3. He gives completion to our salvation. 8, 18—25. 4. He gives successful intercession for us. 8, 26. 27.

Our salvation from vocation through justification to glorification is by God's operation,— and we burst out in a holy hymn of rapturous praise of the love of God, which is in Christ Jesus, our Lord. 8, 28—39.

### IV. Israel's Relation to the Gospel.

1. In the past: a) The privileges were great. 9, 1—5. b) There was an election, 9, 6—13, c) according to God's will, 9, 14—18, d) leading to Gentile salvation, 9, 19—29, e) and Jewish rejection, 9, 30—33.

2. In the present: a) Israel was disobedient to God, 10, 1—15, b) rejecting the Gospel, 10, 16—21.

3. In the future: a) A remnant is saved. 11, 1—10. b) Israel's loss is the Gentiles' gain. 11, 11—24. c) God hath concluded them all in unbelief that He might have mercy upon all. 11, 25—32.

4. The mystery is ended with a doxology to God: "For of Him and through Him and to Him are all things; to whom be glory forever! Amen." 11, 33—36.

These chapters give "the outline of the philosophy of history," and Godet thinks "a more far-reaching glance was never cast over the divine plan of the history of the world."

### V. Practical Results of the Gospel.

1. Complete consecration to the service of God. 12, 1. 2. 2. Humble use of God's gifts. 12, 3—8. 3. Perfect love for the brother. 12, 9—21. 4. Obedience to the government. 13, 1—7. 5. Love of the brother. 13, 8—14. 6. Toleration. 14, 1—12. 7. Self-denial. 14, 13—23. 8. Mutual helpfulness. 15, 1—13. 9. Reference to Paul's apostleship. 15, 14—22.

### The Conclusion.

1. Paul plans to take the collection for the poor to Jerusalem and then to visit the Romans on his preaching-tour to Spain. 15, 23—29. 2. He asks for their prayers. 15, 30—33. 3. He commends Phoebe to them. 16, 1. 2. 4. He salutes many. 16, 3—16. 5. He warns against divisions. 16, 17—20. 6. He sends the greetings of others. 16, 21—24. And the list of names agrees remarkably with the names of members of Caesar's household found in Roman inscriptions. 7. He praises God in his longest and most elaborate doxology. 16, 25—27.

---

While waiting for the first ship to sail east to keep the Passover at Jerusalem on Thursday, April 7, Paul learned of a plot of the Jews to kill him. No doubt the fanatical Jews would stab him in his sleep and slip his body into the sea, as the crew plotted against the poet Arion on the voyage from Tarentum to Corinth. Paul foiled the murderers by returning through Macedonia.

There accompanied him into Asia, Sopater, the son of Pyrrhus of Berea; and of the Thessalonians, Aristarchus and Secundus; and Gaius of Derbe, and Timotheus; and of Asia, Tychicus and Trophimus. These, going before, tarried for us at Troas.

After the Days of Unleavened Bread — Passover of the year 57, April 7—14 — Paul and Luke left Philippi, sailed from Neapolis on Friday, the 15th, arrived at Troas on Tuesday, the 19th, and abode seven days. The last day was a Sunday, and, of course, all hands went to church. This first day of the week was at that time quite generally accepted as the day of worship.

What kind of service did they have?

Bordering on Troas was Bithynia, from which Governor Pliny wrote the Emperor Trajan: "The Christians fill all towns and market-places," and: "The whole of their fault lay in this, that they were wont to meet together on a stated day, before it was light, and sing among themselves alternately a hymn to Christ as God and to bind themselves by a sacrament [or oath], not to the commission of any wickedness, but not to be guilty of theft or robbery or adultery." After this early service they separated and assembled again in the evening to partake of a common meal.

Upon the first day of the week, when the disciples came together to break bread, Paul preached unto them, ready to depart on the morrow; and continued his speech until midnight. And there were many lights in the upper chamber where they were gathered together. And there sat in the window a certain young man named Eutychus, being fallen into a deep sleep; and as Paul was long preaching, he sunk down with sleep and fell down from the third loft and was taken up dead. And Paul went down and fell on him, and embracing him, he said: "Trouble not yourselves, for his life is in him."

When Paul was come up again, and had broken bread, and eaten, and talked a long while, even till break of day, so he departed.

And they brought the young man alive and were not a little comforted.

## FROM TROAS TO MILETUS.

Paul's friends sailed around Cape Lectum, while he, on Monday, left by the southern gate, passed the hot springs, went through the green oak woods, and came by the Sacred Way among the famous tombs, through the ancient gate, to Assos, perched on a high rock, a journey of twenty miles. The road to the harbor was so steep and dangerous that Stratonicus jokes:—
Wilt hurry to thy death? See Assos, then.

THE EMPEROR TRAJAN.

Here the poet Cleanthes was born 350 years before, and here was the Sarcophagus, the wonderful stone that consumed the whole body entombed in it in less than forty days, teeth only excepted.

At Assos we took Paul into the ship and in the afternoon came to Mytilene, the capital of Lesbos, "where burning Sappho loved and sung," also Alcaeus. It was the home of Pittacus, one of the Seven Sages, and the learned Aristotle spent two years here to learn from the learned men. Here also Pompey's Cornelia waited for news about the battle of Pharsalia, August 9, 48 B. C.

SAMOS.

ASSOS.

And we sailed thence and came the next day over against Chios, famous for wine, marble, mastix, and for being one of the reputed birthplaces of Homer.

The next day the shores of Ionia came into sight and Ephesus; but they steered for Samos, so called from the circular harbor. It was famous for its wine —

Fill high the cup with Samian wine!

The tyrant Polycrates, with his ring, was uniformly successful, but in the end he was crucified by the Persian Satrap of Sardis. It was also the home of the great Pythagoras, who was dissatisfied with the tyranny of Polycrates, went to Crotona, and founded one of the Italic schools, from which came Empedocles and also Philolaus, who sold the books of the school to Plato. It was the home of Simonides, singer of Marathon, Thermopylae, Artemisium, Salamis, who took his fifty-sixth prize when eighty years old.

Paul and his company soon reached the roadstead of Trogyllium at the foot of Mount Mycale, where Leotychides and Xanthippus defeated the Persian naval forces in September, 479 B. C., the day of the battle of Plataea. There they spent the night.

THE GATE AT ASSOS THROUGH WHICH PAUL PASSED.

By Thursday noon they were at Miletus, where the Maeander meanders into the sea, thirty-six miles south of Ephesus. It was once the capital of Ionia, the mother of eighty colonies, and is still a place of some importance. It was the home of Thales, one of the Seven Sages, the teacher of Anaximander, who was the teacher of Anaximenes, who was the teacher of Anaxagoras, who went to Athens and became the teacher of Pericles and Euripides. It was noted for its woolens, its theater, its beautiful and witty women, and notorious for the licentious Milesian song and speech.

Paul had determined to sail by Ephesus, because he would not spend his time in Asia. For he hastened, if it were possible for him, to be at Jerusalem the day of Pentecost, May 28.

## PAUL'S INSTRUCTIONS TO THE SHEPHERDS OF THE FLOCK.
### Acts 20, 17—38.

From Miletus, thirty miles, eight hours, he sent to Ephesus and called the elders of the church. And when they were come, about Saturday noon, the 30th, he said to them words of parting.

MILETUS.

### I. A Farewell Speech.

*1. Review of the Past.* — "Ye know, from the first day that I came into Asia, after what manner I have been with you at all seasons, serving the Lord with all humility of mind and with many tears and temptations, which befell me by the lying in wait of the Jews; and how I kept back nothing that was profitable unto you, but have showed you and have taught you publicly and from house to house, testifying both to the Jews, and also to the Greeks, repentance toward God and faith toward our Lord Jesus Christ."

MYTILENE, CAPITAL OF LESBOS.

THE THEATER AT SMYRNA, WHERE POLYCARP WAS BURNED.

Dr. Dodd preached repentance and faith so much that he was nicknamed "Faith and Repentance." Philip Henry adds: "If this is to be vile, I will be yet more vile; for faith and repentance are all in Christianity. If I were to die in the pulpit, I would desire to be preaching repentance; or if I were to die out of the pulpit, I would desire practising repentance. He that repents every day for the sins of every day, when he comes to die, will have the sins of but one day to repent of."

"For I know this, that after my departing shall grievous wolves enter in among you, not sparing the flock. Also of your own selves shall men arise, speaking perverse things, to draw away disciples after them. Therefore watch and remember that by the space of three years I ceased not to warn every one night and day with tears. Take heed, therefore, unto yourselves and to all the flock over the which the Holy Ghost hath made you overseers, to feed the Church of God, which He hath purchased with His own blood."

SMYRNA, WHERE POLYCARP IS BURIED.

When a storm blows up, sailors lower their sails. Paul, however, bravely furled not a single sail, but boldly spread out every inch of sail to have all the sails filled full of every doctrine of God to speed the Gospel ship across the stormy sea to the haven of safety.

The Pope tried to silence Savonarola with the cardinal's red hat. "No other red hat will I have than that of martyrdom, colored with my own blood." Louis XIV said: "I don't know how it is: When I hear my other chaplains preach, I admire them; but when I hear Massillon, I always go away dissatisfied with myself."

2. *The Future of the Church.* — "And now, behold, I know that ye all among whom I have gone preaching the kingdom of God shall see my face no more. Wherefore I take you to record this day that I am pure from the blood of all men. For I have not shunned to declare unto you

all the counsel of God. But none of these coming dangers move me from the path of my duty, neither count I my life dear unto myself, so that I might win my race with joy and the ministry which I have received of the Lord Jesus, to testify the Gospel of the grace of God."

Told the Romanists had burned his New Testament, William Tyndale wrote he had looked for that, and they shall "burn me also; if it be God's will, it shall be so." And it was so.

The king of France offered the Prince of Conde 1) to go to Mass, 2) to die, 3) prison for life. "With regard to the first, I am fully determined never to go to Mass; as to the other two, I am so perfectly indifferent that I leave the choice to Your Majesty."

## II. THE PRESENT OUTLOOK.

*Paul's Own Future.* — "And now, behold, I go bound in the spirit unto Jerusalem, not knowing the things that shall befall me there, save that the Holy Ghost witnesseth in every city, saying that bonds and afflictions await me."

Mr. Schindler's poem tells of the engineer deep down in the ship who cannot see the way, but simply obeys the pilot on deck, who does see the way.

> And so in the wearisome journey
>   Over life's troubled sea,
> I know not the way I am going,
>   But Jesus shall pilot me.
> I know not the way I am going,
>   But well do I know my Guide;
> With childlike trust I give my hand
>   To the mighty Friend at my side.

Francis Xavier said: "If those islands had scented woods and mines of gold, Christians would have courage enough to go thither, nor would all the perils in the world prevent them. They are dastardly and alarmed because there are only the souls of men to be gained. And shall love be less hardy than avarice? 'They will destroy me,' you say, 'by poison.' It is an honor to which such a sinner as I am may not aspire. But this I have to say, that whatever form of torture or of death awaits me, I am ready to suffer it ten thousand times for the salvation of a single soul."

## III. THE CONCLUSION.

"And now, brethren, I commend you to God," — I lay you down beside God. So long I have borne you, I can carry you no longer; I lay the burden down before God's throne. "And to the Word of His grace, which is able to build you up and to give you an inheritance among all them who are sanctified."

The Word of God's grace is the means of God's grace through which we receive God's grace and keep God's grace, and so we will eagerly read and heed the Word of Grace.

"I have coveted no man's silver or gold or apparel." Apparel was a large part of Oriental wealth, and just Ephesus was famous for the

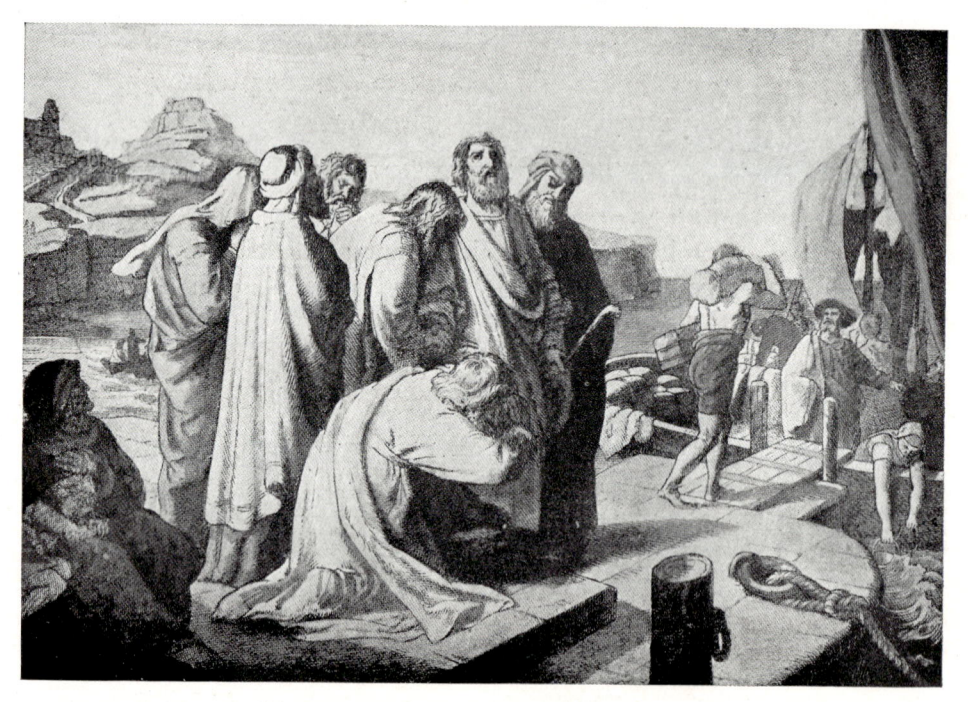

PAUL PARTING FROM THE ELDERS AT MILETUS.

manufacture of fine clothing. This is not silly self-praise, but an earnest warning against avarice.

"Yea, ye yourselves know that these hands have ministered unto my necessities and to them that were with me. I have showed you all things, how that so laboring ye ought to support the weak and to remember the words of the Lord Jesus, how He Himself said, 'It is more blessed to give than to receive.'"

The great philanthropist George Peabody said: "It is sometimes hard for one who has devoted the best part of his life to the accumulation of money to spend it for others; but practise it and keep practising it, and I assure you it comes to be a pleasure." Said a church-member, "The more I give, the more I like to give."

When Paul had thus spoken, he kneeled down and prayed with them all. And they all wept sore and fell on Paul's neck and showered him with kisses, sorrowing most of all for the words which he spake that they should see his face no more. And they went with him to the ship.

## FROM MILETUS TO JERUSALEM.
### Acts 21, 1—16.

Tearing himself away from his friends, Paul sailed with a straight course by Patmos, a pile of rocks like a horse's neck, twenty-eight miles around, to which the Emperor Domitian banished the evangelist John.

On Sunday, May 1, they came to Cos, a garden island, famous for its potteries, wines, silks, and salves; it was of special interest to Luke, for it was the great medical school of Aesculapius and the birthplace of Hippocrates, the first scientific physician. At this famous little place, forty miles south of Miletus, the sailors furled the sails for the night. Opposite is Halicarnassus with the Mausoleum, one of the seven wonders of the ancient world.

PATMOS.

Next day they rounded the Point of Cnidus, famous for its Venus by Praxiteles, for which the abandoned Phryne had posed. They made Rhodes, "the land of roses." The city was built by Hippodamus, the builder of the streets of Piraeus, and was famous for its ship-building, celebrated by Pliny. Here Herod the Great, the Jew, built the beautiful Pythium, a temple of Apollo! Among the three thousand statues was the Colossus of Apollo, 105 feet high, one of the seven wonders of the ancient world, built by Chares of Lindos about three hundred years before. After fifty years an earthquake toppled it over, and Paul could see only the legs on the pedestal, the huge body of bronze lying along the port. In 672 a Jewish junk dealer bought the metal, and nine hundred camels carried away the 720,000 pounds. Theodorus of Gadara, the teacher of Tiberius, had taught in the famous schools of Rhodes. In later years 60,000 Knights of St. John stood out against 200,000 warriors of Solyman the Magnificent.

On the next morning the snowy peaks of Lycia rose to the north, and

RHODES.

the ship headed for the seven capes, pushing out from the green slopes of the Cragus into the sea. Skirting these cliffs and the mouths of yellow Xanthus, they sighted Patara amidst the palms with its famous temple of Apollo and its theater carved from the rock. Here they went on shore, Tuesday, May 3.

Taking another ship, they left Cyprus on the left and landed at Tyre, 340 miles from Patara, made in about two days. Tyre is famous from the startling journey of Jonah; for here, so legend says, he was cast up on the yellow sand. King Hiram of Tyre built the splendid breakwaters and furnished the lumber for Solomon's Temple. 1 Kings 5. His tomb is near the city. Nebuchadnezzar, for thirteen long years, laid unavailing siege to the city and finally was forced to make a treaty of peace with her king. King Ahab married Jezebel of Tyre. 1 Kings 16, 31. Ezekiel prophesied the ruin of the "Joyous City," the "Crowning City." Ezek. 27 and 28; Is. 23, 7. Alexander the Great built a causeway to Tyre on the island,

RUINS OF ANCIENT TYRE.

and it finally fell a terrible victim to his long-baffled rage. Our Savior came into the coasts of Tyre and mentions the city in the warning of Judgment. Matt. 15, 21; 11, 21.

Here Paul tarried seven days while the ship was unloading her cargo, May 7—13. Paul used the time to seek out the Christians at Tyre, who told him through the Spirit that he should not go up to Jerusalem. But Paul would not be turned aside. "We departed and went our way; and they all brought us on our way, with wives and children, till we were out

TYRE.

UNDERWOOD & UNDERWOOD. PTOLEMAIS.

of the city; and we kneeled down on the shore and prayed. And when we had taken our leave one of another, we took ship, and they returned home again."

Even the children went with their parents to see the Apostle off on his voyage and bid him Godspeed. This reveals a new trait in the lovable character of the great church-builder. It reminds us of Luther, the mightiest man of battle and yet the writer of the most exquisite letter to little Johnny.

THE PROPHECY OF AGABUS.

In days of old Tyre was a glorious city, but now?

> Dim is her glory, gone her fame,
>   Her boasted wealth has fled,
> On her proud rock — alas her shame! —
>   The fisher's net is spread.
> The Tyrian harp has slumbered long,
>   And Tyrian mirth is low;
> The timbrel, dulcimer, and song
>   Are hushed or wake to woe. — *W. M. Thomson.*

From Tyre they came to Ptolemais, one of the oldest seaports in the world, the Accho of Judg. 1, 31. It was besieged by the Egyptians before

THE MOUNT OF OLIVES, FROM MOUNT ZION.

the days of Joseph; Sennacherib and Esarhaddon brought their armies against the city. Cleopatra was its queen. Vespasian and Titus took it. It was known as St. Jean D'Acre when the Crusaders Baldwin I and the lion-hearted King Richard conquered it. In 1799 Bonaparte bombarded it in vain against Sir Sidney Smith.

In this famous port Paul spent Saturday with the Christians.

They made the thirty miles to Caesarea and spent Sunday in the house of Philip the evangelist, who was one of the seven "deacons." Acts 6, 5. This house was standing in Jerome's day and shown even in the time of Bede. Philip had four daughters, virgins, who did prophesy.

And as we tarried there many days, there came down from Judea a certain prophet, named Agabus. And when he was come unto us, he took Paul's girdle and bound his own hands and feet and said: "Thus saith the Holy Ghost, 'So shall the Jews at Jerusalem bind the man that owneth this girdle and shall deliver him into the hands of the Gentiles.'"

And when we heard these things, both we and they of Caesarea besought Paul not to go up to Jerusalem.

Then Paul answered, "What mean ye to weep and break mine heart? For I am ready not to be bound only, but also to die at Jerusalem for the name of the Lord Jesus Christ." And when he would not be persuaded, we ceased, saying, "The will of the Lord be done."

Tender and true! Sensitive and self-sacrificing!

So Luther would not be kept from Worms, though the fate of Hus and Savonarola was held up to him; he would go, should there be as many devils there as tiles on the roofs. So Duerer's wonderful knight rides on with set face and fixed eyes, heedless of Death and Satan, trying to hinder him.

> He saw a hand they could not see
> Which beckoned him away;
> He heard a voice they could not hear
> Which would not let him stay.

After those days we packed up our baggage and saddled and went up to Jerusalem, sixty-four miles away. There went up with us also certain of the disciples of Caesarea and brought us to one Mnason of Cyprus, an early disciple, a charter member of the church, with whom we should lodge. After lodging with Mnason Thursday night, Paul reached Jerusalem on Friday, May 27, the day before Pentecost.

## CHAPTER VI.

## PAUL'S IMPRISONMENT AT CAESAREA.

*Acts 21, 17—36.*

O comrade bold, of toil and pain!
  Thy trial, how severe,
When severed first by prisoner's chain
  From thy loved labor sphere!
Say, did impatience first impel
  The heaven-sent bond to break?
Or could'st thou bear its hindrance well,
  Loitering for Jesus' sake? — *J. H. Newman.*

WHEN Paul arrived at Jerusalem for Pentecost on Friday, May 27, 57, the brethren received him gladly. Next day he went to James, with his long white hair falling on his long white robe; and all the elders were present. When Paul had saluted them, he reported in detail what things God had wrought among the Gentiles by his labors. As living fruits of these labors he joyfully pointed to his companions, Luke, Timothy of Lystra, Sopater of Berea, Aristarchus and Secundus of Thessalonica, Gaius of Derbe, Tychicus and Trophimus of Ephesus, now all Christians, from far-away foreign cities.

For these men it was a proud moment in their lives as they now stepped up as a committee and brought forward their leather bags with the money collected for years by Paul's heathen converts for the poor Christians at Jerusalem, whence themselves had received the Gospel of their salvation.

When James and the elders heard it, they glorified the Lord. But they hastily said to Paul: "Thou seest, brother, how many thousands of Jews there are which believe; and they are all zealous for the Law, and they are informed of thee that thou teachest all the Jews who are among the Gentiles to forsake Moses, saying that they ought not to circumcise their children, neither to walk after the customs. What is it therefore? The multitude must needs come together, for they will hear that thou art come."

That would mean accusation, probably violence, possibly death. What would Paul do about it? James was ready with a way out: —

"Do, therefore, this thing that we say to thee. We have four men who have a vow on them. Them take and purify thyself with them and pay their expenses that they may shave their heads — and thus be freed

CASTLE ANTONIA.
Showing Paul speaking to the people. Mount of Olives in background.

from their vow; and thus all may know that those things whereof they were informed concerning thee are nothing, but that thou thyself also walkest orderly and keepest the Law. As touching the Gentiles who believe, we have written and concluded that they observe no such thing, save only that they keep themselves from things offered to idols, and from blood, and from strangled, and from fornication."

Paying the expenses of poor Nazirites was a popular work of charity. Returning to Jerusalem after escaping many dangers, King Agrippa paid out of his private purse the cost of shaving several Nazirites. With four paupers Paul was to stand in the Temple court, oil cake in hand, and then offer five lambs for a burnt offering, five ewes for a sin-offering, five rams, and five baskets of unleavened bread for a thank-offering, the necessary meat-offering and drink-offering, and finally burn the shaved hair in the fire of the altar under the boiling caldron of the peace-offering. Not being a matter of principle, but prudence; not law, but love; patience with the prejudice of Jewish Christians, the advice was taken.

Then Paul took the men, and the next day, purifying himself with them, entered into the Temple to signify the end of the days of purification, until that an offering should be offered for every one of them. When the seven days were almost ended, the Jews who were of Asia, when they saw him in the Temple, stirred up all the people and laid hands on him, crying out: "Men of Israel, help! This is the man that teacheth all men everywhere against the people and the Law and this place; and furthermore brought Greeks also into the Temple and hath polluted this holy place." They had seen Trophimus, an Ephesian, with Paul in the city and at once supposed Paul had brought the Gentile into the Temple also, which was against the rules.

Under the Palestine Exploration Society, M. Clermont Ganneau discovered in the Via Dolorosa a sign which reads: "No Gentile is to enter within the balustrade and fence around the Temple. If any one is taken in the act, let him know that he has himself to blame for the penalty of death that follows."

With such a warning staring him in the face, Paul would not recklessly take a Gentile into the forbidden enclosure. But it was a good accusation. It gave the Jews an excuse for killing Paul for a crime according to their own law without interference from the Roman authorities, even though he was a Roman citizen. This right was conceded by General

PAUL'S IMPRISONMENT AT CAESAREA.

PAUL RESCUED FROM THE JEWISH MOB BY THE CHIEF CAPTAIN CLAUDIUS LYSIAS.

Titus in a speech a few years later, according to Josephus (*Jewish War*, VI, 2). The gathering crowd would put Paul to death at once, but not in the Holy Place, and so they first dragged him out of the grounds and shut the doors and then went about to kill him.

The sentinel on the Tower of Antonia, in the northwest corner of the Temple place, noticed the gathering mob and at once alarmed the garrison. The tribune, Claudius Lysias, promptly took soldiers and

PAUL BOUND BY ROMAN SOLDIERS.

centurions and ran down unto them. When the mob saw the chief captain, they quit beating Paul. The tribune came near and laid his hand on Paul, which was a Roman sign that no other hand must touch him, and commanded him to be bound. In a twinkling Roman handcuffs were on Paul's wrists, linked with a light brass chain to the wrist of two soldiers, who died sooner than let him escape or be harmed, for he was a prisoner of Rome. Turning to the crowding mob, Lysias demanded who he was and what he had done. And some cried one thing, some another. When the tribune could not know the certainty for the tumult, he was disgusted and curtly commanded, "To the castle!"

When Paul came upon the stairs, so it was that he was borne of the soldiers for the violence of the people; for the multitude of the people followed after, crying: "Away with him!" As they had crucified Christ, so they would, thirty years after, now kill the apostle of Christ.

## PAUL'S DEFENSE.
### Acts 21, 37—22, 29.

As Paul was to be led into the castle, he said to the chief captain, "May I speak to thee?" He was greatly astonished and said: "Canst thou speak Greek? Art not thou that Egyptian who before these days madest an uproar and leddest out into the wilderness four thousand men that were murderers?" — *sicarii*, dagger-men.

"I am a Jew of Tarsus in Cilicia, a citizen of no mean city, and I beseech thee, suffer me to speak to the people."

When the chief captain had given him leave, Paul stood on the stairs and beckoned with the hand to show he wished to speak. When there was made a great silence, he spake to them in the Hebrew tongue: "Men, brethren, and fathers, hear ye my defense which I make now to you." And when they heard that he spake in the Hebrew tongue to them, they kept the more silence. Chrysostom says: "What nobler spectacle than that of Paul at this moment! There he stands, bound with two chains, ready to make his defense to the people. The Roman commander sits by to enforce order by his presence. An enraged populace looks up to him from below. Yet in the midst of so many dangers, how self-possessed is he, how tranquil!"

1. Paul spoke of his birth and training as a strict Pharisee, with rare courtesy adding, "as ye all are this day."

2. Paul spoke of his persecuting those of "this Way," the Christians, as they well remembered.

3. Paul told of his conversion while engaged in persecution.

4. Paul told of his commission from God Himself to preach the Gospel to the Gentiles.

"Gentiles!" That stung them to the quick. They gave him audience unto this word and then lifted up their voices and shouted: "Away with such a fellow from the earth, for it is not fit that he should live!"

As they cried out and cast off their clothes and threw dust into the air, like demons possessed, the chief captain commanded Paul to be brought into the castle and bade that he should be examined by scourging, so that the chief captain might know wherefore the people cried so against Paul.

As they stripped and stretched him out on the whipping-post to apply the lash, and as they bound him with thongs, Paul said to the centurion that stood by: "Is it lawful for you to scourge a man that is a Roman and uncondemned?"

When the centurion heard that, he went and told the chief captain, saying, "Take heed what thou doest; for this man is a Roman." Then the chief captain came hurriedly and said searchingly: "Tell me, art thou a Roman?"

"Yea."

And the chief captain answered: "With a great sum obtained I this freedom." Judging from his name, he bought his freedom from the wife of Claudius, who made much money in this manner, as Dio Cassius reports.

Paul replied, and we catch the tone of pride, "But I was free born."

Sudden silence ensued as the pompous captain in astonishment stared at the Apostle, and we fancy Luke smiling as he penned this portion.

Cicero, *Against Verres*, says: "It is a heinous sin to bind a Roman citizen; it is a wickedness to beat him; it is next to parricide to kill him and, what shall I say, to crucify him?"

Then straightway the scourgers departed from Paul; and the tribune also was afraid after he knew that Paul was a Roman, and because he had bound Paul and had ordered torture, against the express decree of Augustus. Says Cicero: "How often has this exclamation, 'I am a Roman citizen,' brought aid and safety even among barbarians in the remotest parts of the earth!"

## PAUL BEFORE THE SUPREME COUNCIL.
### Acts 22, 30—23, 15.

On Tuesday morning, because he would have known the certainty wherefore Paul was accused by the Jews, the tribune loosed Paul from his bands and commanded the chief priests and all their council to appear; and brought Paul down and set him before them. The Emperor Caligula had restored to the Sanhedrin the judging of all religious questions in the "Hall of Xystus."

Paul earnestly beheld the Sanhedrin. Jesus had stood there. John and Peter had stood there when Gamaliel advised to free them. Stephen had stood there and was sent to his death, Paul consenting to his death. Paul perhaps had sat there on his crimson cushion plotting against the Christians. Now Paul himself stood there a criminal at that bar. Perhaps he there saw Simon and Joshua, sons of his old teacher Gamaliel, and the sons of the great Sadducee Ananias, the hater of Jesus.

Paul began: "Men and brethren, I have lived in all good conscience before God until this day."

The high priest Ananias commanded them that stood by him to smite Paul on the mouth for his blasphemy. Then said Paul to him: "God shall smite thee, thou whited wall; for sittest thou to judge me after the Law and commandest me to be smitten contrary to the Law?" "Whited wall" is a proverbial phrase meaning a hypocrite covering his malice with a show of piety.

They that stood by said: "Revilest thou God's high priest?"

Then said Paul: "I wist not, brethren, that it was the high priest; for it is written: 'Thou shalt not revile the ruler of thy people.'" Ex. 22, 8. 9. 28; Deut. 17, 8—13; Ps. 82, 1.

Ananias was appointed about ten years before by Herod. In 52 he was accused by the Samaritans and brought to Rome for trial. He was acquitted and returned and held his office, in all, eleven years — a long period at that time. As the meeting was informal, Ananias did not wear the usual white robe of the high priest, and therefore Paul did not recognize him as such.

Josephus also notes the avarice and cruelty of Ananias. Later his house was burned in a sedition raised by his own son; he was drawn out from his hiding-place and slain by the *sicarii*, the assassins. He would have Paul killed by assassins; he was himself killed by assassins. Paul's prophecy came true.

When Paul perceived that the one part were Sadducees and the other Pharisees, he cried out in the Council: "Men and brethren, I am a Pharisee, the son of a Pharisee. Of the hope and resurrection of the dead I am called in question." When he had so said, there arose a dissension between the Pharisees and the Sadducees; and the multitude was divided. For the Sadducees say that there is no resurrection, neither angel, nor spirit; but the Pharisees confess both.

And there arose a great cry, and the scribes that were of the Pharisees' part arose and strove, saying: "We find no evil in this man; but if a spirit or an angel hath spoken to him, let us not fight against God."

And when there arose a great dissension, the tribune, fearing lest Paul should have been pulled in pieces of them, commanded the soldiers to go down and take him by force from among them and to bring him into the castle. The castle of the conqueror the only safe spot in all Jerusalem for the greatest living Jew!

*The Cheer.* — The night following the Lord stood by him and said: "Be of good cheer, Paul; for as thou hast testified of Me in Jerusalem, so must thou bear witness also at Rome."

*The Conspiracy.* — When it was day, certain of the Jews banded together and bound themselves under a curse, saying that they would neither eat nor drink till they had killed Paul. They were more than forty that had made this conspiracy. They came to the chief priests and elders, and said: "We have bound ourselves under a great curse that we will eat nothing until we have slain Paul. Now, therefore, ye with the Council signify to the chief captain that he bring Paul down to you to-morrow, as though ye would inquire something more perfectly concerning him, and we, or ever he come near, are ready to kill him."

This is amazing to us; it was quite natural to them. It was a rule among the Jews that a private person might kill one who had forsaken the Law of Moses, and that was the accusation against Paul. Josephus tells us ten Jews had sworn to assassinate their King Herod the Great, whom they held an apostate from the Jewish faith. Philo was one of the purest teachers outside of the New Testament, yet he says: "It is highly proper that all who have a zeal for virtue should have a right to punish with their own hands, without delay, those who are guilty of this crime" — falling away from Judaism.

## PAUL, THE PRISONER, BROUGHT TO CAESAREA.
### Acts 23, 16—35.

The conspiracy was carefully and cleverly concocted, yet it was promptly checked. When Paul's sister's son heard of their lying in wait, he went and entered into the castle and told Paul. Then Paul called one of the centurions to him and said: "Bring this young man to the tribune, for he hath a certain thing to tell him." So the centurion took Paul's

**ANCIENT CAESAREA.**

Breakwater with turrets topped with statues, the Sebasteum (circular temple), to the right of it the Praetorium, the former royal palace, where Paul was imprisoned, and the amphitheater.

nephew and brought him to the chief captain and said: "Paul, the prisoner, called me unto him and prayed me to bring this young man unto thee, who hath something to say unto thee."

Then the chief captain took him by the hand and went with him aside privately and asked him: "What is that thou hast to tell me?" And he said: "The Jews have agreed to desire thee that thou wouldst bring Paul down to-morrow into the Council, as though they would inquire somewhat of him more perfectly. But do thou not yield to them; for there lie in wait for him of them more than forty men, who have bound themselves with an oath that they will neither eat nor drink till they have killed him; and now are they ready, looking for a promise from thee."

The chief captain let the young man depart and charged him: "See thou tell no man that thou hast showed these things to me."

Uncle Paul must have been a mighty fine uncle to have so devoted a nephew. "This incident indicates to me just what kind of man Paul was better than all the Pauline literature put together," says breezy Wm. H. Ridgeway.

Lysias called two centurions: "Make ready 200 infantry to go to Caesarea and 70 heavy cavalry and 200 lancers, or light cavalry, at the third hour of the night — 9 P. M. — and provide horses for Paul and his guard and bring him safe to Felix, the Procurator."

He wrote his *elogium,* or judiciary report, after this manner: —

"Claudius Lysias, to the most excellent governor Felix, greeting!

"This man was taken of the Jews and should have been killed by them; then came I with an army and rescued him, having understood that he was a Roman. And when I would have known the cause wherefore they accused him, I brought him forth in their Council; whom I perceived to be accused of questions of their Law, but to have nothing laid to his charge worthy of death or of bonds. And when it was told me how the Jews laid wait for the man, I sent him straightway to thee and gave commandment to his accusers also to say before thee what they had against him. Farewell."

Captain Claudius may have been a bluff Roman soldier, he was surely a diplomatic letter-writer. He very conveniently forgot to write that he had arrested Paul, mistaking him for a notorious rebel. He forgot to mention the order to scourge Paul, a Roman citizen; yes, he wants to make it appear he rescued Paul because he knew him for a Roman citizen, although he had found that out later.

PAUL'S APPEAL TO CÆSAR

Acts 25:11

After about five hours they came to Bethoron, where Joshua had won the great battle against the five Canaanite kings, one of the most magnificent views in all Palestine — beneath them the Plain of Ajalon and Sharon and beyond, the shimmering, silvery sea. This road was traveled by Herod, Pilate, Felix, Festus, Titus, Vespasian, and millions of pilgrims from all the world.

After about four more hours they halted for the night at glorious Antipatris, in a paradise, about forty miles from Jerusalem. At the river Audsche the English and the Turkish armies faced each other so long during 1917 and 1918, and then Allenby marched up this road to capture Jerusalem.

In the morning the infantry return, and the cavalry went on to Caesarea, some twenty-six miles, and delivered the epistle and the apostle to Felix, Wednesday, June 2, 57. When the governor had read the letter, he asked of what province the prisoner was. And when he understood that he was of Cilicia, the governor said: "I will hear thee when thine accusers are also come." And he commanded Paul to be kept in Herod's judgment hall, where he also had his own official residence.

Why would the Governor of Judea try a Roman citizen of Cilicia? As a rule, a prisoner was tried in his birthplace; but the trial could also be held where the crime was committed.

Herod the Great turned the Greek fishing village known as Straton's Tower into a handsome city and called it Caesarea in honor of Augustus. Josephus says: "He drew his model and set people to work, and in twelve years' time finished it. The buildings were all of marble, private houses as well as palaces; but his masterpiece was the port, which he made as large as the Piraeus of Athens — a safe station against all winds and weathers." Immense blocks of stone, fifty feet long, were sunk to twenty fathoms, on the south and southwest, to form a breakwater, leaving a free passage only by the north. This pier had a walk a hundred feet wide bristling with towers, one very imposing and named Drusion, after a member of the imperial family.

Famous for its harbor, Caesarea became the port of Jerusalem; the road of seventy-five miles was splendidly paved with huge blocks of stone, still traced down the mountain slopes. Aqueducts brought water from Mount Carmel, twenty-five miles to the north, and from the Crocodile River.

Herod also dedicated a temple to Augustus, remarkable for its size and splendor, with a colossal statue of the Emperor, not inferior to the Jupiter Olympus, after which it was modeled, and another statue of the Goddess Roma. He also built a forum, and a stadium, and an amphitheater, and a gorgeous palace, and dedicated the city in the year 10 B. C.

Agrippa left Jerusalem for Caesarea to celebrate with games the safe return of Claudius from his triumphs in Britain, July, 43 — January, 45. His robe, made wholly of silver, was dazzling in the bright rays of the morning sun, and the people cried out: "It is the voice of a god and not of a man!" And immediately the angel of the Lord smote him because he gave not God the glory; and he was eaten of worms and gave up the ghost. Acts 12, 20—23, and Josephus. He gave up the ghost in the palace within a week, during which time the Jews, in the dust under his windows, prayed for the life of their "pious" king.

Around this palace the Jews from Jerusalem cried for six days and nights, "Take them away!" — the little silver figures of the emperor on the Roman standards in Jerusalem, by which their holy city was defiled. At last Pilate met them in the theater and sent his soldiers with swords, prepared to slaughter them. The Jews went down on their knees, baring their throats, willing to die rather than have their laws broken. Pilate wavered and in deep disgust let them have their way.

Here also were large synagogs of the Jews, who were so numerous that 20,000 were slain in the streets after Jerusalem was taken by Titus.

Herod's palace was also the Praetorium, the residence of the Roman governor of Judea. The palace was also a prison, and the historian Josephus, when twenty-six, visited priests who lived on figs and nuts, refusing the "unclean" prison fare. In this prison Paul lived from June, 57, to June, 59.

## PAUL BEFORE FELIX.

### Acts 24, 1—26.

Owing his throne to the efforts of the Jew Agrippa II, the Emperor Claudius naturally favored the Israelites. He ordered the Roman officials to respect the Jewish worship and pay it public homage and yearly sacrifice in the Temple in his name. When the high priest Jonathan and the Empress Agrippina seconded the efforts of the Emperor's favorite freedman Pallas to have his brother Antonius Felix, a slave of Antonia, the mother of Claudius, follow Cumanus as governor of Judea, Claudius made the appointment, held from 52—59, though the usual term was only two or three years.

The Jewish rebellion Felix stamped out for the time being by promptly using the utmost cruelty. When the high priest Jonathan protested against his outrages, Felix hired murderers to kill the priest in the very Temple.

In private life he was as bad as in public. Suetonius calls this former slave the husband of three queens. One is not known to us; the second was Drusilla, daughter of King Juba of Mauritania and granddaughter of Antony and Cleopatra; the third was also named Drusilla, the sister of Agrippa II and wife of King Azizus of Emesa, who had turned Jew for her. The charms of the fair Jewess fired the lust of the lewd Felix, and he simply hired the Cyprian sorcerer Simon to get her to leave her husband and live with the brother of Nero's mighty minister Pallas. Felix and Drusilla were living in adultery at Caesarea at this time. She and their son Agrippa perished in the eruption of Vesuvius during the reign of Titus in 79.

The Roman historian Tacitus writes: "In the practise of all kinds of cruelty and lust he exercised the power of a king with the temper of a slave.... He did not think it needful to put any restraint on his desires, but considered his connection with the emperor's favorite as a license for the worst of crimes." (*Annals,* 12, 54; *History,* 5, 9.) Such the judge of Paul.

A speedy trial was a rule of the Roman courts, and so five days after Paul's removal from Jerusalem the high priest Ananias and a lawyer named Tertullus, probably a young Roman practising in the province for practise in the Roman Forum, came down to Caesarea, Sunday, June 6.

*The Accusation.* — When Paul was called forth, Tertullus opened for the prosecution; and he did so very, very shrewdly. Had he left out the usual compliments, he would have offended the judge; had he praised the judge overmuch, he would have offended his clients, who heartily hated Felix. So he sailed on a safe sea by praising the governor for the order he kept in the province.

"Seeing that by thee we enjoy much peace, and that evils are corrected for this nation by thy providence, we accept it always and in all places, most noble Felix, with all thankfulness. Notwithstanding, that I be not further tedious unto thee, I pray thee that thou wouldest hear us of thy clemency a few words."

*The First Charge: Sedition.* — "We have found this man a pestilent fellow and a mover of sedition among all the Jews throughout the world."

This first count was a very serious offense against Roman law and rule and amounted to high treason and therefore placed Paul in great peril.

*The Second Charge: Sectarianism.* — "A ringleader of the sect of the Nazarenes."

*The Third Charge: Sacrilege.* — "Who also hath gone about to profane the Temple; whom we took and would have judged according to our Law. But the chief captain, Lysias, came upon us and with great violence

PAUL BEFORE FELIX AND DRUSILLA.    WILLIAM HOGARTH.

took him away out of our hands, commanding his accusers to come unto thee, by examining of whom thyself mayest take knowledge of all these things whereof we accuse him."

And the Jews assented, saying that these things were so.

*The Vindication.* — Then Paul, after that the governor had beckoned unto him to speak, answered: —

"Forasmuch as I know that thou hast been many years a judge unto this nation, I do the more cheerfully answer for myself."

After this tactful and truthful introduction Paul takes up the charges in order.

*The First Charge: Sedition.* — "There are yet but twelve days since I went up to Jerusalem for to worship. And they neither found me in the Temple disputing with any man, neither raising up the people, neither in the synagog, nor yet in the city. Neither can they prove the things whereof they now accuse me."

Only twelve days, and five of these were used to arrest him and keep him in Caesarea. Raise an insurrection in those few days? Absurd on the face of it! The simple statement of the facts refutes the charge.

*The Second Charge: Sectarianism.* — "But this I confess to thee, that after the Way which they call heresy, so worship I the God of my fathers, believing all things which are written in the Law and in the prophets, and have hope toward God, which they themselves also allow, that there shall be a resurrection of the dead, both of the just and unjust. And herein do I exercise myself to have always a conscience void of offense toward God and toward men."

*The Third Charge: Sacrilege.* — "Now, after many years I came to bring alms to my nation and offerings. Whereupn certain Jews from Asia found me purified in the Temple, neither with multitude nor with tumult. Who ought to have been here before thee and object if they had aught against me. Or else let these same here say if they have found any evil doing in me while I stood before the Council, except it be for this one voice, that I cried standing among them: 'Touching the resurrection of the dead I am called in question by you this day.'"

*The Procrastination.* — Felix knew the accusation was false; he knew the vindication was complete. He knew Paul was innocent, and the judgment should have been, "Not guilty; the prisoner is discharged."

Not so. In order to please the Jews, Felix adjourned the case and gave as an excuse, "When Lysias, the chief captain, shall come down, I will know the uttermost of your matter."

Felix commanded a centurion to keep Paul and to let him have liberty and that he should forbid none of Paul's acquaintance to minister or to come to him. No doubt Philip, the "deacon," and others visited him.

The bearing and speech of Paul must have made a deep impression on Felix, and so after certain days, when he came with his wife Drusilla, who was a Jewess, he sent for Paul and heard him concerning the faith in Christ.

What a congregation — Felix and Drusilla!

What a preacher — St. Paul!

What a sermon — righteousness, chastity, and Judgment to come!

The effect? Felix trembled. His conscience confirmed the truth of God's Word as preached by Paul. Did he repent? "Go thy way for this time; when I have a convenient season, I will call for thee." Felix sent God away, put Him off till a more convenient time — which never came. He preferred his sins to his soul! He lost his soul and also his sinful pleasures.

> The Apostle spake of Judgment, just,
>   And certain unto men as death;
> Prince Felix felt as if the thrust
>   Of deadly arrows stayed his breath:
> "I'll hear thee at convenient time,"
>   He said, his terror to dissemble;
> But when can guilt conveniently
>   Invite the truth that makes it tremble?

"To-morrow and to-morrow creeps in this petty pace from day to day to the last syllable of recorded time; and all our yesterdays have lighted fools the way to dusty death." — *Macbeth*.

> To-morrow, he promised his conscience,
>   To-morrow I mean to believe,
> To-morrow I'll think as I ought to,
>   To-morrow my Savior receive;
> To-morrow I'll conquer the habits
>   That hold me from heaven away.
> But ever his conscience repeated
>   One word, and one only — "To-day!"
> To-morrow, to-morrow, to-morrow,
>   Thus day after day it went on,
> To-morrow, to-morrow, to-morrow,
>   Till youth like a vision was gone,
> Until age and his passion have written
>   The message of fate on his brow,
> And forth from the shadows came death
>   With the pitiless syllable — "Now!"

Like Felix, many more have trembled, but not repented; the "convenient season" never came, and they went to their doom. "To-day, if ye will hear His voice, harden not your hearts." Ps. 95, 7; Heb. 3, 8. 14.

> Procrastination is the thief of time.
> Year after year it steals till all are fled,
> And to the mercies of a moment leaves
> The vast concern of an eternal time. — *Young*.

Felix also hoped Paul would give him money to set him free. For this reason he sent for Paul the oftener and talked with him. This was directly against the Julian law *De Repetundis,* expressly forbidding a judge receiving anything for a person's imprisonment or liberation. Like Felix then, so some to-day try to get money out of the preacher, out of the Church, out of Christ. Some join the Church with business schemes, for revenue only.

The Jews claimed Caesarea as a Jewish city, for Herod had built it. The Syrians said Herod had built for the Gentiles, and so they claimed it. The Jewish Josephus admits: "The Jewish inhabitants, who were proud of their wealth and despised the Syrians, pursued the latter with insults to provoke them to acts of violence." There was street-fighting almost every evening. When Felix hastened to disperse the mob, the Jews committed further outrage. Then the Procurator charged them with his soldiers and killed many, and gave up the houses of the ringleaders for plunder. He referred the dispute to the emperor.

Claudius had been murdered by the poisoned mushrooms of his loving wife Agrippina, and Nero was the new emperor. Nero's mistress was Poppaea, a Jewish proselyte, and she procured the recall of Felix. Before quitting Palestine, "he left Paul in chains" to please the Jews and make them a bit lenient in their charges against him. He sent priests in chains to Rome, where they languished in prison for three years before Josephus got them freed.

Pallas had been banished in 56, and the new imperial treasurer, Claudius Etruscus, passed for a loyal minister, who would deal sharply with his subordinates. Felix barely escaped death, but he had to disgorge his great wealth. He died in obscurity.

Cornelius had sent for Peter to Caesarea (chap. 10); Felix left Paul in chains in Caesarea, — one Roman soldier condemns the other Roman soldier.

## PAUL BEFORE FESTUS.

*Acts 24, 27—25, 12.*

Porcius Festus, the new governor, came to Caesarea in the year 59 and already after three days went up to Jerusalem to get to know the people he was to rule.

The new high priest, named Ishmael, appointed by Agrippa II in 59, and the chief of the Jews informed Festus against Paul and besought him and desired favor against him that he would send for Paul to Jerusalem, laying wait in the way to kill him. But Festus replied: "It is not the manner of the Romans to deliver any man to die before that he who is accused have the accusers face to face and have license to answer for himself concerning the crime laid against him. Therefore Paul shall be kept at Caesarea, and I shall myself depart shortly thither, when the chief men among you may accompany me and accuse the prisoner, if there be any wickedness in him."

CAESAREA. ST. PAUL'S PRISON.

After ten days Festus returned to Caesarea and the very next day held court to try Paul.

*A New Trial.* — The Jews who came down from Jerusalem stood round about and laid many grievous complaints against Paul, which they could not prove. Paul answered for himself: "Neither against the law of the Jews, neither against the temple nor yet against Caesar have I offended anything at all." But Festus, willing to do the Jews a pleasure, answered Paul: "Wilt thou go up to Jerusalem and there be judged of these things before me?"

Paul replied: "I stand at Caesar's judgment-seat, where I ought to be judged. To the Jews have I done no wrong, as thou very well knowest. For if I be an offender or have committed anything worthy of death, I refuse not to die. But if there be none of these things whereof these accuse me, no man may deliver me unto them. I appeal unto Caesar."

Then Festus: "Hast thou appealed unto Caesar? Unto Caesar shalt thou go." Every Roman citizen had the right to appeal to Caesar against the tyranny of provincial magistrates, and the *Lex Julia* strictly forbade needless delay in bringing the case before the court at Rome. Suetonius tells us when Galba governed Spain, he refused an appeal. Mommsen shows an appeal had to be allowed by the governor. This one was allowed; so Festus thought this an important case.

*King Agrippa Drawn into the Case.* — While Agrippa II was basking in the Claudian favor at Rome, his father Herod Agrippa I, in the midst of pomp and pride, was smitten with a dread disease and died a disgraceful death at Caesarea.

On the score of Agrippa's youth — sixteen years — the emperor excused himself from keeping his promise to give Agrippa his father's kingdom and sent Cuspius Fadus as procurator to Judea, which thus became a Roman province in the year 44. Four years longer Agrippa lived in such debauchery in Rome that even the pagan satirist Juvenal spoke scathingly of his scandalous life. On the death of his uncle Herod he received the little province of Chalcis in 48, with the right of overseeing the Temple and appointing the high priest. In 52 he received the tetrarchy of Philip; in 55, various other cities. His yearly income was about $125,000, — not so bad for those days.

The eldest daughter of Agrippa I, Bernice, was famous for her dazzling beauty and notorious for her immorality. After a brief betrothal to a nephew of Philo she was married to her uncle, King Herod of Chalcis, to whom she bore two sons. She became a widow at twenty-one and lived with her brother Agrippa in incest.

This precious pair fared forth from Caesarea Philippi to Caesarea Stratonis to pay a state visit to congratulate the new procurator on his promotion. When they had been there many days, Festus spoke of Paul's case to Agrippa: "They brought none accusation of such things as I supposed, but had certain questions against Paul of their own superstition and of one Jesus, who was dead, whom Paul affirmed to be alive."

CAESAREA.

Then Agrippa said to Festus: "I would also hear the man myself." "To-morrow thou shalt hear him."

In Athens, Paul had seen the stone statue of Bernice; in Caesarea he was to see her in the flesh.

*The Pomp of the Royal Court.* — On the morrow, when Agrippa was come and Bernice, with great pomp, and was entered into the place of hearing, with the chief captains and principal men of the city, at Festus' command Paul was brought forth. Great pomp, indeed, was seen by Paul. Festus and his court, King Agrippa II and Queen Bernice, in all the gaudy splendor of Oriental royalty. The Fifth, Tenth, and Fifteenth Legions of the line, besides five cohorts, or auxiliary troops, with squadrons of cavalry, were usually stationed at Caesarea, and the gleaming armor and gay attire of the army officers with the furred gowns and flowing robes of the municipal officials, must have presented a picturesque spectacle.

Festus said: "King Agrippa, and all men who are here present with us, ye see this man about whom all the multitude of the Jews have dealt with me, both at Jerusalem and also here, crying that he ought not to live any longer. But when I found that he had committed nothing worthy of death and that he himself hath appealed unto Augustus, I have determined to send him. Of whom I have no definite charge to write to my lord. Wherefore I have brought him forth before you, and specially before thee, O King Agrippa, that, after examination had, I might have somewhat to write. For it seemeth to me foolish to send a prisoner and not withal to signify the crimes laid against him."

Luke has been criticized for making Festus call Nero *kurios* (lord), saying that title was not given to the emperor till the time of Domitian, after Paul's days. But recovered records prove it was already given to Claudius and very commonly to Nero. Again the critics are wrong, again Luke is right.

## PAUL BEFORE KING AGRIPPA.

*Acts 25, 13 — 26, 32.*

Then Agrippa said to Paul: "Thou art permitted to speak for thyself."

Paul stretched forth the hand, in the manner of Greek orators, and answered for himself: "I think myself happy, King Agrippa, because I shall answer for myself this day before thee touching all the things whereof I am accused of the Jews, especially because I know thee to be an expert in all customs and questions which are among the Jews; wherefore I beseech thee to hear me patiently." This is not flattery or a mere compliment. Rabbinical writers note Agrippa's knowledge of the Jewish law.

Paul again told the story of his youth and his conversion and labors among the Gentiles and went on: "Having therefore obtained help of God, I continue unto this day, witnessing both to small and great, saying none other things than those which the prophets and Moses did say should come: that Christ should suffer and that He should be the first that should rise from the dead and should show light unto the people and to the Gentiles."

At the mention of the resurrection Festus sneered loudly: "Paul, thou art beside thyself. Much learning doth make thee mad."

Quite natural. Festus was living one life in one world, Paul was living another kind of life in a wholly different world. If Festus was living the life, Paul surely was not, was wasting his life, was mad. But if Paul was not mad, then Festus was. And that is the inference Paul lets Festus draw.

"Paul, thou art mad!" This argument of Festus has been heard many a time since. "Heretic! Fool! Fanatic! Madman! Antichrist!" were the arguments papists hurled at the head of Luther. Many missionaries have heard the same argument. It is the only argument there is against Christianity. In the British House of Commons the mission of William Carey to India was publicly called "the mission of a madman." "Little detachments of maniacs" is what even the Rev. Sydney Smith called foreign missionaries. The great wit had not wit enough to see a great thing.

PAUL BEFORE AGRIPPA.

"I am not mad, most noble Festus, but speak forth the words of truth and soberness. For the King knoweth of these things, before whom also I speak freely; for I am persuaded that none of these things are hidden from him; for this thing was not done in a corner. King Agrippa, believest thou the prophets? I know that thou believest!"

Agrippa said: "With little thou persuadest me to become a Christian."

Agrippa — a Christian! Capital joke. The royal jester was doubtless rewarded by the broad smiles on the faces of his glittering company.

But Paul was not disturbed, and he quickly retorted: "I would to God that, with little or with much, not only thou, but also all that hear me this day were such as I am — except these chains."

"With little thou wouldst make me a Christian," said King Agrippa. Of course, it is little, always is, with people like Agrippa. The argument of Christianity is always too little to convert men like Agrippa to give up their darling sins. The brilliant Senator John Ingalls of Kansas thought the Ten Commandments unpractical for politics. Many a business man wants his family to go to Church, but Christianity is too "little" for him. What sin is he living in?

"Almost" saved is altogether lost. Think it over.

*The Royal Charter* had sailed around the whole world in safety and was then wrecked in Moelfra Bay, on the coast of Wales, in sight of home. The first officer's wife had supper on the table and was awaiting him when she heard of his drowning. Almost home, but drowned!

>  "Almost persuaded," harvest is past!
> "Almost persuaded," doom comes at last!
> "Almost" cannot avail;
> "Almost" is but to fail!
> Sad, sad, that bitter wail —
> "Almost, *but lost!*" — *P. P. Bliss.*

The king rose up and the governor and Bernice and they that sat with them; and when they were gone aside, they talked between themselves, saying: "This man doeth nothing worthy of death or of bonds." Said Agrippa to Festus: "This man might have been set at liberty if he had not appealed unto Caesar."

This was the beginning of the trial to take place before the Supreme Court at Rome and must be regarded as a test case; for if Paul "was acquitted, the issue of the trial was a formal decision by the Supreme Court of the empire that it was permissible to preach Christianity. The trial, therefore, was really a charter of religious liberty, and therein lies its immense importance," says Ramsay.

During his term of office Festus dispersed the *sicarii,* the professional assassins with the dagger. He died in 62.

Agrippa, at the outbreak of the Jewish war, received the Christians into his territory and treated them kindly at Pella. Did the speech of Paul at Caesarea have some effect on the king? He was pro-Roman and after the destruction of Jerusalem lived at Rome till the end of the century.

Origen, the great Christian scholar, lived at Caesarea, and Eusebius, the father of church history, was bishop here. Here Baldwin I found the green crystal vase in the beginning of the twelfth century, which gave rise to the legend of the Holy Grail, the cup used by Christ in the Last Supper. No one has given us a more beautiful version of the story of the Holy Grail than James Russell Lowell as he describes the search of the haughty young nobleman through many lands for the precious cup. At last, after a lifetime of wandering —

> A poor old man, worn out and frail,
> He comes back from seeking the Holy Grail.

He finds a loathsome leper by the brink of the spring, and sharing with him his crust of coarse brown bread and water out of his wooden bowl, he finds that the poor wooden bowl from which he had given the leper drink is itself the true Holy Grail, and the voice of the Christ speaks to him through the leper, saying: —

> Who gives himself with his gifts feeds three:
> Himself, his hungering neighbor, and Me.

## CHAPTER VII.

## PAUL'S JOURNEY TO ROME.

*Acts 27, 1—12.*

AUGUST, 59, TO FEBRUARY, 60.

> Though the strained mast should quiver as a reed
>    And the rent canvas, fluttering, strew the gale,
> Still must I on; for I am as a weed,
>    Flung from the rock, on ocean's foam to sail
> Where'er the surge may sweep, the tempest's breath prevail.
>                                *Lord Byron.*

WHEN the Emperor Vespasian left his son Titus to take Jerusalem, he sailed from Alexandria to Rhodes, traveled through Greece, crossed the Adriatic, and then went through Italy to Rome. And when Titus returned, he sailed in a merchantman and touched at Rhegium and Puteoli. At the end of 61 Josephus made the same journey, but the ship went down with six hundred people.

Why did ships not make a short cut and sail in an almost straight course from Alexandria to Malta and the foot of Italy? The prevailing westerly winds made it almost impossible, and it was safer to go in a roundabout way to Asia Minor and then cross over toward Italy.

*All Aboard!* — In such roundabout way Paul was taken to Rome as a state prisoner, in company with other prisoners, all in charge of Julius, centurion of an Augustan cohort, or Imperial Guard. This was a corps attached to each provincial legion to communicate between the Emperor and his forces abroad, mainly to carry dispatches and convey prisoners. They were known as *Peregrini*, soldiers from abroad, and, when at Rome, were quartered in the Castra Peregrinorum on the Caelian Hill, joining the emperor's palace on the Palatine Hill. Aristarchus, a Macedonian of Thessalonica, and Luke were permitted to go with Paul — perhaps as his slaves, just as Arria, the wife of the Stoic Thrasea Paetus, was allowed to go with him only as his slave from Illyricum to Rome.

*Sail!* — About August 17, 59, they sailed in a ship bound for Adramyttium, near Troas.

SIDON.

## PAUL'S JOURNEY TO ROME. 241

*Refreshments at Sidon.* — The next day we touched at Sidon, sixty-seven miles away, the oldest commercial city of the world. From here Hiram shipped the lumber for Solomon's Temple, and from here came Jezebel, the wicked queen of Ahab. Here Julius courteously treated Paul and gave him liberty to go to his friends to receive medical attention.

*Change Ships at Myra.* — And when we had launched from Sidon, we sailed under Cyprus, to the north of it, because the winds were contrary. When we had sailed over the sea of Cilicia and Pamphylia, we came to

**SIDON.**
Lebanon in the Background.

Myra, a city of Lycia, after fifteen days. Myra seems to have been the great port for the direct cross-sea traffic to the coasts of Syria and Egypt. It was the seat of the sailors' god, to whom they offered their prayers before starting on the direct, long course and paid their vows on their safe arrival. This god survives as St. Nicholas of Myra, the patron saint of sailors. There the centurion found a ship of Alexandria sailing into Italy; and he put us therein. Such a grain freighter, *The Goddess Isis,* was driven by stress of weather into the port of Piraeus, and the Athenians were amazed at her great size. Lucian describes it in *The Ship:* —

"But what a ship it was! The carpenter said it was one hundred and eighty feet long and forty-five feet wide and from the deck down to the pump at the bottom of the hold forty-five and a half feet. And for the rest — what a mast it had! And what a yard it carried! And with what a cable was it sustained! and how gracefully the stern was rounded off, and was surmounted with a golden goose — the sign of a corn ship! And at the other end, how gallantly the prow sprung forward, carrying on either side the goddess after whom the ship was named! And all the rest of the ornament — the painting, and the flaming pennants, and, above all, the anchors, and the capstans, and the windlasses, and the cabin next the

SOUTH COAST OF CRETE.

stern — all appeared to me perfectly marvelous. And the multitude of sailors one might compare to a little army! And it was said to carry corn enough to suffice for a year's consumption for all Attica! And this unwieldy bulk was all managed by that little, shriveled old gentleman with a bald pate, who sat at the helm, twisting about, with a bit of handle, those two ponderous oars on each side which served as rudders."

*On to Fair Havens.* — Leaving Myra, they made slow progress for a hundred and forty miles, for the wind was against them, and bore up to Cnidus, where the Athenian Conon defeated the Spartan Pisander in 394 B. C.

The moment they tried to round the cape, the northwest wind would strike the ship full force, and so they put about and with difficulty rounded the Cape of Salmone, on the east of Crete, and made Fair Havens, where they cast anchor, on the south coast of Crete, five miles west of the city of Lasea, the ruins of which were discovered by the Rev. George Brown on January 16, 1856. Had they tried to double the promontory of Matala a few miles west, the northwester would have blown right into their teeth; and so they remained in the two sheltered bays of Fair Havens, waiting for a favorable wind. The fast of the great Day of Atonement, October 5, was past; in other words, the autumnal equinoctial storms were raging, and sailing was now dangerous and navigation closed for the season after November 11 to February 8.

Telemachus heard Nestor tell how he and Menelaus sailed safely till they saw

> Malea's misty tops arise,
> Sudden the Thunderer blackens all the skies,
> And the winds whistle, and the surges roll
> Mountains on mountains, and obscure the pole.
> The tempest scatters and divides our fleet.

Macaulay says: —

> So flies the spray of Adria
> When the black squall doth blow.

*Paul's Advice.* — A council was held. Julius presided, though only a military officer; but the ship was now in the service of the imperial government. Paul admonished them: "Sirs, I perceive that this voyage will be with hurt and much damage, not only of the lading and ship, but also of our lives."

Nevertheless the centurion believed the master of the ship more than those things which were spoken by Paul; although he was not a mere landsman, but quite a sailor, having already been shipwrecked three times. The fact that Paul, though a prisoner, could give any advice at all shows in what estimation he was held, shows his greatness. It does not need a strong imagination to imagine the jokes the sailors and soldiers cracked at the expense of a preacher advising sailors in the matter of sailing.

*Taking a Chance.* — Because the haven was not commodious to winter in, the more part advised to depart thence also if by any means they might reach Port Phoenix, or Phenice, and to winter there, only a few hours' sail around the Cape of Matala.

## PAUL SHIPWRECKED.
### Acts 27, 13—41.

When the south wind blew softly, supposing that they had obtained their purpose, they left Fair Havens and sailed close to the shore of Crete. But when they reached the cape, there came from the 7,000 feet high Mount Ida a sudden typhonic squall, a northeaster, called Euroclydon, or Euraquilo. "The wind comes down from those mountains fit to blow the ship out of the water," said a skipper to Sir William Ramsay.

*Struck by a "Twister."* — When the ship was seized in this cyclone and whirled around and could not look the wind in the face, we let her drive and ran under a small island named Clauda, or Cauda, now Gozzo, twenty-three miles away. Here the water was a little less rough, and they with much work hoisted aboard the little boat till now in tow. Next they frapped the ship — wound strong cables around her to keep her from straining and springing a leak and sinking.

*A Fearful Run.* — Lastly, fearing lest they should be driven into the Syrtis, — sandbanks at Tripoli, where Aeneas and many others were shipwrecked, — they made all snug, and with her right side to the gale they drifted at the rate of about thirty-six miles in twenty-four hours, and this for about thirteen days makes a fearful run of about four hundred and sixty-eight miles.

And we, being exceedingly tossed with a tempest, the next day lightened the ship; they threw overboard everything they could spare, for the ship had likely sprung a leak in spite of the frapping. On the third day the united passengers and crew "cast out with our own hands the mainyard of the ship," an immense spar nearly as long as the ship, which lightened the vessel to some extent.

*Dreary Darkness.* — And when neither sun nor stars in many days appeared and no small tempest lay on us, all hope that we should be saved was then taken away.

*Exhortation.* — But after long abstinence Paul stood forth in the midst of them and said: "Sirs, ye should have hearkened unto me and not have loosed from Crete and to have avoided this trouble and loss. And now I exhort you to be of good cheer; for there shall be no loss of any man's life among you but of the ship. For there stood by me this night the angel of God, whose I am and whom I serve, saying: 'Fear not, Paul; thou must be brought before Caesar; and, lo, God hath given thee all them that sail with thee.' Wherefore, sirs, be of good cheer; for I believe God that it shall be even as it was told me. Howbeit, we must be cast upon a certain island."

In one of the most dramatic scenes in His picturesque life, Christ said, "Why are ye fearful, O ye of little faith?" Matt. 8, 26. In a similar situation His great Apostle strengthened his fellow-passengers. When all others seemed cowed and cowering, the poor prisoner-preacher Paul comes forth as the strong man to give strength to the others. He is the unconquered captain of his soul, and he virtually captains the captain of the sailors and the captain of the soldiers. As their superior Paul plainly and pointedly rebukes them for having flouted his advice at Fair Havens and for having thus brought all this trouble on them all, and then calmly promises them their lives and anchors his faith in God's Word.

PAUL EXHORTING HIS FELLOW-PASSENGERS TO BE OF GOOD CHEER.

At the edge of a watery grave Paul trusts the Word of God. That is faith. "God is our Refuge and Strength, a very present Help in trouble. Therefore will not we fear, though the earth be removed, and though the mountains be carried into the midst of the sea; though the waters thereof roar and be troubled, though the mountains shake with the swelling thereof." Ps. 46.

> Amid the howling, wintry sea
> We are in port if we have Thee. — *Keble.*

Just so in the troublous times of the Reformation it was the preacher Luther that was the real leader of the leaders of Europe, and he also founded his faith on the Word of God and in the upheaval of the world courageously shouted his famous battle-hymn: —

>A mighty Fortress is our God,
>A trusty Shield and Weapon;
>He helps us free from every need
>That hath us now o'ertaken.

"Fear not, you carry the fortunes of Caesar," said the mighty Julius to the trembling sailor in the Adriatic. "Fear not, you carry the Gospel of Christ," said Paul, in effect, to the panic-struck sailors and soldiers in his boat in the same sea. They were all saved for the sake of the saving Gospel and the Apostle. For the sake of only ten righteous God would have spared even Sodom and Gomorrah; for all the good they enjoy the children of the world are indebted to the children of God.

On the way to the West Indies, Zinzendorf's ship was about to sink in a storm, and in prayer the missionary was assured by God of the safety of the passengers, assured so certainly that he could hearten all on board. On his first trip to China, Hudson Taylor's ship was becalmed and drawn to the shore where cannibals joyfully expected to feast on the helpless passengers. Taylor received assurance his prayer was heard. He told the officers to hoist the sails and was laughed at. After a few moments a breeze sprang up, the sails were set, and the ship sailed to safety.

*Breakers Ahead!* — When the fourteenth night was come, as we were driven up and down the Adria — yes, Adria, and Luke did not fall into error. Ptolemy, the geographer, calls Adria that part of the Mediterranean between Sicily and Crete.

About midnight the shipmen deemed that they drew near to some country — they heard the breakers of the low rocky point of Koura — and sounded and found it twenty fathoms — 120 feet. And when they had gone a little farther, they sounded again and found it fifteen fathoms — 90 feet.

*A Fearful Night.* — Then, fearing lest we should have fallen upon rocks, they cast four anchors out of the stern and wished for the day. So realistic is this chapter that an old sea-captain, on hearing it read, here cried out: "Luff, ye lubbers! Land-lubbers, luff!" Few authors have such a compliment paid them. Reading this chapter in the morning, Lord Nelson anchored his ship by the stern at Copenhagen in 1804.

*Paul Foils a Plot.* — And as the shipmen were about to flee out of the ship, when they had let down the boat into the sea, under color as though they would have cast anchors out of the foreship, Paul said to the centurion and to the soldiers: "Except these abide in the ship, ye cannot be saved." Then the soldiers cut the ropes of the boat and let her fall off.

Where was the captain of the soldiers and the captain of the sailors? The preacher's eagle eye and quick wit saw the danger and saved the day. Paul did not lose heart, nor his head, nor his nerve; he was the soul of that storm-tossed company — captain, chaplain, steward, all in one.

THE BAY OF ST. PAUL, FROM THE SOUTH.
In the center is the island of Salmonetta. At the west "two seas met" and the wreck occurred.

*Encouragement.* — While the day was coming on, Paul besought them all to take meat: "This day is the fourteenth day that ye have tarried and continued fasting, having taken nothing. Wherefore I pray you to take some meat, for this is for your safety; for there shall not a hair fall from the head of any of you."

*A Wonderful Breakfast.* — And when he had thus spoken, he took bread and gave thanks to God in the presence of them all; and when he had broken it, he began to eat. Then were they all of good cheer, and they also took some meat. And when they had eaten enough, they lightened the ship by casting out the wheat into the sea. They cast out the staff of life to save the earthly life, and you will not cast out your earthly junk to save your eternal life?

*Terra Incognita (i. e., unknown land).* — And when it was day, they knew not the land. This is not surprising, for St. Paul's Bay is on the northeastern shore of Malta, out of the usual course of ships. They discovered a bay with a sandy beach, into which they were minded, if it were possible, to thrust in the ship. They cut the ropes and left the anchors in the sea; they dropped the steering paddles and thus controlled the ship; they hoisted the foresail and made for the shore.

*A Shipwreck.* — They drifted rapidly on a ridge where two seas met, between the small island Salmonetta and the mainland. The prow stuck fast in the clay, but the stern went to pieces with the violence of the waves.

*Kill the Prisoners!* — Remembering they were answerable with their lives for their prisoners, the soldiers counseled to kill them, lest any of them should swim out and escape. But the centurion, willing to save Paul, kept the soldiers from their purpose.

ST. PAUL SHIPWRECKED.   DORE'.

*Two Hundred and Seventy-Six Overboard!* — The centurion commanded that they which could swim should cast themselves first into the sea and get to land; and the rest, some on boards and some on broken pieces of the ship.

*All Safe!* — And so it came to pass that they escaped all safe to land, soldiers and sailors, passengers and prisoners, saints and sinners, two hundred and seventy-six souls.

On August 10, 1810, the British frigate *Lively* fell on these same breakers in a dark night and was lost.

When they were escaped, they knew that the island was Melita, or

Malta. Here, some think, Calypso, daughter of Atlas, had enslaved Odysseus, as Homer tells us. In 1530 Charles V gave it to the Knights of St. John, since known as the Knights of Malta, with the Maltese cross, who defended Christendom against the Turks. Also, the Maltese cats come from this island.

*Sympathy from Barbarians.* — On Malta the natives, of Punic origin, from Barbary, showed us uncommon kindness; for they kindled a fire and

ST. PAUL CASTING OFF THE VIPER.

received us, every one, because of the present rain and because of the cold. No doubt the shipwrecked band were refreshed with oranges, figs, and olives, which abound on Malta.

*Stung!* — And when Paul had gathered a bundle of furze-roots and laid them on the fire, there came a viper out by reason of the heat and fastened on his hand. Infidels have denied the presence of serpents on Malta, but in 1820 the Rev. S. S. Wilson killed a serpent near the spot where Paul had shaken one from his hand.

*Paul a Murderer?* — When the rustics saw the beast hang on his hand, they said among themselves: "No doubt this man is a murderer, whom, though he hath escaped the sea, yet Justice hath not suffered to live." Justice, Nemesis, or Zeus, the avenger of wrong. Just as a Greek epigram tells of a criminal saved from a watery grave on the coast of Libya, only to meet his punishment by being killed while asleep by a serpent.

*Surprise.* — But Paul shook off the beast into the fire and felt no harm. Still the natives looked for the time when he should have swollen or fallen down dead suddenly. As Shakespeare says of the asp-bitten Cleopatra —

> Trembling she stood and on the sudden dropped.

*Paul a God?* — After they had looked a great while and saw no harm come to him, the Maltese changed their minds and said that he was a god.

In the case of Paul, God again proved that He protects and provides and preserves; and He has done so many times since. A sorcerer poisoned the food of Nommensen on Sumatra. When it did not hurt the missionary, the sorcerer confessed his crime and asked what he must do to be saved.

*Service.* — Close by was the town, now called Alta Vecchia, the residence of Publius, the Protos of the island, likely a legate of the Propraetor of Sicily. He received us, and lodged us three days courteously. And it came to pass that the father of Publius lay sick with fever and dysentery. To him Paul went in and prayed and laid his hands on him and healed him.

*The First Mission Dispensary.* — So when this was done, others also who had diseases in the island came and received medical treatment; who also honored us with many honors — also money. And when we departed, they loaded us with such things as were necessary. "Thanks, to men of noble minds, is honorable meed," says Shakespeare. "Epicurus says: 'Gratitude is a virtue that has commonly profit annexed to it!' And where is the virtue, say I, that has not? But still the virtue is to be valued for itself and not for the profit that attends it," says Seneca.

> Borne upon the ocean's foam,
> Far from native land and home,
> Midnight's curtain, dense with wrath,
> Brooding o'er our venturous path,
> While the mountain wave is rolling
> And the ship's bell faintly tolling —
> Savior! on the boisterous sea
> Bid us rest secure in Thee.
>
> Blast and surge, conflicting hoarse,
> Sweep us on with headlong force;
> And the bark, with tempest's urge,
> Moans and trembles at their scourge;
> Yet should wildest tempests swell,
> Be Thou near, and all is well —
> Savior! on the stormy sea
> Let us find repose in Thee.

Ramsay writes: "Only the rarest conjunction of favorable circumstances could have brought about such a fortunate ending to their apparently hopeless situation; and one of the completest services that has ever been rendered to New Testament scholarship is James Smith's proof that all these circumstances are united in St. Paul's Bay." Mr. James Smith of Jordan Hill repeatedly sailed the same sea and by careful search found Luke correct in every particular and thinks Luke "at some period of his life exercised his profession at sea. No one unaccustomed to sea-life could have described the events connected with it with such accuracy as he has done." And Dr. Breusing, Director of the Bremen Navigation School, says: "The most valuable nautical document preserved to us from antiquity is the description of the sea-journey and shipwreck of the Apostle Paul. Every seaman recognizes at once that it must have been written by an eyewitness."

It is the most remarkable record of travel which has come down to us from ancient times.

On February 10 the Maltese still celebrate the "Naufragio," the shipwreck, with civic and church processions and joyous cries of "Evviva San Paolo!" "Long live St. Paul!"

At the time of Paul's shipwreck Josephus, the Jewish historian, was also on his way from Palestine to Rome and shipwrecked; out of 600 people 520 were drowned.

## FURTHER PROGRESS TOWARD ROME.
### Acts 28, 10—13.

After three months — from the middle of November to the middle of February — we departed in a ship of Alexandria, which had wintered in the isle, whose sign was *The Twin Brothers,* the Dioscuri, Castor and Pollux, sons of Zeus by Leda, who were translated into the sky and as the "shining stars" had a good influence on the ocean and so were the patron gods of the sailors.

> Safe comes the ship to haven,
>   Through billows and through gales
> If once the Great Twin Brethren
>   Sit shining on the sails.

*Seeing Syracuse.* — After a run of eighty-six miles the ship lay for three days at Syracuse — made up of five cities. The walls were twenty-two miles in circumference, and the city rivaled Carthage in wealth, according to Strabo. Cicero calls it "glorious Syracuse, greatest of Greek cities, and fairest of all cities." It was a colony of Corinth and for years almost mistress of the world. The Athenians besieged it in vain and lost their power forever. After their generals surrendered and were killed, six thousand troops were imprisoned in the caves from which the stones were quarried to build the imperial city. This disastrous expedition under Nicias and Demosthenes has been called the most important event in Greek history by Thucydides. The most interesting of these Latomies, as the quarries are called, is one 200 feet long and 75 feet high, the shape of an S, called

SYRACUSE.

"The Ear of Dionysius," because the slightest whisper can be heard all over, like in the Tabernacle at Salt Lake City, and thus Dionysius could detect the plots of the prisoners. Surely a natural dictaphone. Timoleon was thanked for restoring the liberties to the people from the tyrant Dionysius II. Here is the scene of the friendship of Damon and Pythias. Here some of the tragedies of Aeschylus were first rendered under the eyes of the poet himself. Here Pindar's odes were sung and the idyls of Theocritus chanted. Here is Hiero's altar, 640 feet long and 60 wide, on which 450 oxen were yearly sacrificed to Zeus for the overthrow of the

SYRACUSE.
Greek theater of fifth century B. C. in foreground.

tyrant Thrasybulus. Here the river god Alpheus chased the nymph Arethusa, and Diana changed her into the famed Fountain of Arethusa, where fish play among the papyrus stems. Here are catacombs larger than those at Rome; here was the celebrated statue of Venus Anadyomene. Here the great scientist Archimedes lived and labored and was killed by a soldier when the Romans took the town and brought the rich plunder to Rome to begin to debauch the great city. Archimedes said give him a place to stand, a fulcrum strong enough, and a lever long enough, and he could

RHEGIUM.
Mount Etna across the Strait of Messina.

move the world. What Archimedes wished for and could not do, Paul had and did do.

They say the Gospel was brought here in 44 by Marcian, and Paul preached at the temple of Bacchus, which became the church of San Giovanni. The temple of Minerva, praised by Cicero, is now the cathedral.

*A Strange Sight.* — Beyond Syracuse the eyes of Paul saw a strange sight, his first active volcano, symmetrical, snow-capped Etna, wreathed with its own sulphuric vapors.

*At Rhegium.* — By tacking, they came to Rhegium in Italy and remained one day. This place and Messina across the strait were wrecked by the earthquake of 1908. At Rhegium stands a stately cathedral with the inscription: "By tacking, we came to Rhegium."

*Between Scylla and Charybdis.* — Fifteen miles from Rhegium, Paul saw sticking out from the Italian shore a rock pictured as a fearful monster, barking like a dog, with twelve feet and six long necks, and Vergil says: —

> Then catch one glimpse of Scylla's cell
> And hear those grisly hell-hounds yell.

STRAIT OF MESSINA.

On the Sicilian side Paul saw Charybdis, "a sea monster which three times a day sucks in the sea and discharges it again in a terrible whirlpool," "like water caldroned o'er a furious fire"; "here Charybdis holds her boisterous reign." Homer has it: —

> Dire Scylla there a scene of horror forms,
> And here Charybdis fills the deep with storms.
> Scarce the famed Argo passed these raging floods,
> The sacred Argo, filled with demigods.

Ovid says Scylla was the beautiful daughter of a sea-god, who incurred the jealousy of one of the gods, who then changed her into a sea-monster;

THE RAGGED ROCKS OF SCYLLA TO THE EAST OF THE STRAIT OF MESSINA.
To the west was the Whirlpool of Charybdis.

CAPRI, WITH THE TWELVE VILLAS OF TIBERIUS.

**PAUL'S DEFENCE BEFORE AGRIPPA**

Acts 26:23

a second change made her a rock perilous to sailors. Some poets said Charybdis was an old woman, who devoured cattle of Hercules, and as a punishment Zeus cast her into the sea, where her appetite changed from cattle to ships and sailors.

Despite these dangers the ship set sail in a stiff southern breeze and scudded safely through, and Paul saw the active volcano of Stromboli on one of the Lipari islands.

*Capri.* — Next Paul saw Capri, famous for its blue grotto. It was the home of the Sirens and became the home of the Caesars. Augustus built palaces, baths, and aqueducts there and made it the lovely abode of his old age and left it to Tiberius, who spent his time on this island since the year 27. He built twelve villas, adorned with theaters and statues in groves and gardens, lived a month in each in turn, and turned them into dens of crazy cruelty and debasing debauchery. He gathered the most beautiful women from the whole empire and debauched them in the twelve palaces dedicated to the twelve Olympian gods, especially in the Villa of Jove on Capo, the eastern cape. From a cliff rising to a sheer height of nearly one thousand feet he would hurl his victims, after prolonged tortures, down into the sea. The least suspicion was enough to bring on this fate for slave or senator. Perhaps Pilate thought of this when the Jews threatened, "Thou art not Caesar's friend!" To-day the fisherfolk call this cliff Salto Timberio, the Leap of Tiberius, and they still call him Cattive Timberio, the terrible Tiberius.

TIBERIUS.

## PAUL SETS FOOT ON THE ITALIAN SHORE.
*Acts 28, 13. 14.*

Rounding the promontory with the temple of Minerva, Paul beheld what the poet Shelley calls the most beautiful bay in the world. This is considered the most beautiful spot of the most beautiful land in all the world. The ancients named it for Parthenope, a siren here risen from the sea. The people there say this is a part of Paradise brought down by Lucifer when driven from heaven, and when Jesus came here, He wept, and from the tears dropped into the sand a vine grew, which gives the famous wine called "Lacrimae Christi," the tears of Christ.

In this beautiful bay the aged Augustus cruised for his health and gave gold to the sailors of the Alexandrian cornship with garlands and incense.

Caligula was not so gentle. When a crowd admired the imperial galley, the imperial monster had them promptly drowned in this beautiful bay. Murder was his pastime. He murdered his brother and forced his father-in-law to cut his throat with his razor. He threw crowds of people into the arena to the wild beasts in order to enjoy the cries of his victims. He wished the whole Roman nation had but one neck, then he could cut their throat at one stroke! His horse wore diamond necklaces and clothing of the imperial purple and was housed in a marble palace. Woe to the neighbors that disturbed the slumbers of this horse!

NAPLES AND VESUVIUS.

To the left was Cape Misenum, where Lucullus had his famous villa, and where Tiberius died, and where the imperial fleet rode at anchor, commanded by the elder Pliny when Pompeii was destroyed by the eruption of Vesuvius.

*Vesuvius.* — Dominating all the bay loomed up in the center the towering Vesuvius with smiling vineyards to the top, and nestling at the base Pompeii to the right and Herculaneum to the left.

*Naples.* — In the bend of the bay is Neapolis, Newtown, now Naples, with the famous gardens of Lucullus, where Augustus visited and Vergil wrote his finest poems.

Here is the green hill of Posilipo, "Freedom from Sorrow," which was tunneled by Augustus. Seneca grumbled about the dust, the darkness, and the bad odors of this tunnel. On the hillside was the home of

ISLAND OF NISIDA.

Cicero and also of Vergil, who here wrote his *Georgics* and *Aeneid*. Dying at Brundisium (Calabria), he begged Augustus, with whom he was traveling, to be buried on this hill. On a slab we read his own epitaph: —

> In lovely Mantua was my childhood's home
> Till my ambition lured me forth to Rome;
> Flocks, fields, and heroes have inspired my breast;
> And now on Naples' sunny slope I rest.

His ashes were placed on Mount Posilipo with the inscription: "Mantua's son and prey of Calabria. Parthenope now holds me, who sang of herds, fields, and war."

They say Paul visited the tomb, and a verse sung in churches during the Middle Ages runs: —

> When to Vergil's tomb they brought him,
> Tender grief and pity wrought him
>   To exclaim with pious tears:
> 'What a saint I might have crowned thee,
> Had I only, living, found thee,
>   Poet, first and without peers.'

So much is true — the Gospel ennobles all art.

Here is Baiae, imperial Rome's most pretentious and notorious resort,

HILL OF POSILIPO.
On the slope of this hill Emperor Augustus had a villa, and in his time a tunnel was made through the ridge.

where the fashionable idlers from Rome built their palaces out into the sea, to the great disgust of Horace. Here were the famous sulphur springs, that drew the sick from many quarters.

"No gulf in the world outshines lovely Baiae," sings Horace. Here the Roman fleet will ride at anchor when the commander Pliny the Elder will lose his life at the outbreak of Vesuvius in 79.

Nisida, the little island where Brutus had a villa, where he and Cicero met for the last time after the murder of Caesar at Pompey's pillar, and where Portia, the wife of Brutus, killed herself on hearing of her husband's death at the battle of Philippi.

To the left Ischia rests on the rebellious giant Typhoeus, who now and then writhes in agony and shakes the island in an effort to throw off the crushing load. Renan called it his "dear volcano," rivaling even Capri in its witching beauty.

Close by was Bauli, the favorite villa of Nero, where he, with Seneca and Burrus, plotted the murder of his own mother Agrippina only a few

MOUNT VESUVIUS.
From across the Bay of Naples.

years before the arrival of Paul. Agrippina planned her vices and crimes here. When she heard that Nero schemed to kill her, she said, "Let him kill me; if he but reign!" Here the Lucrine Lake supplied the delicate oysters to the pampered palates of Roman epicureans. Here the colored sails of the countless pleasure yachts flitted about like butterflies. Here are the remains of the floating bridge built by the crazy Caligula across the bay over which he rode in Alexander's chariot, drunk with cruelty and debauchery. He debauched women, his own sisters and the wives of other men. He turned the imperial palace into a brothel to make money. He needed it. In 37 he inherited from Tiberius about 500,000,000 Roman coin and squandered them in one year.

The finest statues of the gods were brought from Greece, the heads were knocked off, and Caligula's was put on. In a temple stood his own

SEASHORE OF BAGNOLI, POZZUOLI (PUTEOLI).

divine statue, which was dressed daily as he was dressed. He went through the streets of Rome with his beard gilded, and handling the lightning like Jove! The whole world had to worship this crowned idiot like a god!

*Puteoli.* — As they neared Puteoli, they saw the vast pile which hung over the sea and belonged to Julius Caesar, and on the slope of the hill

LOOKING ACROSS THE BAY FROM POZZUOLI TOWARD NISIDA.

above stood the villa of Cicero, who was too patriotic to approve, and too timid to resist, the guilty ambition of Caesar. Puteoli was eight miles northwest of Naples and the greatest port of Italy, especially for wheat from Egypt, the granary of Rome, 140 miles away. Here stood a large pier of twenty-five arches, of which thirteen ruined ones remain; at this pier the vessels discharged their passengers and cargo. Curious crowds commonly came to see the sight. In a letter of Seneca we may see the

THE BAY OF PUTEOLI, NOW POZZUOLI.

scene: "Suddenly to-day Alexandrian vessels, which are wont to be sent forward to herald the arrival of a fleet, appeared. They call them letter-carriers, or packets, and the sight of them is welcome to all Campania. All the crowd collects upon the mole of Puteoli and recognizes Alexandrian corn-vessels from a whole fleet of others by their sails, — for they alone are permitted to enter the harbor with their topsail set. As soon as they come between Capreae and the promontory of Minerva, others are ordered to be content with the lower sail; the topsail is the mark of an Alexandrian ship. Then all the town made ready to hasten to the water's edge to watch the sailors dancing on the quays, or to gloat over the wonders which had traveled thither from Arabia, India, and perhaps even from Cathay...." (*Ep.* 77.)

Two hundred and fifty years before, an embassy from Carthage had landed at Puteoli to sue for peace from Rome; Paul landed to bring peace to Rome, the only true peace — "peace through the blood of the Cross." St. Paul's Chapel stands just behind the old pier to mark the spot where Paul set foot on Italian soil. Not many years later Titus landed here after the destruction of Jerusalem, and not many years after that Ignatius wished to land here to follow the footsteps of Paul on his way to his martyrdom in Rome.

PIER WHERE PAUL LANDED.

Here Paul saw a statue of Tiberius, reared about this time in honor of the rebuilding of the fourteen Asian cities overthrown by an earthquake. Here stood the splendid temple of Serapis, of which ruins remain to this day, as also of the theater in which Nero acted. Among the ruins of Pompeii was found an inscription reading, "Rejoice in the fire, O Christian," which proves there were Christians in this region at the time, and that they were known as Christians. Paul searched out the Christians at Puteoli and for seven days enjoyed their kindness.

Still standing are thirteen columns which supported the great pier where Paul landed at Puteoli, the greatest commercial city of all Italy, also a "miniature Rome," as Cicero calls it.

## THE LAST STRETCH OF THE JOURNEY TO ROME.
*Acts 28, 14. 15.*

On the eighth day after landing, Paul left Puteoli for Rome, one hundred and seventy miles away. On the Via Consularis he passed the temple of Serapis. Going between the two mountains beyond the city, he crosses the famous and fertile fields of Campania. After a march of nineteen miles he spends the night at Capua, famous for its mighty ancient amphitheater and its statue of Venus.

He leaves on the Via Appia, built by the Censor Appius Claudius in 312 B. C. during the Samnite War. In 280 the blind man by a great speech had hindered a peace with Pyrrhus. He was also Rome's first author and composed a collection of wise sayings. Eight hundred years later this "Queen of Roads," as Statius calls it, was still in such perfect state as to astonish Procopius, secretary of General Belisarius. Procopius writes: "To traverse the Appian Way is a five days' journey for a good walker. It leads from Rome to Capua. Its breadth is such that two chariots may meet upon it and pass each other without interruption, and its magnificence surpasses that of all other roads." Procopius goes on to tell us Appius had the material brought from a great distance, "so as to have all the stones hard and of the nature of millstones." Then he had the stones smoothed and polished and cut in corresponding angles, "so as to bite together in jointures without the intervention of copper or any other

PEDESTAL OF STATUE IN HONOR OF TIBERIUS AT PUTEOLI.
Erected for aid given the fifteen cities of Asia destroyed by the earthquake of A. D. 17.

material to bind them; and in this manner they were so firmly united that, on looking at them, we would say they had not been put together by art, but had grown so upon the spot." Mile-stones were all along the way; every forty feet was a seat; about every twenty miles was a "mansion," or post-station, where horses, mules, and vehicles were kept for travelers and government dispatches. From Capua twenty-tix miles west to the sea at Sinuessa and Mount Massicus, whose wines were sung by Vergil and Horace, and whose vines are still the largest in all Italy. Suddenly comes the splendid view of the Gulf of Gaeta, the home of Cardinal Cajetanus, who will examine Luther in Augsburg in 1518.

In the spreading marshes of the Liris River at Minturnae, Marius was captured, the conqueror of the Cimbri and Teutons. All the coast is lined with the marble villas of the rich Romans.

They halted at Formia, one of the loveliest spots in Italy. Here was Cicero's Formianum, where Antony's ruffians murdered the great orator. His monument was passed the next morning on the way through the mountains, the most romantic part of the road. There, for instance, is Itri, a nest in the rocks, the home of the notorious Fra Diavolo.

THE VILLA OF THE GENTILII ON THE VIA APPIA.

About noon they are through the mountains and reach Fondi, and across the plain they can make out the Volscian Mountains running into the sea at Terracina, seventy-five miles from Rome.

The road squeezes itself through between the sea and the gigantic cliffs, the famous pass of Lautulae. Here the Romans heroically fought the Samnites in 315 B. C.; here Quintus Fabius Maximus halted Hannibal on his march on Rome; and here Paul passed on to Rome. On a high peak will stand the castle of Theodoric the Goth and dreamily look down upon the sea.

To the left boldly juts out into the sea the Cape of Circe, the home of the mighty sorceress of Homer's hymns.

After two and a half miles Paul crossed the stream which flows from the Fountain of Feronia — "And where Feronia's grove and temple stand," says Vergil. (*Aen.*, VIII, 800.)

Servius says: "This goddess delighted in freedom and took deserving slaves under her protection; and they received their liberty by being seated on a chair in her temple, on which was inscribed: —

" 'Let slaves who have behaved well sit down here and rise up free.' "

The Grove of Feronia was on the edge of the Pontine Marshes, and Paul was towed on a barge through the canal.

"Where the wet road the Pontine Marsh divides." (Lucian, III, 85.)

Strabo says travelers generally went through the canal by night.

Procopius calls it Decanovius and says the Goths encamped on it at Regeta, thirty-five miles from Rome, when they elected Vitiges their king in 536 B. C. The canal still exists, though Trajan in his third consulship built a road.

THE MAUSOLEUM OF AUGUSTUS IN CAMPUS MARTIUS.
One of the obelisks now stands before the Quirinal, the other before Santa Maria Maggiore.

*The Forum of Appius.* — Paul landed at Appii Forum, where Appius Claudius founded a market for the country people when he built "the Queen of Roads," of which the great Caesar himself had once been a curator. Suetonius says: "Claudius Drusus erected a statue of himself, wearing a crown, at Appii Forum." A hundred years before, Horace was here with Vergil and Maecenas on the way to Brundisium to reconcile Augustus and Mark Antony. He found the water was utterly bad. The place was full of boatmen and extortionate tavern-keepers.

Julius was an imperial officer, and the *parochi*, or public entertainers, had to supply him and his with "wood and salt," or "bed and board."

During the night the slaves bantered the boatmen and the boatmen the slaves, and the troublesome mosquitoes and the croaking frogs kept sleep from their eyes. They left in the evening and went through the nineteen-mile canal in fourteen hours —

> "At ten, Feronia, we thy fountain gain;
> Then land and bathe." — (*Sat.*, 1.)

Four buildings, one a miserable inn, is all that remains of Foro Appio. The forty-third mile-stone is still there. Here Paul was met by Christians who had come from Rome to greet him.

*Three Taverns* is ten miles beyond the Market of Appius. At Antium on the sea, where Nero was born, Cicero had a villa, and on his way to Formiae he stopped at Three Taverns. While the horses were being changed, he tasted the wine and wrote a letter to Atticus on the festival of Ceres, April 12, 58 B. C. Here more Christians from Rome came to greet the Apostle. "When Paul saw these, he thanked God and took courage." Maclaren remarks here that Luther was braced for the Diet of Worms by the bluff soldier George von Frundsberg, who clapped the monk on the back and spoke a hearty word of cheer.

*Lanuvium,* founded by Aeneas, the birthplace of P. Sulpicius Quirinius, the Cyrenius, governor of Syria, mentioned in Luke 2, 2.

To the right the Alban Hills with the Monte Cavo, topped by the temple of Jupiter, and the famed Lake Nemi.

*Roma Aeterna!* "I must see Rome," Paul had written. At Aricia he saw the city of his desire, "the grandeur that was Rome," sixteen miles distant in the Campagna.

> 'Tis sunset on the Palatine. A flood
> Of living glory wraps the Sabine hills,
> And o'er the rough and serrate Apennines
> Floats like a burning mantle.

Now that Paul saw Rome, what were his emotions? We do not know. We know the feelings of Paul's greatest disciple. Fifteen hundred years later Luther came from the cold North and, on seeing Rome, fell on his knees and cried out rapturously, "Hail, holy Rome, I salute thee!"

The tomb of Aruns, son of Lars Porsena of Clusium.

The tomb of Pompey, whose villa later belonged to Emperor Domitian and is now the town of Albano, near the Alban Lake.

Solid villas, and slighter "houses of pleasure," and temples, and converging roads, and stately, stretching aqueducts, all in the midst of meadows, and vineyards, and gardens, all made beautiful by God's nature and man's art, and the world's gold.

At eleven and a half miles stood the tomb of Clodius, suspected of wrong with Pompeia, Caesar's wife, who must be above suspicion.

Up hill and down dale for six miles from Aricia to Bovillae, ten miles from Rome, taken by Coriolanus, says Plutarch, and Tacitus tells us: "A chapel was consecrated to the Julian family and statues to the deified

THE PONTE MOLLE, MILVIAN BRIDGE.

Over this bridge Constantine returned to Rome after defeating Maxentius at Saxa Rubra, Red Rocks, farther up the Tiber on October 28, 312. Here Consul Cicero, at the beginning of December, 63 B. C., found on the Allobroges the proofs of Catiline's conspiracy. Here Charles the Great, on November 24, 800, crossed over to be crowned on Christmas Day. Here, in 1462, Pope Pius II, at the head of his cardinals, amid thousands of white-clad, palm-bearing priests and prelates, received from the Greek Bessarion the head of St. Andrew and erected a chapel with the large statue of the saint by the greatest sculptor of the age, Paolo di Mariano. Here Luther, in December, 1510, crossed over to Rome.

Augustus at Bovillae." From here the whole Roman knighthood bore the body of Augustus in triumph to Rome.

Here the road falls into a plain and runs in straight line and is lined on both sides with graceful and pleasing tombs with busts and statues amid trees and flowers — the vast, moundlike tombs of the Etruscans, the graceful miniature temples of the Greeks, the round Roman sepulchers like Cecilia Metella's, the massive simple sarcophagi like Scipio's. Some plain, some sculptured; some square, some round; red brick, and white limestone, and black lava, and gray slate, and red and gray granite, and marble white, pink, green, and black. And nightingales in cypress-trees flooding the night with melody.

At the eighth mile, on the right, the villa of Persius, the satirical poet, who will die November 23, 62; a beautiful brick tomb will rise there.

Another half mile, to the right, the fine brick tomb of Quintus Verannius, consul in 49, who died in Britain in 55.

THE FIFTH MILE FROM ROME ON THE VIA APPIA.   CANINA.

To the left the temple of Hercules, from the time of the republic. Caius Cossutius, a freedman of Epaphroditus, Nero's secretary, restored it in March, 61, about the time Paul was passing there. Domitian will again restore it, and the face of the god will look like Domitian.

Near the seventh mile the scene of the celebrated battle between the Roman Horatii triplets with the Latin Curiatii triplets, marked by the tomb of the two Horatii on the spot where they were killed.

At the sixth mile is the massive round tomb of Cotta, the tomb of

Messella Corvinus, the historian and poet, who died in A. D. 11, erected to him by Marcus Aurelius Messallinus Cotta, consul in A. D. 20.

At the fifth mile are the tombs of the three Curiatii "in different places, as they fought," says Livy.

On the right is the tomb of Pomponius Atticus, the friend of Nepos and Cicero, buried February 28, B. C. 33.

At the fourth mile the village Pagus Lemonius and Seneca's villa in

THE PANTHEON.
Built by Agrippa.

the "great gardens," as Juvenal has it, or "suburban country," as Tacitus puts it. In a few years he will kill himself at the word of Nero; the tomb will be built soon after 65.

Away to the right the great aqueduct of Claudius, just built in 50; 155 arches still standing. The great villa of the Quintilii.

At the third mile Paul passed the great circular tomb of Caecilia Metella, wife of Lucius Cornelius Sulla, the dictator.

One mile from Rome, to the right, the tombs of the glorious Scipios, the oldest that of L. Scipio Barbatus, consul in 298 B. C.

PART OF ROMAN FORUM.
BY E. BECCHETTI.

Temple of Jupiter (Capitol). Tabularium. Temple of Concord. Basilica of Julia. Temple of Saturn. Golden Mile-stone. Rostra. Temple of Vespasian. Umbilicus of Rome. Temple of Rome. Arch of S. Severus. Column of Duilius.

Also to the right, the columbaria of the freedmen of Caesar's household. Many will have names found in the New Testament. Is it possible we can still look upon the ashes of some of Paul's converts?

They crossed the Almo, a little stream, and entered the capital through the Porta Capena in the wall of Servius Tullius. Over it ran the Aqua Appia, and "the Capenian Gate drips with large drops," says Martial. Here the patricians and fashionables took their walks or drives in the evening, as they do now on the Pincian Hill. Through this gate had passed victorious generals and Caesars with their legions, and captives, and spoils of war, ambassadors and kings, the guests of the empire, from beyond the Euphrates, the funeral pomps of Caesars and patricians.

Horace writes: —

> What conflux issuing forth or passing in;
> Praetors, proconsuls to their provinces
> Hasting, or on return, in robes of state,
> Lictors and rods, the ensigns of their power,
> Legions and cohorts, turms of horse and wings,
> Or embassies of regions far remote,
> In various habits, on the Appian Road. . . .
> Dusk faces with white silken turbans wreathed.

Matthew Arnold says: —

> In his cool hall, with haggard eyes,
>   The Roman noble lay;
> He drove abroad in furious guise
>   Along the Appian Way.

To the left, filling the valley between the Aventine and Palatine hills, stood the Circus Maximus. The applause once so disturbed the Emperor Caligula on the Palatine that he sent his soldiers to drive the spectators away. Here the Appian Way turns into the Road of Triumph, on which victors brought captive kings with the spoils of war. Between the Palatine and Esquiline they tread the Via Sacra and go down the sloping Sacer Clivus to the Golden Mile-stone, which gave mileage to the world, and the Rostrum, which gave law to the world. All roads lead to Rome, to this Forum Romanum, the heart of Rome and therefore the heart of the world.

Under the portico on one side stood the Latin and Roman kings in bronze, from Aeneas to Tarquinius Superbus; under the other were ranged the Roman heroes, all in triumphal robes; in the center rose a colossal statue of Augustus. Here stood the immense Basilica Julia, begun by Caesar and finished by Augustus, and opposite the Basilica Aemilia.

Temple of Venus and Roma.
Arch of Fabian.

Palatine.
House of the Vestals.

Statue of Vespasian.

Temple of Castor and Pollux.

Basilica of Julia.

Temple of Julius Caesar.

PART OF ROMAN FORUM.
BY E. BECCHETTI.

Ahead of him Paul could see the hundred steps leading up the Capitoline Hill to the shrine of Jupiter Tonans, "adorned with all the refinements of art and blazing with the plunder of the world. In the center of the temple, with Juno on his left and Minerva on his right, the Thunderer sat on a throne of gold, grasping the lightning in one hand and in the other wielding the scepter of the universe."

On the left rose the Palatine Hill, which gave the name of "palace" to the house of Caesar on it, where stood preserved Romulus's lowly cottage thatched with reeds. The gleaming temple of Apollo stood within the royal precincts, and spacious gardens stretched down towards the Circus Maximus behind, surrounded by Caesar's portico.

In the Campus Martius is Pompey's theater, the first one of stone, some parts still remaining. There stands also the Mausoleum of Augustus, also the Pantheon of Agrippa. The bronze of that dome we may see to-day forming the sacred baldachino of St. Peter and the orthodox cannon of St. Angelo.

The barracks of the ten thousand picked Pretorian Guards were located by Tiberius outside the walls to the northeast of the city,

AGRIPPA, SON-IN-LAW OF AUGUSTUS, BUILDER OF THE PANTHEON.

where a few years before the British King Caractacus had been led in triumph. A detachment of the Pretorians had their quarters in connection with the palace, directly beneath it. Here the courtly Julius delivered his prisoners to the Stratopedarch. This may have been the Prefect of the Pretorian Guard, at this time Burrus. Several soldiers whiled away their idle time by scratching their names on the plaster of the barrack wall, where we can scan them to-day; perhaps the eyes of Paul saw these scrawls as he was led into prison. Others think Paul was given into the custody of the Princeps Peregrinorum, the officer of the soldiers from abroad, who conducted prisoners to Rome and had their camps on the Coelian Hill or on Tarquin's Field, near the Viminal Hill, to the northeast.

Thus ended the greatest triumphal procession Rome had ever seen; nay, having eyes, she did not see.

"I must also see Rome," Paul had said. Acts 19, 21. Now he was in Rome, January 61.

> I am in Rome! Oft as the morning ray
> Visits these eyes, waking at once I cry,
> Whence this excess of joy? What has befallen me?
> And from within a thrilling voice replies,
> Thou art in Rome! — *Rogers.*

ST. SEBASTIANO GATEWAY, APPIAN WAY, THROUGH WHICH PAUL MUST HAVE PASSED.

The city was on both banks of the yellow Tiber covering the famous seven hills in a circuit of about twelve miles. There were open spaces, like the Forum and the Campus Martius, but the streets were narrow and crooked and flanked with the high *insulae,* or crowded tenements. No vaulting domes or lofty spires relieved the dull sky-line.

The population was about one and a half million, one half slaves, who did all the work. There was no middle class. The most of the other half were pauper citizens, clamoring for "bread and games" from the rulers as their share of the spoils of the war of conquest of the world. Certain wealthy land-owners had as many as 20,000 slaves.

*The Jews in Rome.* — As early as the year 63 B. C., when Pompey had conquered Palestine, several thousand Jews were sold as slaves in Rome. Others came freely to do business. These lived in the Ghetto, east of the Tiber. Julius Caesar showed them kindness, and Augustus gave them religious liberty and let them share with the Romans in the distribution of wheat. If this fell on their Sabbath, they could come on Sunday. But

PAUL REACHES ROME IN CHAINS.

they were a troublesome and dangerous element, and in the year 19 Tiberius banished them from Rome. He deported 4,000 arms-bearing men to the sulphur mines of Sardinia, and so there were about 10,000 Jewish men in Rome, according to the estimate of Pierre Batiffol. In 52 Claudius also banished them from Italy. They soon came back and formed a numerous and prosperous community. In the days of Paul they numbered above 60,000, and they had seven synagogs. They crossed the Tiber on the narrow bridge of black stones built a hundred years before by Fabricius, whose name you can still read on it. Martial complained he couldn't sleep anywhere for the noise of the Jewish pedlers. (*Sat.*, 12, 57.) Juvenal sees the Jewish fortune-teller interpreting dreams for a trifling tip —

> Her hand is filled but sparingly; the Jew
> Will sell you cheap the vision of your choice.

They forced their way into the public bath and secured the best seats; doubly absurd when they tried to hide their Jewish origin. Horace, Cicero, Perseus, and Tacitus sneer at them. And yet many of the higher Romans embraced Judaism, for instance, Poppaea, Nero's wife. Nero's favorite actor, Aliturus, was a Jew.

## PAUL'S FIRST MEETING IN ROME.
### Acts 28, 17—29.

Only three days after his tiresome journey the tireless apostle called the chief of the Jews together, and when they were come, he said to them: "Men and brethren, though I have committed nothing against the people or customs of our fathers, yet was I delivered prisoner from Jerusalem into the hands of the Romans, who, when they had examined me, would have let me go because there was no cause of death in me. But when the Jews spake against it, I was constrained to appeal to Caesar; not that I had aught to accuse my nation of. For this cause therefore have I called for you, to see you and to speak with you, because that for the hope of Israel I am bound with this chain."

*Willing to Hear.* — They said to him: "We neither received letters out of Judea concerning thee, neither any of the brethren that came showed or spake any harm of thee. But we desire to hear of thee what thou thinkest; for as concerning this sect, we know that everywhere it is spoken against."

The Christians were spoken against, and that everywhere, in Asia and in Europe. The Christians were spoken against, and that by everybody, by the Jews and by the heathen. That shows they were strong men, men of principle, men who practised what they preached, who lived their faith, suffered for their faith, died for their faith.

"And when they had appointed him a day, there came many to him

PAUL PREACHING IN ROME.

A. BAUR.

into his lodging; to whom he expounded and testified the kingdom of God, persuading them concerning Jesus, both out of the Law of Moses and out of the prophets, from morning till evening. And some believed the things which were spoken, and some believed not."

Paul expounded, and testified, and persuaded out of, the Bible. The Bible was to him the very Word of God. The Word of God was the basis and also the sum and substance of his preaching. Paul, with all his learning and with all his experience and with all his keen logic and with all his loving heart and noble enthusiasm, preached the Gospel of Jesus Christ from the Word of God — and yet "some believed not." O the hardness of the human heart! As then, so to-day: do what we may, some believe not.

*Paul's Parting Shot.* — When they agreed not among themselves, they departed, after that Paul had spoken one word: "Well spake the Holy Ghost by Esaias, the prophet, to our fathers, saying, 'Go unto this people and say, Hearing ye shall hear and shall not understand; and seeing ye shall see and not perceive; for the heart of this people is waxed gross, and their ears are dull of hearing, and their eyes have they closed, lest they should see with their eyes, and hear with their ears, and understand with their heart, and should be converted, and I should heal them.' [Is. 6, 9. 10; Matt. 13, 14. 15; Mark 4, 12; Luke 8, 10; John 12, 40.] Be it known, therefore, unto you that the salvation of God is sent to the Gentiles and that they will hear it."

God is Love; yet even He is forced to abandon people to their self-chosen doom: the sight fills us with solemn awe.

"They will hear it" is a word of reproach, rebuke, and condemnation to the hardened Jews. Is it not also a stick to stir up indifferent Christians?

"They will hear it" is a word of triumphant faith in the conquest of the enemy heathen world. Is it not also a tonic to stimulate and strengthen us in our foreign mission work?

"They will hear it" — prophecy has become history. We of the heathen have heard it; let us be heartily thankful for the grace of God, who granted us the Gospel of Christ for our soul's salvation.

And when Paul had said these words, the Jews departed and had great reasoning among themselves.

"Paul dwelt two whole years" — February, 60, to February, 62 — "in his own rented lodgings and received all that came in unto him, preaching the kingdom of God and teaching those things which concern the Lord Jesus Christ, with all confidence, no man forbidding him."

"No man forbidding him" — triumph!

> Look in and see Christ's chosen saint
> In triumph wear his Christlike chain!
> Nor fear lest he should swerve or faint —
> "His life is Christ, his death is gain." — *Keble*.

The most important little book of history in the world ends with a note of triumph — "No one forbidding him!"

## CHAPTER VIII.

## PAUL'S IMPRISONMENT AT ROME.

WE must now without our trusty guide grope our way as best we may from the notices in the later epistles and the hints of tradition. Julius Caesar, in 26 B. C., built the Septa Julia, a voting place, and in one of its rooms Paul is said to have been kept for a short time. On the site of this government building stands the Church of Santa Maria in Via Lata, St. Mary's in Broadway, founded by Sergius in the eighth century and rebuilt by Innocent VIII in 1485. Here is shown the chain with which, and the pillar to which, Paul was bound. "But the Word of God is not bound," reads the inscription. Later Paul lived in his own rented rooms, where now stands the small church of S. Paolo o Paolino allo Regola, near the Ghetto, near Ponte Sisto and the theater of Balbus. Rented rooms the headquarters of the kingdom of God on earth!

By a long, light chain Paul's right wrist was linked to the left hand of a Pretorian guardsman. Josephus tells us when Tiberius flung Agrippa I into prison, Antonia bribed the Pretorian Prefect Macro to place him under a kind centurion, and at meals he had his hands unchained. Let us hope Paul enjoyed like little favors. Paul was chained to a soldier by day and to two by night, and this for two years! Many soldiers were thus forced to observe closely the life and labor of Paul when alone and with visitors. Can we imagine Paul not preaching Christ to his guards? Can we not imagine the soldiers in their guard-room discussing Paul and Paul's Christ? Can we doubt some of them were converted? Sent abroad through the empire, they scattered the seed of the Gospel throughout the world. *Thus Paul turned even his prison into a Practical Missionary Seminary.* It is so we understand Paul's words that his imprisonment had "fallen out rather to the furtherance of the Gospel, so that my bonds in Christ are manifest in all the Praetorium and in all other places." Phil. 1, 12. 13. That helps to explain the large number of Christians in the Roman army, over which Tertullian later exults. Paul was chained to the Pretorians, and the Pretorians were chained to Christ. Mommsen tells us the Praetorium is the whole body of persons connected with the sitting in judgment, the Supreme Imperial Court, the prefect, or both prefects, of the Pretorian Guard, representing the Emperor in his capacity as the fountain of justice, together with the assessors and high officers of the court.

Not only in the soldiers' barracks beneath, but also in Caesar's palace above was the influence of Paul felt. "Chiefly they that are of Caesar's household" salute the Philippians. 4, 22. Aulus Plautius, the conqueror of Britain, in 57 or 58, tried his wife, Pomponia Graecina, for "foreign superstition" — Christianity, as some think. A generation later the Emperor Domitian condemned Flavius Clemens and his wife, Flavia Domitilla, members of the imperial family, for "atheism" — Christianity, as even Gibbon says.

Seeing Paul's imprisonment was so mild, "many of the brethren in the Lord, waxing confident by my bonds, are much more bold to speak the Word without fear." Phil. 1, 14—18. And so Paul's influence reached out into the city also.

From the various bits of evidence pieced together, Signor de Rossi thinks some of the Gens Cornelia were converted, at least Pudens and Claudia and their daughters

SHIELDS.
PAUL PLEADING WITH HIS CENTURION.

Pudentiana and Praxedis. The church of Santa Pudentiana stands on the site of the house of Pudens on the Viminal Hill, near the royal palace. Another convert was Clement, a fellow-laborer with Paul, and his name is in the book of life. Phil. 4, 3.

Some of the preachers preached the Gospel of Christ from pure motives, but others not sincerely, hoping to add affliction to Paul's bonds.

Did that worry Paul? With sublime grandeur of soul he asks, "What of it? Only that in every way, whether in pretense or in truth, Christ is preached; and therein I rejoice, yea, and will rejoice." Phil. 1, 18.

Like Paul, Henry Martyn was abused by Persian Moslems for the sake of Christ, and he rejoiced: —

> If for Thy sake upon my name
> Shame and reproach shall be,
> All hail, reproach, and welcome, shame!
> Good Lord, remember me.

"There is a deep joy in actually suffering physical violence for Christ's

THE CAMP OF THE PRETORIANS.

sake," said David Hill after a Chinese rioter had almost broken his arm with a club.

As long as he can magnify Christ, Paul is magnificently indifferent to life and death. "For to me to live is Christ and to die is gain." If he lives, he will continue to labor for Christ; if he dies, he will be with Christ, — he hardly knows which to choose.

In a few years the Christians were "a great multitude," as the historian Tacitus tells us.

Luke was with Paul in prison for two years at Caesarea and for two years more at Rome — what better time, and place, and opportunity, and sources of information to write his gospel and the Acts? Beside the beloved physician, Paul had Timothy, his well-beloved son in the faith; Aristarchus of Thessalonica, who had risked his life for Paul at Ephesus and had been his companion from Caesarea to Rome; Tychicus from Ephesus was there for a time; Epaphroditus from Philippi; Epaphras from Colossae; Mark, who had regained Paul's confidence; Demas, who later forsook Paul; Jesus Justus, one of the circumcision, a comfort to Paul; Onesimus, the runaway slave; Epenetus, Amplias, Stachys, Tryphena and Tryphosa, Aquila and Priscilla, his dear Persis, and Mary, "who had toiled so much for the Church."

This prison of Paul was the Roman Hall of Fame, and these obscure followers of a "wretched superstition," as Tacitus calls the Gospel, are the real Immortals. The words of the Roman writers of that period are mostly lost; what few remain are read by a few scholars — who reads Seneca? — but the Gospels according to Mark and Luke and the Acts of Luke and the epistles of Paul are living and life-giving to millions in all languages among all nations throughout the world from that day to this day and from this day till Judgment Day.

Annaeus Seneca, Spaniard, was exiled to Corsica by Messalina in 41, recalled in 49 to become the tutor of Nero, and was now the greatest living statesman in the world. It is interesting that in 1867 a funeral tablet was found at Ostia reading: "Sacred to the memory of Marcus Annaeus Paulus Petrus, son of Marcus Annaeus Paulus." Lanciani holds this proof positive that the Annaei, the family of Seneca, were Christians.

## THE EPISTLE TO PHILEMON.

While Paul was at Ephesus, Philemon of Colossae turned Christian; likely Apphia was his wife and Archippus their son. They lent their house for a meeting-place for the little congregation, and so Paul calls them his "fellow-workers" and Archippus his "fellow-soldier."

In this household a slave named Onesimus, or "Profitable," became "Unprofitable" by running away. He found his way to Paul at Rome, who converted him and sent him back in the company of Tychicus with a letter to secure a pardon and assure a welcome from the injured owner.

The Epistle to Philemon gives us three portraits, miniatures like Meissonier's.

"ST. PAUL'S PRISON," ROME.

## I. PHILEMON

is a man of strong faith in the Lord Jesus, and this living faith shows itself in practical works of love toward all the saints, for the hearts of the saints have been refreshed through him. This loving faith gave much joy and comfort to Pastor Paul, who had converted Philemon, and Paul cordially calls him brother.

## II. ONESIMUS

was a thief: he had stolen himself, Philemon's personal property, and likely some money to help him depart for parts unknown.

The Phrygian slaves were commonly counted the worst of all. This unpromising material came to Paul, and he turned it into a Christian and therefore into a real man.

Paul calls him "my child, whom I have begotten in my bonds; my very heart, whom I would fain have kept with me that in thy behalf he might minister unto me in the bonds of the Gospel." Surely the Unprofitable had again become Profitable.

In his body Onesimus was Philemon's slave; in spirit he was Christ's freeman. Free in Christ, Onesimus returned to Philemon to face lifelong slavery or even crucifixion. Duty to his heavenly Master showed Onesimus his duty to his earthly master, and he walked the rugged road of duty. Here is conversion, a turning around; he turned back from Rome to Colossae.

## III. ST. PAUL

shows the ease and refinement of the Christian gentleman in this personal and private epistle, which is full of courtesy and grace, beginning and ending with grace. Paul practised what he preached; this little letter is a practical illustration of his advice: "Let your speech be alway with grace, seasoned with salt." Col. 4, 6.

The earnest appeal of the epistle is made in a half playful manner, and a gentle smile lights up the grave features of Paul. It is Paul, the aged, who asks a favor; he has not long to live to ask many more. It is Paul, the prisoner of Christ Jesus, who makes a plea for the slave of Philemon, who is a believer in Christ Jesus.

Paul promises to make good for Onesimus: "Charge the whole amount to my account. I, Paul, write it with my own hand; I will repay it." And thus Paul turns his letter into his bond.

Paul had saved the soul of Philemon and "therefore had boldness in

Christ to enjoin that which is befitting," had a good right to make heavy demands on him. But with exquisite delicacy the Apostle foregoes his right to demand, and "for love's sake I rather beseech thee."

Onesimus had been hopelessly lost to Philemon. It was Paul who had rescued the lost, lost in a twofold sense, had made a useful man of him, had made the Unprofitable to be again Profitable. By the rights of discovery, nay, by the rights of authorhood, Onesimus rightly belonged to Paul. But Paul would not urge his rights as man to man, but as brother to brother, as a Christian to a Christian; Paul would only beseech Philemon for a favor.

And what is the favor? To receive Onesimus no longer as a slave, but as a Christian, more than a slave, a brother beloved, especially to me, but how much rather to thee both in the flesh and in the Lord — as a fellow human being and as fellow-Christian. If, then, thou countest me a partner, receive him as myself.

"Brother, let me have joy of thee in the Lord; refresh my heart in Christ. Having confidence in thine obedience, I write unto thee, knowing that thou wilt do even beyond what I say." And, of course, we have the same confidence.

Paul adds: "Prepare me also a lodging; for I hope that through your prayers I shall be granted unto you." It seems that Paul was not long after released from prison.

Not many years later the Younger Pliny sent to his friend Sabinianus a similar plea for an offending freedman, which is justly praised as a most graceful specimen of letter-writing come down from pagan antiquity; yet in simple dignity, refined courtesy, large sympathy, personal affection, and, of course, Christian spirit, Paul's letter deserves the palm; in fact, we think it the finest letter ever written.

Jerome, Erasmus, Grotius, Bengel, Lightfoot, Renan, Sabatier, Ewald, Meyer, Von Soden, Dodds, and others outdo one another in chanting the praise of this idyllic epistle; but to our thinking Luther is the meistersinger. Listen to his hearty, soulful, spiritual song: "This epistle showeth a right noble, lovely example of Christian love. Here we see how Paul layeth himself out for poor Onesimus and with all his means pleads his cause with his master and so setteth himself as if he were Onesimus and had himself done wrong to Philemon. Even as Christ did for us with God the Father, thus also doth Paul for Onesimus with Philemon. . . . We are all His Onesimi, to my thinking."

214  PAUL'S VOYAGE

Acts 27:35

Slavery was a cancer on the ancient heathen world. When Paul tells Philemon to receive the slave Onesimus "as a brother beloved," he inserts a solvent that in time loosed and removed the cancer from the social body. "Slave-girls like Blandina in Gaul and Felicitas in Africa, having won for themselves the crown of martyrdom, were celebrated in the festivals of the Church with honors denied to the most powerful and noblest born of mankind," says Lightfoot. In Paul's day slavery was everywhere, in our day it is nowhere.

Now Epaphras, Paul's "dear fellow-servant," came to Rome and told the prisoner of the conditions in those regions. He praised their faith and charity, but also spoke plainly of the threatening Gnosticism. This was a mixture of dreamy imagination and rigorous rites. It was doctrinal and practical, affecting creed and conduct. It robbed Christ of His divine glory and the Christian of his divine comfort.

Paul does not combat the heresy by fierce denunciation nor by his personal authority, but by the noblest form of controversy, which is the plain presentation of the pure truth. He lays the ax to the root of the trouble by showing the perfect sufficiency of Christ for our salvation.

Paul dictated to Timothy, and sent by Tychicus,

## THE EPISTLE TO THE COLOSSIANS.

### PART ONE.

#### 1. CHRIST.

On the pinions of the Spirit we swiftly soar to the zenith of heaven, and the full-orbed Christ comes gloriously into our ken, and our heart is filled with the dynamic truth that Christ is the Image, or Character, of the invisible God. 1, 15. In Him dwelleth all the fulness of the Godhead bodily. 2, 9.

1. Christ is the Creator and Sustainer of the universe; for all things have been created through Him and unto Him, and also in Him all things consist, or hang together. 1, 15—17.

2. Christ is the Redeemer; for in Him we have redemption through His blood, even the forgiveness of sins. Having made peace through the blood of the cross, He hath reconciled us, who had been enemies; and He is the Beginning, the First-born from the dead, and so He is the Head of the body, the Church, that in all things He might have the preeminence.

## 2. THE CHRISTIAN.

Ye are made full, ye are complete, in Him who is the Head of all principality and power.

1. In relation to God, Christ is God's image, at once God's representation and manifestation; and so we need no other teacher.

2. In relation to the universe, Christ is the Mediator between God and all created things; Christ is before all creatures and Lord of all creatures; Christ is the band, or tire, which holds all the wheel of the universe together, and so there is no room for other mediators.

3. In relation to the Church, Christ is the one Head, and the Church is His one body, and so there is no room for any third party to come in between the Christian and his Savior. Christ is all in all in all respects. We worship "Him first, Him last, Him midst, and without end."

And you, being in time past alienated and enemies in your mind in your evil works, yet now hath He reconciled in the body of His flesh through death, to present you holy and without blemish and unreprovable before Him.

This is the Christ whom Paul preached. Christ in you, the hope of glory, whom we preach, warning every man, and teaching every man in all wisdom, that we may present every man perfect in Christ Jesus. 1, 27. 28.

This is 1) the message of Paul's Gospel, 2) the method of his ministry, 3) the mark at which he aimed. It is 1) the proclamation, 2) the person, 3) the purpose of Paul's preaching. It is 1) the person Paul presented, 2) the threefold plan of procedure, 3) the purport of his effort.

## PART TWO.

### THE WARNINGS.

#### 1. THE WARNING AGAINST FALSE PHILOSOPHY.

In Christ dwelleth all the fulness of the Godhead bodily. That is the glorious truth. Now, then, as ye have received Christ Jesus, the Lord, so walk ye in Him, rooted and built up in Him, and stablished in the faith, as ye have been taught, abounding therein with thanksgiving.

Therefore, beware lest any man capture you through philosophy and vain deceit, after the traditions of men, after the rudiments, or elements, or a-b-c of the world, and not after Christ.

We have been made full in Christ; we have all and need nothing else. If we have Christ, we have religion, the true philosophy, and need no other philosophy, nothing that is not after Christ, according to Christ, in harmony with Christ.

Clear-eyed and keen-minded Martin Luther says in his Table Talk in words that have hands and feet: "See to it that thou know no God and worship no God except the Man Christ Jesus; but lay hold of Him alone and continue hanging with thy whole heart upon Him and let all thoughts and speculations about the Majesty go their way. In this business look straight at the Man alone, who presents Himself to us as Mediator and says, 'Come unto Me, all ye that labor and are heavy laden.'"

Do they say the body is itself evil? The sufficient reply is: The fulness of the Godhead dwelleth in Christ bodily. In the body of His flesh Christ achieved our reconciliation and made us holy and without blemish and unreprovable before Him in faith.

### 2. The Warning Against False Ceremonies.

Ye have been made full in Christ, therefore you need nothing else. Therefore yield not to the false teachers who would force you to be circumcised like the Jews; for in Holy Baptism you have already been circumcised by the circumcision made without hands.

Let not the false teachers enslave you with the Jewish rules of *kosher* foods and feasts and the Sabbath; for they all are but the shadows, and Christ is the substance. If you have Christ, you have the substance and need not the shadow. All these ordinances Christ has blotted out, torn, canceled, nailed to the cross; they are outworn, out of date.

Ye are made full in Christ, therefore let no man rob you of your prize by a voluntary humility and worshiping of angels, which the false teachers would shove in to separate the Christians from their Christ. In order to escape this deadly void of visions, "hold fast the Head, from whom all the body, being supplied and knit together through the joints and bands, increaseth with the increase of God."

### 3. The Warning Against False Confidences.

Ye are made full in Christ, therefore be not entangled in the meshes of a rigid and mechanical asceticism, which demands, "Handle not, nor taste, nor touch." Christianity is not slavery to such human rules, but liberty from such human rules imposed as if they were of God. These doctrines and precepts of men have a show of wisdom and humility and severity to the body; but, after all, they are not of any value against the indulgence of the flesh. Monkery and nunnery of any kind cannot save us. Rites do not make righteous. Symbols and ceremonies are more apt to sensualize the spirit than spiritualize the senses. Ritualism will obscure Christ rather than secure Christ.

Then, what does save us? "Seek the things that are above, where Christ is, seated on the right hand of God." Walk in Christ, in Christ alone. This is the scope of the epistle, says Bengel. Christ relieves us of the need of all paltry panaceas.

Christ suffered in His body to save the world, and Paul rejoices in the bodily afflictions he endures in carrying on the work of Christ in saving the Church by the ministry of preaching the Gospel. Shall we not rejoice in the real sacrifices we bring to carry on the work of the Savior in saving the people?

Matthew Arnold's friend in the slums of London's East End had some of the rejoicing spirit of Paul: —

> 'Twas August, and the fierce sun overhead
>   Smote on the squalid streets of Bethnal Green,
>   And the pale weaver, through his window seen
> In Spitalsfield, looked thrice dispirited.
>
> I met a preacher there I knew and said,
>   "Ill and o'erworked, how fare you in this scene?"
>   "Bravely!" said he; "for I of late have been
> Much cheered with thoughts of Christ, the Living Bread."

Christ's Gospel is the mystery long hid, but now revealed to initiate the whole world into Christ, teaching every man all wisdom, to present him perfect, through all degrees, in Christ, in whom are all the treasures of wisdom and knowledge hidden.

In Christ there are no high-caste and low-caste, no high-degree and low-degree members. The Church is democratic — all wisdom for every man.

But a surface survey will not suffice. Toil and moil, dig and delve, like miners for the mine of treasures hid in Christ.

But — continue in the faith, grounded and steadfast, and be not moved away from the hope of the Gospel which ye heard, which was preached in all creation under heaven. Earthquakes are not to topple us from our foundation; storms are not to root us up out of the ground; floods are not to loosen us from our anchorage and moorings and set us adrift.

### PART THREE.

#### The Results.

##### 1. In General.

1. Negatively: Strike dead your sinful members on earth, put off the old man. 3, 5—9.

2. Positively: Put on the new man and use God's Word. 3, 10—17.

##### 2. In Particular.

Each and every one is to do his duty in his particular place and calling: 1) wives, 3, 18; 2) husbands, 3, 19; 3) children, 3, 20; 4) fathers, 3, 21; 5) servants, 3, 22—25; 6) masters, 4, 1; 7) all together, 4, 2—6.

#### Conclusion.

Personal matters and greetings. 4, 7—18.

## THE EPISTLE TO THE EPHESIANS.

Paul wrote the Colossians, 4, 16: "When this epistle is read among you, cause that it be read also in the church of the Laodiceans; and that ye likewise read the epistle from Laodicea." This may refer to the Epistle to the Ephesians, which likely was a circular letter to be read at Ephesus, at Laodicea, at Colossae, and perhaps at other places.

### THE INTRODUCTION

has seven clauses, "which rise like a thick cloud of incense higher and higher to the very throne of God."

### PART ONE.

#### The Doctrine of the Church.

*Chaps. 1—3.*

##### 1. The Eternal Plan.

Paul at once takes wing and makes his flight backward into eternity and swiftly soars upward into heaven and peers into the council chamber of the glorious Trinity and finds the conception of the Church was in the mind of God from eternity. Before the foundation of the world God hath chosen us in Christ; from eternity He predestined us unto the adoption of children by Jesus Christ unto Himself, according to the good pleasure of His will; from eternity He predestinated us according to the purpose of Him who worketh all things after the counsel of His own will.

In this eternal plan all the three persons of the Holy Trinity have a share. The Father hath chosen us in Christ and made us accepted in the Beloved. In Christ we have redemption through His blood, the forgiveness of sins, according to the riches of His grace. Believing in Christ, we were sealed with that Holy Spirit of promise who is the earnest of our inheritance until the redemption of the purchased possession.

Follows an earnest prayer that, "having the eyes of your hearts enlightened," ye may know fully the wealth and glory of your heritage and the power of God in raising Christ from the dead and making Him the Head of His body, the Church, which is the "fulness of Him who filleth all things with all things."

### 2. The Eternal Power.

The Apostle returns to earth and sees God's power and process of building the Church in this world age.

1. God hath quickened you, breathed into your nostrils His Holy Spirit, and so you became a living soul. God hath quickened you, who were dead in trespasses and sins; wherein in time past ye walked according to the course of this world, according to the prince of the power of the air, the spirit that now worketh in the children of disobedience, among whom also we all had our conversation in times past in the lusts of our flesh, fulfilling the desires of the flesh and of the mind; and were by nature the children of wrath, even as others. At that time ye were without Christ, having no hope, and without God in the world.

But God, who is rich in mercy, for the great love wherewith He loved us, even when we were dead in sins, hath quickened us together with Christ,—by grace are ye saved,—and hath raised us up together and made us sit together in heavenly places in Christ Jesus. This is the effectual working of His power.

2. This great grace of God is intended for the Gentiles as well as for the Jews; for Christ broke down the middle wall of partition and made the two parts one new man, one body unto God, through the cross; and preached peace to the one as well as to the other; and Gentiles as well as Jews, through Christ, have access in one spirit unto the Father. Both Jews and Gentiles are now fellow-citizens with the saints; both are of the house-

hold of God; both are stones built upon the foundation of Jesus Christ unto one holy temple in the Lord, one habitation of God through the Spirit.

The saints are the units; in Christ the units are unified and form a unity. This union is shown in four pictures.

1) Christ is the Savior, 5, 23, and the saved are united to Him.

2) Christ is the Corner-stone, 2, 20, and the saints are the stones built upon Him.

3) Christ is the Husband, 5, 25, and the Church, as His Bride, is united to Him.

4) Christ is the Head, 1, 22; 4, 15; 5, 23, and, as His Body, the Church is united to Him.

The Christians are "in Christ," Paul says one hundred and seventy-six times in his letters, thirty-six times in Ephesians, eleven times in the first sentence. No wonder it has been said Paul's theology could be summed up in these two words, "In Christ."

3. The process by which the power of God builds up the Church is that of preaching the Gospel. The Gospel is the mystery now revealed to God's holy apostles and prophets by His Spirit to preach to all men the unsearchable riches of Christ and the manifold wisdom of God, to make all men see what is the fellowship of the mystery, that Christ may dwell in your hearts by faith; that ye, being rooted and grounded in love, may be able to comprehend with all saints what is the breadth, and length, and depth, and height; and to know the love of Christ, which passeth knowledge, that ye might be filled with all the fulness of God.

### 3. THE ETERNAL PURPOSE.

Paul again, on heavenly wing, flies forward and upward and scans the eternal purpose God has for His Church. God has chosen His Church "to the praise of the glory of His grace wherewith He graced us in the Beloved," 1, 6. 12. 14; "that in ages to come He might show the exceeding riches of His grace, in His kindness toward us, through Christ Jesus. For by grace are ye saved, through faith; and that not of yourselves; it is the gift of God; not of works, lest any man should boast. Now, unto Him that is able to do exceeding abundantly above all that we ask or think, according to the power that worketh in us, unto Him be glory in the Church by Christ Jesus throughout all ages, world without end. Amen." 2, 7—9; 3, 20. 21.

## PART TWO.

### The Appeal to the Church.
*Chaps. 4—6.*

#### 1. The Appeal for Unity.

Christ, by the cross, made peace and unity; therefore keep this unity. The simplest duty based on the sublimest truth. "I, then, the prisoner of the Lord, exhort you to walk worthily of the calling in which ye were called." That is the clear key-note of the whole following appeal.

*1. The Unity of the Spirit.*

Give diligence to keep the unity of the Spirit in the bond of peace. Peace is the bond to bind together the Christians.

*2. The Unity of Faith.*

Strive to keep the unity of faith amid all the varieties of the different gifts God graciously gives to build His Church on earth. All are to serve us to grow unto a perfect man, unto the measure of the stature of the fulness of Christ, to grow up into Him in all things, who is the Head, even Christ.

*3. The Unity of Life.*

Strive for unity of life in the practise of the Christian virtues, though the heathen held them vices. Put off the old man, which is corrupt according to the deceitful lusts; put on the new man, which after God is created in righteousness and true holiness, sincerity, gentleness, self-control, honesty, and diligence, clean speech, mutual kindness, forgiving one another, even as God for Christ's sake hath forgiven you.

These duties of love are duties of light, — then walk as the children of light. 5, 1—20. As examples of his meaning the Apostle shows the mutual duties of husband and wife, 5, 22—33; of parents and children, 6, 1—4; of masters and servants, 6, 5—9.

#### 2. The Appeal for War.

The clanking of the long chain which coupled his right wrist to the soldier's left may have led Paul now to use the military language in which he couches his final appeal.

Finally, my brethren, be strong in the Lord and in the power of His might. Put on the whole armor of God that ye may be able to stand against the wiles of the devil. For we wrestle not against flesh and blood, but against principalities, against powers, against the rulers of the darkness of this world, against spiritual wickedness in high places. Wherefore take unto you the whole armor of God, that ye may be able to withstand in the evil day and, having done all, to stand. Stand, therefore, having your loins girt about with truth and having on the breastplate of righteousness and your feet shod with the preparation of the Gospel of peace; above all, taking the shield of faith, wherewith ye shall be able to quench all the fiery darts of the Wicked. And take the helmet of salvation and the sword of the Spirit, which is the Word of God; praying always with all prayer and supplication in the Spirit and watching thereunto with all perseverance and supplications for all saints and for me, that utterance may be given unto me, that I may open my mouth boldly, to make known the mystery of the Gospel, for which I am an ambassador in bonds; that therein I may speak boldly as I ought to speak.

THE CONCLUSION

gives a personal matter and a double benediction.

---

While Colossians and Ephesians are alike in some respects, they differ in others. In Colossians we hear the crash and clash of arms; in Ephesians we have peace and prayer and the paeans of praise. In Colossians we are on a field of battle; in Ephesians we are on holy ground; we put off our shoes, we enter the silence of the sanctuary to kneel in meditation and worship.

Paul was sitting in a Roman prison, at the same time he was sitting in heavenly places with Christ, and, like in Philippi, he was singing in prison. Ephesians is a solemn liturgy, instruction passing into prayer, creed soaring to the loftiest of evangelic psalms. It is the epistle of the ascension and the heavenlies, an ode to Christ and His spotless bride, the Church; the Song of songs and the Alps of the New Testament.

Calvin intended to make Ephesians the basis of his theology. Bunyan's *Pilgrim's Progress* got its suggestion and much of its inspiration here. Chrysostom says the epistle "overflows with lofty thoughts and doctrines," while Grotius thinks it "equals its sublimity of ideas with words more sublime than any human language ever possessed," and so Coleridge correctly classes it "the divinest composition of man." Farrar writes: "In the depth of its theology, in the loftiness of its morals, in the way in which the simplest moral truths are based upon the profoundest religious doctrines, this epistle is unparalleled." We might continue this cantata much longer, but let us end with a recitative by Luther: "It is one of the noblest books in the New Testament, which shows thee Christ and teaches thee everything necessary and good for thee to know."

## THE EPISTLE TO THE PHILIPPIANS.

When the Christians at Philippi heard Paul was in prison at Rome, they promptly raised a collection and sent it by Epaphroditus to cheer their beloved preacher, who had saved their souls by the Gospel of Christ Crucified.

Epaphroditus became Paul's fellow-worker and fellow-soldier in the Gospel. He worked so hard that in time he fell sick and was nigh unto death; but God in mercy restored him. 2, 25—30. Now he was going home, and Paul sent with him a letter of thanks for the gift. At the same time Paul uses this golden opportunity to appeal for unity, which was lacking mainly between Euodias and Syntyche, otherwise most excellent women, who labored with Paul in the Gospel. 4, 2. 3.

### PART ONE: THE APPEAL.
#### I. THE MIND OF CHRIST.

1. Christ was in the form of God, was really and truly God. Yet He was not minded to count that as a prize to be grasped for selfish satisfaction, as a soldier snatches the spoils of war for personal pleasure and profit. To His mind it was nobler to give service than to get service. To His mind it was more blessed to give than to receive. In His mind we find the inspiration of the royal motto, *"Ich dien'* — I serve."

2. That mind is embodied in action, definite and practical action. As a result of that mind Christ emptied Himself, divested Himself of the unbounded, continual use of His divine majesty; and became not a great one among men, but a servant; not a head servant, but the lowest of all; He became obedient, obedient even unto death, yea, the death of the cross. He humbled Himself until He could humble Himself no lower.

Christ, the Son of God, died the most shameful death on the accursed cross as our Substitute and Representative, the Just for the unjust, to bring us to God.

Mind readers? Yes, mind readers. We can readily read the very mind of Christ Himself, for here is the apocalypse, the revelation, the unveiling of the mind of Christ. It is a devotional volume. Let us kneel and worship in grateful adoration.

3. The reward of this humiliation? Exaltation. Wherefore also God highly exalted Him and gave unto Him the name which is above every name, that in the name of Jesus every knee should bow, of things in heaven and things on earth and things under the earth, and that every tongue should confess that Jesus Christ is Lord, to the glory of God the Father. 2, 5—11.

Here is the lowest depth of the deepest mystery of theology, and it is at once the basis of the most spiritual worship and the most potent incentive to the sanest and most strenuous social service in all the wide world. Here is the cold logic of the thinker, the lyric passion of the poet, and the practical enthusiasm of the reformer. The intellect, the heart, and the will in a threefold cord unite to Christ.

> From the throne of highest glory
> To the cross of deepest woe,
> All to ransom guilty captives! —
> Flow my praise, forever flow!

## II. THE MIND OF THE CHRISTIAN.

Having shown the mind of Christ, Paul bids the Christians show the same mind.

1. The mental attitude is the same. Whatever privilege a Christian has, he does not count it a prize to be grasped, as a victor snatches the spoils of war for selfish profit or pleasure; but he counts his privilege a sacred trust, to be lovingly used for the good of others also.

2. This mind will be embodied in a life. As Christ sacrificed Himself that there might be a saving Gospel, so the Christian will sacrifice himself to spread that saving Gospel. That alone is a life worthy of the Gospel of Christ.

The mind of Christ was the mind of Paul. He sacrificed all his bright prospects on earth and humbled himself to become a persecuted preacher of the Gospel of Christ. "I have suffered the loss of all things and do count them but dung that I may win Christ."

With all his good works, Paul puts no trust in his good works. "Not that I have already obtained or am already made perfect; but I press on. Like a racer running a race, forgetting the things behind, every meta marking the laps in the course of the Circus Maximus, pressing forward, and only forward, toward the grandstand, with the judge holding the palm of victory for the winner of the goal, so I run the race on the road of righteousness toward the goal unto the prize of the high calling of God in Christ Jesus. 3, 3—14.

This mind of Paul is to be the mind of all Christians. "Brethren, be ye imitators of me and mark them that so walk, even as ye have us for an example." They are to keep step with Paul like soldiers on parade.

Though they lived in Macedonia, these Philippians were not Macedonians, but a colony of Romans and citizens of Rome and governed by the laws of Rome, 700 miles away. So we Christians live in a sinful world, but we are not of the sinful world. Our citizenship is in heaven, whence also we wait for a Savior, the Lord Jesus Christ; who shall fashion anew the body of our humiliation that it may be conformed to the body of His glory, according to the working whereby He is able even to subject all things unto Himself. 3, 15—21.

The mind of Christ was the mind of the Philippians, in a measure, and Paul thanks God for their help in the Gospel. But they are to grow in this mind. I pray that your love may abound yet more and more, . . . being filled with the fruits of righteousness. . . . Stand fast in one spirit like an immovable phalanx of Roman veterans, with one soul striving athletically for the faith of the Gospel, fearless and brave as in a contest or conflict. 1, 3—11. 27—30. Be of the same mind, having the same love, being of one accord; doing nothing through faction or through vainglory, but in lowliness of mind each counting the other better than himself; not looking each of you to his own things, but each of you also to the things of others. 2, 1—4. 12—16.

Whatsoever things are true, whatsoever things are honorable, whatsoever things are just, whatsoever things are pure, whatsoever things are lovely, whatsoever things are of good report; if there be any virtue, and if there be any praise, think on these things. The things which ye both learned and received and heard and saw in me, these things do; and the God of peace shall be with you. 4, 8.

This has been called "Attic salt"; that is no compliment — in all Attica there never was salt of such flavor and aroma.

3. What is to brace and support the Christian in his life of sacrificing service? The mind of Christ. For the joy that was set before Him, Jesus

endured the cross, despising the shame, and is set down at the right hand of the throne of God. Heb. 12, 2. 3. As Christ, so the Christian. In his Philippian prison Paul had sung songs in the night; and he had not lost the habit, for in his Roman prison he writes: I joy and rejoice: do ye also joy and rejoice. This triumphant note bursts through this letter again and again. It comes from a man in chains and in prison. The sunflower holds its head high facing the full flood of the sunlight and laughing and praising the Lord all the day. Paul was like the sunflower: if things went well, he looked his King full in the face and rejoiced in Him. The night-blooming cereus sends blossoms of beauty from thorny stems in dank and dark cellars. Paul was like this plant: if things went ill, even in chains in a dank and dark prison, old, worn, and weary, he shot out beautiful blossoms. "Joy," "rejoice," "peace," "content," "thanksgiving," sparkle twenty times in one short letter.

Not long before Paul's imprisonment Cicero was exiled, but he could choose his own house, live in luxury, have troops of admiring friends around him; yet he forgot all the philosophy he had been preaching and in almost every letter broke out in unmanly wailing. While Paul was in prison, Seneca was exiled to Sardinia. Though he had immense wealth, high rank, great reputation, powerful friends working for him, the great Stoic philosopher forgot all his philosophy and gave way to weak wailing and groveled at the feet of an ex-slave and with fulsome flattery piteously begged him for help to return to Rome. As these, so others in olden times and in modern times. Contrast with these the mighty man in the aged, feeble, bent, scarred body of Paul! A victor, though in chains; a monarch, though in a dungeon; rejoicing and bidding others rejoice, though on the road to death; apostolic dignity amid adverse circumstances; heavenly contempt for the ills that flesh is heir to. Our faith is the victory that overcometh the world. Great religion, this Christianity!

## PART TWO: THE THANKS.

Paul closes his "love-letter" with warm words of thanks for the kind gift. "Not that I speak in respect of want; for I have learned in whatsoever state I am to be content. I know how to be abased, and I know also how to abound; in everything and in all things have I learned that secret both to be filled and to be hungry, both to abound and to be in want.

I can do all things in Him that strengtheneth me." 4, 10—13. On Christ we are dependent; of everybody else and everything else we are independent. Zeno of Greece and Seneca of Rome did not succeed in even saying such things. Paul said them and, what is infinitely more, lived them. This is not Stoic hardness, but Christian victory over circumstances. Paul could have walked down the streets of Athens with Socrates and sincerely say with that sage, "How many things there are which I can get along without!" In the spirit of Paul, Francis of Assisi cried out, "O brother, we are not worthy of such vast treasure!" — a piece of bread and a cup of cold water. Having slept for weeks on bare floors, John Wesley said, "Brother Nelson, let us be of good cheer. I have one whole side yet, for the skin is off but on one side."

Unbelievers may persecute a preacher, but Christians are to receive a faithful pastor "in the Lord with all gladness and hold such in reputation," in honor. The pastor has a right to expect right treatment from a Christian congregation. 2, 29. "Ye did well that ye had fellowship with my affliction. Not that I seek for the gift, but I seek for the fruit that increaseth to your account." 4, 14—17. Paul had done spiritual sowing and had a right to expect earthly reaping.

What these Philippian Christians did for their preacher all Christian churches are to do for their preachers, who save immortal souls by the Gospel of Christ.

The Philippians had given themselves to God and to Paul, and their personal religion was a purse-and-all religion. They had sent money to Paul twice at Thessalonica and once to Corinth and now at Rome. Phil. 4, 16; 2 Cor. 11, 9. They had sent money to the needy Jews at Jerusalem. And they gave according to their ability, and beyond their ability, in their deep poverty. They were not begged for their gift; it was they who begged Paul to receive their gift. God loveth a cheerful, that is, a hilarious, giver. God loved them, Paul loved them, we love them. As gracious givers they have erected a supreme monument to themselves. And this gift was a blessing to the giver and to the receiver and also "an odor of a sweet smell, a sacrifice acceptable, well-pleasing to God."

And this gift shall be a blessing to the givers even in the future — "My God shall supply every need of yours according to His riches in glory in Christ Jesus." It is Paul that is the real benefactor.

The Philippian church lived without a history and perished without a memorial — except the immortality it gained by this exquisite letter of thanks for a little gift of money. Has the world's literature anything nearly the equal of this occasional letter, this human document, this "love-letter"?

---

Paul had been delivered by the Centurion Julius to Burrus, the Prefect of the Praetorium, to await the coming of the accusers from Jerusalem and the scattered Jewish communities with the bill of indictment. Paul, the appellant, had to get from the judge *litterae dismissoriae* or *apostoli*, a brief stating the reasons for his appeal, with the needed documents.

A few years before, Claudius had laid down a law to free a prisoner if accusers did not appear in, say, eighteen months. Two years had now come and gone, and yet no accusers appeared, and the indictment was quashed and Paul set free. Felix and Festus had both seen the hollowness of the Jewish charges, and the Imperial Court of Appeals seems to have seen it also. This was either in the spring of 62 or, as Lanciani says, November or December, 63.

# CHAPTER IX.

## PAUL'S FOURTH MISSIONARY JOURNEY.

> A captive to the fowler's artful snare,
> Barred from his wonted flights in mountain air,
> The eagle folds his wing.— Lo! once again
> Dawns the bright day of freedom from the chain —
> Upward he springs to heaven with new delight
> And soars and soars till lost to mortal sight.

SO Paul flew as a bird set free from the cage and hastened to preach the Gospel. A few years ere this Paul had expressed his desire to go to Spain, and thirty years after, Clement of Rome wrote the Corinthians Paul had preached "on the confines of the West," Spain, as Dubowy proves. *Muratori's Fragments* of 170 expressly states Paul went to Spain, and Renan writes: "Weighty reasons induce us to believe that he carried out his project of a journey to Spain."

It seems Paul also went to Crete and left Titus in charge of the churches there. Titus 1, 5. In the second century Dionysius of Corinth wrote a letter to the Christians in Gnossus and Gortyna on that island.

At Ephesus, Paul ended the troubles in the church by putting out of the church Hymenaeus, Philetus, and Alexander, and then left Timothy in charge of the work.

While still in prison, Paul had asked Philemon to prepare him lodgings, and at this time the Apostle visited Colossae, Laodicea, and Hierapolis.

While still in prison, Paul promised to visit the Philippians as soon as possible, and in all probability he kept that promise now.

Possibly from Corinth, Paul sent Artemas to relieve Titus, who was to meet the Apostle at Nicopolis, where he would winter.

From Lechaeum, the western port of Corinth, Paul sailed for Nicopolis, "The City of Victory," the capital of Epirus, built by Augustus in memory of his great naval victory at Actium over Mark Antony and Cleopatra on September 2, B. C. 31, which made him master of the world.

The place where the tent of Augustus had stood was paved with stones and ornaments, with the iron beaks of Antony's ships; next to it rose a temple of Apollo and the statues of the muleteer Eutychus and his mule Nikon, whom Augustus met as a good omen on the morning of the battle.

Nicopolis was a Roman colony, a free city, a city of the first rank, filled with splendid monuments erected by foreign princes to flatter Augustus; Herod the Great was foremost in his munificent gifts.

Amid their interminable labyrinth of broken columns, ruins of temples, baths, theaters, towers, gateways, and aqueducts a small building in the form of a pagan temple is the most interesting, which, tradition asserts, was used by St. Paul as a house of prayer.

From "The City of Victory" Paul set out to get more victories for his great Captain. He preached in Epirus, in Illyria, and in Dalmatia; for otherwise Paul would hardly have sent Titus hither. 2 Tim. 4, 10.

After this we find Paul in Troas, guest of Carpus, where he left his cloak, books, and parchments. 2 Tim. 4, 13. Here, probably, he was arrested and hurried to Ephesus to be tried by the Proconsul Barea Soranus.

The ruins of Paul's prison are still shown at Ephesus, and Ignatius, the bishop of Antioch, in 150, likens himself to Paul in that he also was sent from Ephesus to Rome to suffer martyrdom. Possibly Paul again, as a Roman citizen, appealed to Caesar; possibly the noble Barea Soranus did not like to execute Paul and, as Pliny did with Christians, sent him to Nero. Possibly Soranus sailed with his distinguished prisoner; at any rate, he was killed for his virtues in Rome by Nero in 66.

From Ephesus they set out for Miletus, where Trophimus was left sick; at Corinth Erastus remained behind. From Lechaeum they sailed for Aulon in Illyria, crossed over to Brundisium, and on the Appian Way went on to Rome. They found the Porta Capena carefully guarded, owing to the recent attempt on Nero's life; but being bound for the palace, they found ready admission.

About this time Paul wrote

## THE FIRST EPISTLE TO TIMOTHY,

telling him how to behave in the house of God.

### I. IN GENERAL.

Timothy is warned against all doctrines differing from the Gospel as fables and endless genealogies, causing quarrels and disputes and having no practical value. The end of the charge is love out of a pure heart and a good conscience and faith unfeigned. This is the one important thing, and when people quit this, they turn aside to vain talking. 1, 3—7.

To be sure, the Law is good if a man use it lawfully — to open the eyes of the sinner, to see his sinfulness, in order to lead him to the glorious Gospel. 1, 8—11.

The Gospel is so glorious that Paul thanks Christ for turning him from ignorance and leading him to faith in Him and making him His servant. 1, 12—14.

And what is this glorious Gospel? Faithful is the saying, and worthy of all acceptation, that Christ Jesus came into the world to save sinners, of whom I am chief.

For this salvation Paul glorifies God and charges Timothy to war a good warfare and faithfully preach this glorious Gospel of salvation. 1, 15—20.

The Gospel is intensely practical. If we heartily believe it, we will make supplication, adoration, intercession, and thanksgiving, a) for all men in general, and b) in particular for all men in authority, that we may lead a quiet and peaceable life in all godliness and honesty. This life — godly toward God and honest toward men — is good and acceptable to God, our Savior, who would have all men to be saved and come to the knowledge of the truth.

What is truth?

There is one God, and one Mediator between God and men, the man Christ Jesus, who gave Himself a ransom for all, to be testified in due time. 2, 1—8.

Again it is shown this preaching is practical. Preach that Christ gave Himself a ransom for all, and you open the fountain of love, and a stream of good works will flow out to make fruitful the world.

Men will pray in holiness, without wrath and doubting. Prayer will be ethical, not mechanical. Prayer will come from a heart without wrath against man and without doubt against God.

And women will adorn themselves — do not forget that! But they will adorn themselves in modest apparel, with shamefacedness and sobriety; not with braided hair and gold or pearls or costly raiment, but (which becometh women professing godliness) through good works. Woman's dress is not to be conspicuous and suggestive, especially not in places of public worship. And here she will not be loud and forward and masterful;

she will not be a public preacher. Holy woman's holy sphere is the holy home; she will shine as the godly mother of her godly children. 2, 8—15.

Such holy men and women are produced by the glorious Gospel, and so the preaching of this Gospel is "a good thing," as Paul calls it. Not everybody is fit for this glorious work, and so Paul gives some qualifications a pastor must have for the work. 3, 1—7.

Even such men are not able to do the church-work alone; they need helpers. Not everybody is fit to be a helper, and so Paul points out the qualifications of the deacons. 3, 8—13.

Such pastors and such helpers are to labor in the house of God, which is the Church of the living God, the pillar and ground of the truth. 3, 15.

What truth?

Without controversy great is the mystery of godliness: —
God was made manifest in flesh,
Was declared righteous in spirit,
Was made visible unto messengers,
Was proclaimed among nations,
Was believed on in the world,
Was taken up in glory. 3, 16.

### II. IN PARTICULAR.

From the foregoing glorious Gospel some will fall away, preaching the doctrine of devils, but Timothy is to battle against all false teaching with the Gospel, preach it with zeal, study, and diligence. 4, 1—16.

He is told how to carry himself toward men and women, old and young; especially towards widows, both old and young. 5, 1—16.

The pastors are to be held in double honor and to receive proper support, for the laborer is worthy of his hire. 5, 17. 18.

After more pastoral advice to Timothy, 5, 19—6, 2, Paul denounces the ignorant insolence and grasping greed of false teachers, 6, 3—5, and shows that godliness with contentment is great gain, 6, 6—10, and in this Timothy is to be steadfast till the appearing of our Lord Jesus Christ, 6, 11—16.

Since godliness with contentment is great gain, the rich Christians are not to be high-minded nor trust in uncertain riches, but in the living God, and do good, be rich in good works, ready to distribute, willing to communicate, laying up in store for themselves a good foundation against the time to come, that they may lay hold on eternal life. 6, 17—19.

O Timothy, be faithful to the truth and watchful against false teaching! Grace be with thee!

---

About this time also Paul wrote

## THE EPISTLE TO TITUS.

### I. The Placing of Pastors.

Titus had been left in Crete to "set in order the things that are wanting and ordain elders in every city."

This was a difficult field; for according to a general proverb the Kretans, the Kappadokians, and the Kilikians were the three worst K's of the ancient world.

The Cretans were such finished liars that "to cretize" means to lie. J. Rendel Harris says they got their reputation as liars when they claimed the chief god Zeus was dead and buried on their island.

Plutarch tells us "they stuck to money like bees to their combs." Leonides adds this touch: "The Cretans are always brigands and piratical and unjust. Who ever knew justice among Cretans?" Though quite quarrelsome among themselves, they always managed to unite against an outside foe, and from this we get our "syncretism." Himself a Cretan, Epimenides, in the sixth century B. C., says in his poem *On Oracles:* "The Cretans are always liars, evil wild beasts, lazy gluttons." This is quoted by Callimachus in his *Hymn to Zeus* and by Paul in this epistle, who adds: "This witness is true." 1, 12. 13.

Surely in such a difficult field uncommonly able ministers were needed to build up the Church and defend it against the enemies, and after the greeting, 1, 1—4, Paul gives the Qualifications of Pastors. 1, 5—16.

### II. The Preaching of Pastors.

"Speak thou the things which become sound doctrine."

Aged men, aged women, young women, young men, and slaves — all are to be sober-minded and each one obedient in his or her own particular position in life. All of them, even slaves, are to adorn the doctrine of God, our Savior, in all things. 2, 1—10. This holy life is produced by the Gospel, and the Gospel is intended to produce this holy life.

"For the grace of God hath appeared, bringing salvation to all men, training us to the intent that, denying ungodliness and worldly lusts, we should live soberly — toward ourselves — and righteously — toward our neighbor — and godly — toward God — in this present world; looking for the blessed hope and appearing of the glory of the great God and our Savior Jesus Christ, who gave Himself for us that He might redeem us from all iniquity and purify unto Himself a people for His own possession, zealous of good works." 2, 11—15.

Our past redemption, our present duty, and our future hope; our duty to ourselves, to our neighbors, and to our God are all fused in this one wonderful word of the Epiphany of Grace.

Again Paul calls for all kinds of Christian virtues, and again Paul points out the one good root of all good fruit.

When the kindness of God, our Savior, and His love toward man appeared, not by works done in righteousness, which we did ourselves, but according to His mercy, He saved use through the washing of regeneration and renewing of the Holy Spirit, which He poured out on us richly, through Jesus Christ, our Savior, that, being justified by His grace, we might be made heirs according to the hope of eternal life. Faithful is the saying, and concerning these things I desire that thou affirm confidently, to the end that they who have believed God may be careful to maintain good works. These things are good and profitable unto men. 3, 1—11. The philanthropy of God produces philanthropy in man. These are two gems of the purest water. The aged master's hand had not lost its cunning.

On the arrival of Artemas or Tychicus to relieve him, Titus was to hurry from Crete to meet Paul at Nicopolis, where he would winter.

## THE CAESAR TO WHOM PAUL APPEALED.

"I appeal unto Caesar!" Paul protested. "Hast thou appealed unto Caesar? Unto Caesar shalt thou go!" Festus retorted. Acts 25, 11. 12. Now that Paul was to stand before Caesar, let us look at that Caesar from whom Paul looked for a fair trial.

Cn. Domitius Ahenobarbus — Redbeard — was a vicious man and married the dissolute sister of the Emperor Caligula and said cynically, "Nothing but what was detestable and dangerous to the public welfare could ever be produced from him and Agrippina." True prophet! They produced Nero. They say his mother asked fortune-tellers about him, who told her Nero would be emperor and kill his mother. "Let him kill me, if only he'll be emperor!"

When her own brother, the Emperor Caligula, had to banish her, and her husband died in 40, their son Lucius, born at Antium on December 15, 37, went to live with the wanton Domitia Lepida, worthy mother of the dissolute Messalina, the first wife of the Emperor Claudius, and so shame-

MESSALINA.    BRITANNICUS.
CLAUDIUS.    OCTAVIA.

less that all Rome knew of her adulteries. While Claudius was at Ostia, she forced the handsome Silius to leave his young wife and publicly before many witnesses "married" him. Narcissus told Claudius on the way home Messalina went to her mother's on the Pincian Hill, who advised the precious daughter to kill herself. She couldn't; a soldier ran her through with a sword. When Claudius was told of her death, he silently emptied his goblet of wine.

A barber and a dancer were put in charge of the boy's education.

When Cassius Cerea killed Caligula on January 24, 41, Agrippina returned and married the orator Crispus Passienus and after his death became the fourth wife of her uncle, the Emperor Claudius, in 49.

On February 25, 50, he adopted Lucius as son and joint heir and named him Nero Claudius Caesar Drusus Germanicus.

In 41 the Spaniard Seneca had been banished to Corsica by Messalina. After eight years Agrippina called him back and made him tutor of Nero; Afranius Burrus, a Gaul by birth, had charge of the military training. Early in 53 Claudius married his own thirteen-year-old Octavia to his fifteen-year-old stepson.

At the Trojan games in the Circus Maximus, Nero got more applause than Britannicus, the Emperor's own son, and this influenced Nero; all his life he was stage-struck and thirsted for applause.

When the loving Agrippina put her beloved Claudius out of the way in a pleasant way with poisoned mushrooms on October 13, 54, the Emperor's own son, Britannicus, was pushed back, and the seventeen-year-old Nero was pushed upon the throne of the Roman World Empire on October 13, 54.

Nero himself pronounced the grandiose funeral oration over Claudius, which had been composed by Seneca.

In his *Apocolocynthosis,* Seneca has Apollo say to Nero: —

> Let him overpass
> The span of mortal years, Prince with my face,
> My fairness; skilled as I in speech and song.
> He brings an age of joy to mortal men
> And breaks the silence that held Justice dumb.
> Now, Rome, thy sovereign comes, and thou shalt see
> Thy Nero; bright his glance with gentle fire;
> Proud springs his neck beneath his curling hair.

Nero was of medium stature, strong of limb, had fine features, a ruddy complexion, blue eyes, and wore his light hair in tresses, like a girl; and when he visited Greece, it was even bound in a fillet at the back of his neck. Later he was big of body, thick of neck, and dull of eye, Suetonius tells us. He was usually attired in the most fantastic dress and never wore the same robe twice.

Painting, singing, sculpture, poetry, music, oratory, and charioteering filled his whole time.

Upon one of his rehearsals a solemn thanksgiving to the gods was

312　PAUL'S FOURTH MISSIONARY JOURNEY.

NERO.

KAULBACH.

decreed, and it was resolved to dedicate a part of his verses in letters of gold to Jupiter Capitolinus. On a day of the athletic games Nero shaved his beard, placed it in a box of pure gold, enchased with precious stones, and consecrated it to the same "Father of gods and men"!

Seneca was the first author of the age and the power behind the throne.

"Seneca, the teacher of virtue, was banished by Claudius for an intrigue with Julia and afterwards lived in adultery with Agrippina. He denounced tyrants and was the tutor of a tyrant; he sneered at the companions of kings and was never away from the palace. He attacked flatterers and paid such court to Messalina and the freedmen that he afterwards suppressed the works on this subject. He blamed the rich and amassed 75,000,000 denarii ($12,500,000); he bewails luxury, and to entertain his friends, owned a set of five hundred sandal-wood tables with legs of ivory. Finally, he was a preacher of morals who kept boys for his pleasure, and even initiated Nero in such courses." So says Dio Cassius, the historian.

Seneca and Burrus guided the young Emperor, and the empire fared well. On coming to power, Nero promised to return to the ways of Augustus. By omitting no opportunity of liberality, clemency, or courtesy, he made good his promise, according to his bitter biographer Suetonius. He ended or lessened the more oppressive taxes; he kept down the spy system; he treated the Senate with respect; he refused the servile honors heaped upon him; he softened the courts of justice, so that death penalties were rare, — when asked to sign a death warrant, the young Emperor sighed, "How I wish that I could not write!"

After forty years of monstrous atrocities under monster fiends like Tiberius, Caligula, and Claudius, these first five years seemed like the very age of gold, and they were wistfully remembered in the terrible times to come. The Emperor Trajan is often quoted as wishing his own reign might equal in dignity the first five years of Nero's; but this is wrong; at most he refers only to Nero's building operations.

Agrippina was ambitious; still beautiful, she stooped to the most shameless deeds to gain her end. She tried to sit on the throne with Nero. Being a great-grandson of Augustus and therefore a possible rival, Lucius Silanus was put out of the way. His brother Junius, the Proconsul of Asia, a harmless fellow nicknamed "The Golden Sheep," was poisoned at a friendly banquet. Nero's stepbrother Britannicus, son of Claudius and

Messalina, a boy of fourteen, might claim the throne, and so Locusta was ordered to mix the poison which was given at a friendly family gathering.

Seneca addressed to Nero the work "On Mercy" in order to remove the bad impression the cold-blooded murder left on the god-fearing Stoic.

Nero soon tired of his virtuous wife Octavia and in 55 lived with the Greek flower girl Acte, a former slave. After three years he tired of her and took up with Poppaea, Rome's greatest beauty, the granddaughter of the famous general Poppaeus Sabinus. Poppaea had been the mistress of Burrus and Tigellinus, divorced from one husband and now the wife of Marcus Salvius Otho. Nero took from his friend his fair wife and comforted him with the fair province of Lusitania — a fair exchange; he married her in 62.

Britain had been made a province in 43; Suetonius Paulinus took Mona — Anglesey — in 61; many Romans were slaughtered, but Suetonius Paulinus gained a victory, and Queen Boudicca, or Boadicea, killed herself. King Polemo presented Pontus to Rome, and the Cottian Alps came on the death of Cottius.

The powerful Pallas, a former slave and brother of the Governor Felix, who had held Paul in Caesarea, amassed a fortune of $15,000,000, and the Senate honored him for the law forbidding free Roman ladies to marry slaves. He was now dismissed, and that told the world Agrippina's rule was ended.

The keen-eyed Burrus said: "Keep him from the taste of blood; the wild beast within him, once awakened, will grow insatiable." True prophet of evil. A Greek saying ran, "Chaos, when I am dead." "No! chaos, while I live!" shouted Nero.

In 59 Nero was at Baiae, near Naples; he invited his mother to Bauli; he gave a feast in her honor; at parting he folded her in his arms and kissed her; the tutor Anicetus was to take her in a boat and drown her; she saved herself by swimming. Nicetus was sent to Bauli, broke into her bedchamber, and soldiers killed her with clubs and swords.

Seneca told the Senate Agrippina had sent Agerinus to murder Nero and, hearing of the failure, had committed suicide.

On the way to the Capitol the Romans receive Nero with joy; thank-offerings burn in the temples; the Senate assembles in the curia and declares in the name of Rome that Agrippina's death is a boon to the state. Thrasea Paetus was the single one to blush to share in this hideous farce; in 62 even he in the Senate called Nero an admirable prince.

But Nero said that sleeping and waking he saw furies with fiery torches and swinging their scourges. He called magi from the East to exorcise and appease his mother's spirit; all in vain. He dared not go to the Eleusinian mysteries and hear the herald cry: "Let the sin-oppressed and guilty remain far off!"

Placards on statues and the basilicas called Nero the Orestes, mother murderer. Antistius recited verses insulting to Nero — and was only banished. Nero divorced his virtuous wife Octavia and banished her to Pandataria. Anicetus swore she had committed adultery with him; she was killed; her head was sent to Rome to be a feast to the eyes of Poppaea, who embraced the Jewish faith, and was driven stark naked through Rome in a chariot by Nero. Her statues were set up to adorn Rome. She bore Nero a daughter, who died after three months; she was placed among the gods and given a temple and priests. Later Nero kicked Poppaea to death; others say he only poisoned her.

People like Seneca, Burrus, Gallio, and Lucan had to be stage-managers for the fool emperor who was stage-struck and insisted upon singing with his cracked and husky voice, or playing upon his golden lyre with his trembling hands, or dancing with his spindle legs under his big belly, or reciting poetry of his own home-spun variety. If the people did not applaud, soldiers forced them to do so. Like a spoiled child he always cried for the first prize, and Lucan had to sing his victories in polished verses, only to be killed for all his pains. These performances were given in Nero's own circus on the Vatican. He ran a chariot race in the Circus Maximus. His chariot of ivory white and burnished metal with four jet-black horses and tossing plumes was the finest of all entries. Nero's transparent robe of shimmering gold was clasped to his shoulders with amethysts, which was also the color of his racing ribbons. He drove, smiling, to the first position. At the drop of the white handkerchief the racers were off with a yell and the crack of their whips. Nero's racing colors fluttered in the lead — the other racers knew what was good for their health. They maneuvered to keep from passing the Emperor; they jockeyed for second place. The people caught on and laughed. Yelling like a madman, Nero passed the winning post.

Bending on one knee, he blushingly felt the green wreath pressed upon his long, tangled yellow curls.

All knew he was fierce, and all but himself knew he was a farce.

A comic cartoon has him as a butterfly driving the fiery steeds of the chariot of state.

During one of Nero's artistic performances Vespasian fell asleep and for the heinous crime of not applauding had to pay dearly.

Strange to say — or isn't it strange? — the parts Nero liked most to play were those of Orestes and Alcmaeon — the two mother murderers.

Cornelius Sulla and Rubellius Plautus were killed. Narcissus, one of Rome's best men, was cast into a damp dungeon to starve. In 62 Burrus was poisoned, and Nero was suspected. Now Tigellinus ruled in the place of Burrus and Seneca.

Tigellinus gave a feast in honor of Nero on an artificial floating island in Agrippina's lake, likely on the Campus Martius, a feast so unspeakably vile that even the Rome of that day was shocked; Henry Sienkiewicz treats it in *Quo Vadis?*

A few days later Nero dressed himself as a bride in saffron veil and publicly married the boy Pythagoras for the vice of pederasty, in 64.

## THE BURNING OF ROME.

It was 418 years, 418 months, and 418 days after the Gauls had burned Rome when a fire broke out in the night of the 18th to the 19th of July, 64, three years after Queen Boadicea had burned London. The blaze started at the eastern end of the Circus Maximus, with its 150,000 seats, and raged for six days.

Nero came from his favorite seaside residence of Antium and ordered some buildings torn down to stop the fire. Suddenly it blazed up afresh in the Aemelian gardens of Tigellinus and raged for three days more.

From the Tower Maecenas on the Esquiline Hill, mentioned by Horace, Nero gazed his fill at the furious fire, ravished by the beauty of the flames, — such were his very words, — decked himself in theatrical toggery, and in his thin voice sang of the Fall of Troy to his everlasting guitar. The song may have been from his own poem *Troica*, for Juvenal sneers Orestes was better than Nero; for

> Never sang on the stage Orestes,
> Never *Troica* wrote.

Of the fourteen "regions," or wards, of Rome three were completely burned, seven severely damaged, only four untouched; masses of men had perished; most had lost their all; a few enriched themselves, giving themselves out as government officials. To top all, the plague carried off above 30,000 citizens.

The houses of the Emperor Tiberius, Caligula, and others on the Palatine were so prodigious and sumptuous that our word "palace" comes from that famous hill; but Nero scoffed at the efforts of his forebears and boasted he would show the world what a Nero could do.

He turned the public calamity to his private profit and pleasure. In mad haste he built his dream palace, the Golden House, and turned the surrounding waste into a huge park — fertile fields, pools, artificial solitudes, terraces, and perspectives, everything which in the heart of a city might produce the illusion of the countryside.

Nero's Golden House was richly overlaid with gold and everywhere adorned with the dazzling glitter of precious stones and mother-of-pearl. In the vaulted roofs of his banqueting rooms were several little tables of ivory

THE SILENT WITNESS OF NERO'S "LIVING TORCHES."
Now in front of St. Peter's.
From Piranesi.

so contrived as to turn around and scatter flowers and hollow pipes to shower down perfumed oils upon the guests. His principal dining-room was round and in perpetual motion, day and night, like the celestial sphere. His baths were continually flowing, either with sea-water, or else fed from the sulfureous springs of Tivoli. The golden stalls for his chariot horses and the porticoes and columns extended a mile in length. "Now I can live like a human being!" In the vestibule stood his statue, 120 feet high, and this colossal image gave the name to the Colosseum, the Flavian Theater, later built on this site. The statue was in bronze compounded of gold and silver, the work of Zenodorus, the greatest Greek sculptor of his time and, according to Pliny, a master of bronze casting.

Raffael and Giovanni da Udine went through the rubbish of centuries down to the ruins of this Golden House and brought with them, in mind, the sketch for the wall pictures you may see to-day in the arcades of the court of Damasus in the Vatican.

The *insulae* — tenements — of ungainly height, along narrow and crooked streets, were rapidly replaced by sightly stone structures along broad and regular streets with arcades. Rich rewards were given according to the speed with which people rebuilt in keeping with plans laid down by Nero. The provinces were plundered to meet the great expenses. Nero's freedman Acratus was sent into Asia to strip even the temples of the gods of the finest statues and paintings to adorn the Emperor's Golden House.

In 65 Piso conspired against Nero; Melichus disclosed the plot in hopes of a rich reward. The suspects were slaughtered and their wealth taken. Lucan, the poet of the *Pharsalia* and nephew of Gallio and Seneca, had to kill himself. Gallio had to kill himself. Seneca had to kill himself. Thrasea Paetus and Barea Soranus had to kill themselves. The poet Petronius Arbiter had to kill himself. Corbulo, half-brother of Caesonia, one of the wives of Caligula, had triumphed twice over Tiridates, yet he had to kill himself.

Large rewards were given to stimulate accusers; those of Thrasea Paetus each got about $225,000. All the efforts of Nero to heal the hurt of Rome were of no avail.

The sanctuary consecrated to Luna by Servius Tullius; the altar of Hercules, Evander's handiwork; the temple dedicated by Romulus to Jupiter Stator; Numa's palace; the Penates of the Roman people; the masterpieces of Greek art, trophies of so many victories — all were wiped away!

The blow had pierced Rome's heart. The people frowned and scowled, and murmured and muttered and pointed to Caesar as the Great Incendiary.

Nero tried to turn their thoughts to religious ceremonies. The Sibylline Books were opened and their orders obeyed; prayers to Vulcan, to Ceres, to Proserpine, lustrations of the Roman ladies, supplications, holy vigils.

All in vain! The demand for the culprit daily waxed more menacing and rose to the very ears of Nero.

Like a lost man Nero scanned the earth for a scapegoat. — The Christians! Ha! the hated and despised Christians — they did it!

## NERO'S TORCHES.

The Roman historian Tacitus writes: "Neither these religious ceremonies nor the liberal donations of the prince — Nero — could efface from the minds of men the prevailing opinion that Rome was set on fire by his own orders. The infamy of that horrible transaction still clung to him.

NERO'S LIVING TORCHES.

H. VON SIEMIRADZKI.

In order, if possible, to remove the imputation, he determined to transfer the guilt to others. For this purpose he punished with exquisite torture a race of men detestable for their evil practises, by vulgar appellation called Christians. . . . Nero proceeded with his usual artifice. He found a set of profligate and abandoned wretches, who were induced to confess themselves guilty; and on the evidence of these men a number of Christians were convicted, not, indeed, upon clear evidence of their having set fire to the city, but rather on account of their sullen hatred of the whole human race. They were put to death with exquisite cruelty; and to their sufferings Nero added mockery and derision. Some were covered with the skins of wild beasts and left to be devoured by dogs. Others were nailed to the cross; numbers were burned alive; and many, covered over with inflammable substances, were lighted up when the day declined to serve as torches during the night. For the convenience of seeing this tragic spectacle the emperor lent his own gardens. He added the sports of the circus and assisted in person, sometimes driving a curricle and occasionally mixing with the rabble in a coachman's dress. At length the cruelty of these proceedings filled every heart with compassion. Humanity relented against the Christians; for it was evident that they fell a sacrifice, not for the good of mankind, but to glut the rage of one man alone." — *Annals*, chap. 15.

Suetonius gives unreserved praise to Nero for having deluged the world with the blood of a new and mischievous sect.

This Neronian sport was held in the early days of August, 64.

Juvenal blames Tigellinus for this horrible persecution of the Christians, for he says: —

> Paint Tigellinus, and your fate will be
> To burn with brimstone at the martyr's tree,
> While, as the flames consume the living brand,
> A crimson rill runs trickling o'er the sand.
>
> *Satires*, 1, 155.

The gardens of Nero were on the Vatican Hill, inherited from his mother Agrippina. Caligula built the circus and in it by torchlights beheaded the Senators Papirius and Bassus with their wives.

Here had been the four-acre farm of Cincinnatus, called from the plow to become the savior of Rome.

Sulpicius Severus writes: "This was the beginning of the persecution of the Christians; afterwards laws were passed forbidding their religion, and by virtue of certain edicts, which were published abroad officially, it was no longer lawful to be a Christian."

215  PAUL SHIPWRECKED ON MALTA

Acts 28:5

DIANA OR CHRIST?

The first edict was issued by Nero likely soon after the massacre in his Vatican Gardens.

The persecution spread from Rome into the provinces. The Christians were asked to offer sacrifices to the Emperor and to the heathen idols and to curse and deny the name of Christ; upon refusal they were punished, even with death. Thus they suffered "as Christians," 1 Pet. 4, 16; they suffered for the simple fact that they were Christians.

The firmness with which they bore their sufferings and death was the admiration of even pagan idolaters, and many of them were turned to Christ, and so "the blood of the martyrs became the seed of the Church," as Tertullian beautifully phrases it. Martial has this: —

| When Mutius dared upon command | The silly herd! Far braver he |
|---|---|
| To thrust into the fire his hand, | Who, standing at the martyr's tree, |
| With shouts the people rent the skies | Can yet defy the rabble's cries |
| To laud the noble sacrifice. | And say, "I make no sacrifice." |

### PAUL ARRESTED.

Paul was arrested for the crime of being a Christian and dragged to Rome for trial as an evil-doer. He was put in prison — some say the Mamertine. This was a cell 24 by 16 feet; under it there was another gloomy, circular dungeon dating from Servius Tullius and so called the Tullianum. Here Jugurtha died of starvation after six days of torture; here were strangled the followers of Catiline, Vercingetorix, etc.; the corpses were taken out to be exposed on the Gemonii and then cast into the Tiber.

So rigid was Paul's confinement that Onesiphorus, who had refreshed Paul at Ephesus, now found him only after a diligent search, 2 Tim. 1, 16. 17; 4, 19; so bitter the cold that Paul begged for his cloak left at Troas with Carpus, 2 Tim. 4, 13.

*The Trial.* — Appeals from the provinces in civil causes were heard in one of the basilicas about the Forum by one of the Emperor's delegates; but Paul's was a criminal case, and such were usually heard by Nero in person.

Tiberius and Claudius had heard these cases in the Forum, but following the example of Augustus, Nero judged them at the palace on the Palatine in the temple of Apollo, connected with the Greek and the Latin library, and the whole enclosed by a splendid portico.

But the Palatine now lay in ashes, and so Paul was likely led to Nero's Golden House on the Coelian and Esquiline hills.

THE LAST PRAYER.

## PAUL BEFORE NERO.

The Emperor, "of power equal to the gods," in the words of Juvenal, wearing the imperial purple, headed by twelve lictors with the fasces and attended by a strong German guard, entered and took his seat on the tribunal and presided. On lower benches sat his twenty assessors, or jurors, including the two consuls, magistrates, and senators. Each had three tablets: one marked A — *Absolvo,* not guilty; another C — *Condemno,* guilty; the third N. L. — *Non liquet,* adjournment for further hearing.

The emperors generally simply sanctioned the judgment of the jurors, but Nero often gave sentence according to his whim.

Paul was brought into the court filled with a motley crowd of various nationalities from the four corners of the earth.

The accusation was made — by Alexander, the coppersmith? Paul says he "laid many evil things to my charge; . . . he greatly withstood our words."

And Paul? "At my first answer, or hearing, no man stood by me, but all men forsook me. I pray God that it may not be laid to their charge. But the Lord stood by me, that through me the Gospel might be fully preached and that all the Gentiles might hear."

So ably did Paul conduct his own case, so convincingly did he speak, that for the time he was not condemned. "I was delivered out of the mouth of the lion." 2 Tim. 4, 14—17. "The lion is dead," announced the jailer to Agrippa at the death of Tiberius, and Queen Esther went "before the lion" — Xerxes. Paul was remanded to prison for further action.

In prison Paul, the aged, was rather lonely. Crescens had been sent to Galatia, Titus to Dalmatia, Tychicus to Ephesus. "All they that are from Asia have turned away from me. Demas has forsaken me, having loved this present world. Only Luke is with me. Often has he consoled me, nor was he ashamed of my chains." No wonder Paul urges his beloved Timothy to hurry from Ephesus before winter. And it is pleasant to read he longs for Mark, "for he is profitable to me for the ministry." Mark had reformed, and Paul had restored him. Paul sends greetings from Eubulus, Pudens, Claudia, Linus, and "all the brethren." 2 Tim. 4, 9—12. 21. Let us hope they refreshed him in the privacy of prison, though they dared not publicly protect him in court.

# CHAPTER X.

# PAUL'S DEATH AND HIS INFLUENCE.

WITH the headsman's sword hanging over him, Paul wrote THE SECOND EPISTLE TO TIMOTHY, his last will and testament, his swan-song; wrote it "not so much with ink as with Paul's own blood. It is the solemn subscription of the Pauline doctrine and faith," says Calvin. After the greeting and

THE EMPEROR HADRIAN AND HIS ARCH AT JERUSALEM.

thanksgiving Paul exhorts his beloved young friend to stir into flame the gift of God and suffer hardship with the Gospel of God, who saved us with a holy calling, not according to our works, but according to His own purpose and grace, which was given us in Christ Jesus before times eternal, but hath now been manifested by the appearing of our Savior Christ Jesus, who abolished death and brought life and immortality to light through the Gospel, whereunto I was appointed a preacher and an apostle and a teacher. For which cause I suffer also these things; yet I am not ashamed; for I know Him whom I have believed, and I am persuaded

**PYRAMID OF GAIUS CESTIUS.**
Paul passed this pyramid on his way to martyrdom on the Ostian Way.

that He is able to guard that which I have committed unto Him against that day. 1, 6—12.

Timothy is to suffer hardship as a good soldier of Jesus Christ, as Paul suffered hardship unto bonds, as a malefactor; but the Word of God is not bound! 2, 1—13.

Note the tone of exultation.

Then follow rules how pastors are to conduct themselves. 2, 14—26.

False teachers will arise and lead people away from Christ, "but abide thou in the things which thou hast learned. From a babe thou hast known the sacred writings, which are able to make thee wise unto salvation through faith which is in Christ Jesus. Every scripture inspired of God is also profitable for teaching, for reproof, for correction, for instruction which is in righteousness, that the man of God may be complete, furnished completely unto every good work." 3—4, 5.

Now comes the wonderful, triumphant, exulting shout of victory of the Grand Old Man: "I am already being offered,— for sacrifice, poured out as a drink-offering,— and the time of my

CHURCH OF ST. PAUL AT THE THREE FOUNTAINS.
Here the Apostle was beheaded.

departure is come. I have fought the good fight, I have finished the course, I have kept the faith; henceforth there is laid up for me the crown of righteousness, which the Lord, the righteous Judge, shall give me at that day; and not to me only, but also to all them that have loved His appearing. . . . The Lord will deliver me from every evil work and will save me unto His heavenly kingdom: to whom be glory forever and ever! Amen."

At the second hearing, before governors, as Clement of Rome writes, Paul was found guilty, condemned to death, returned to prison. A delay of ten days was usual to enable the Emperor to grant a pardon; but Nero

WALL OF WAILING, JERUSALEM.

often hustled his victims off to death in an hour, and Helius surely would not let much water flow down the Tiber between the condemnation and the execution.

A centurion at the head of his Pretorian guard leads Paul out of prison, through the Porta Ostiensis, by the pyramid of Caius Cestius, along the Via Ostiensis, for about a mile and a quarter, turns southeast on the

RUINS OF THE ROMAN FORUM.

Via Ardeatina for three quarters of a mile to a hollow, strips, scourges, and beheads him with a sword.

> No more to tread the desert's burning sand
>     Or climb the pass where mountain snows congeal!
> No more to brave the robber's ruffian band,
>     Or plow the stormy seas with treacherous keel!
>     No more the ignominious lash to feel,
> Or drag the galling chain! — Now dawns the day
>     That sets to long-tried faith the welcome seal;
> And lightened of its weary load of clay,
> The spirit rests with Him who "wipes all tears away."

THE EARLIEST REPRESENTATION OF PAUL'S MARTYRDOM
ON THE SARCOPHAGUS OF BASSUS.

Tradition also says three fountains sprang up at the three places where Paul's head touched the ground, and so the place is known as Tre Fontane, or Fountains. The waters are claimed to be healing, and so they are called Aquae Salviae, or Health Springs. They say Lucina buried the body in her burial-ground about a mile from the Ostian Gate.

Constantine, the first Christian emperor, encased the bones in solid metal, 5 by 5 by 5, and built a church over the grave. In 388 Valentinian, Theodosius, and Arcadius began to enlarge the church, which was finished in 395 by Honorius. His sister, Galla Placidia, wife of Atawulf, king of the Goths, covered the arch with glorious mosaics. The magnificent church is adorned with twenty-four columns of the wonderful purple-veined Phrygian marble, likely taken from the Basilica Paulli, mentioned by Pliny the Elder.

Of this church Prudentius writes: —

> Imperial splendor all the roof adorns;
> Whose vault a monarch built to God and graced
> With golden pomp the vast circumference.
> With gold the beams he covered, that within
> The light might emulate the beams of morn.
> Beneath the glittering ceilings pillars stood
> Of Parian stone, in fourfold ranks disposed;
> Each curving arch with glass of various dye
> Was decked: so shines with painted mead
> In spring's prolific day." — *Passio Beat. Apost.*

On July 28, 1838, there was found Constantine's marble casing of the coffin with the inscription: —

PAULO

APOSTOLO MART

## THE IMPERIAL ARTIST ON TOUR.

The Parthian prince Tiridates conquered Armenia, but Gnaeus Domitius Corbulo, one of the greatest generals of the Roman Empire, at last conquered him, and in 66 "the King of Kings" came to Rome, kneeled before Nero to receive the crown, and said: "My lord, as thy slave am I come unto thee, who art my god, to worship thee as the sun itself. I will be what thou makest of me, for thou art my lot and my fortune."

The splendid spectacle did not remove the resentment against Nero, though it cost him 416,000,000 sesterces, say, $12,000,000.

At the close of 66 Nero left the whole business of the vast empire to the former slave Helius, a worthy understudy of his worthy master, and went to seek new laurels in the home of art, "for the Greeks were the only people who had an ear for music and the only fit judges of him and his art."

In his company were several thousand young men wearing the gold ring of knighthood. The baggage was carried in a thousand wagons, some of which were *carrucae dormitoriae,* or Pullman palace sleeping cars, richly decorated with silver and ivory; one was even called the "Golden Car," Nero's private sleeper. The drivers were clad in scarlet, the horses shod with silver, the runners broidered with gold. The cities of Greece were decorated to receive Nero. In order to accommodate him, the festivals of various years were all held in one. The people flocked to the sacred sport to see the imperial victories.

ST. PAUL ON TOP OF THE COLUMN OF MARCUS AURELIUS.

In 1888 M. Holleaux found the speech Nero made at Araephia in Boeotia. — How did Nero win his prizes? He simply killed one singer who dared sing better than Caesar. After that Caesar won all the singing contests! In a chariot race he tumbled off his car twice, was replaced, could not stand, never reached the goal — yet was crowned victor! Thus he received 1,800 prizes, even the Olympian olive crown, and then proclaimed the "liberty of Greece." Liberty! He killed wealthy Greeks for their money and stole statues — five hundred from Delphi alone. He married Sporus, a man.

"Our Lord and God" were the titles given to this Roman emperor and later to the Roman Pope.

Helius sent warnings of trouble brewing in various parts of the empire. Nero came to Naples in the fall of 67 — and played games. On March 19 he heard of the revolt of Julius Vindex,

PAUL'S DEATH AND HIS INFLUENCE. 333

CONSTANTINE PROMISES VICTORY TO HIS SOLDIERS IN THE SIGN OF THE CROSS.
GIULI ROMANO.

the Governor of Gaul. Nero thought he could get rid of the trouble by deposing the traitor with a stroke of the pen. He would finish the games and wasted a week.

The conquering artist drove leisurely to Rome as an Olympian victor, drawn by white horses in the newly gilt chariot used by Augustus in his triumph over Antony and Cleopatra. He entered Rome through a breach in the wall and 1,808 men hung 1,808 wreaths of victory upon the obelisk

NERO.    TITUS.

in the Circus of Nero — the obelisk now standing in front of St. Peter's Church.

As the procession moved solemnly through the Forum to the temple of Apollo on the Palatine Hill, victims were slain, and the way was strewn with saffron, flowers, and sweetmeats.

"Hail, Olympionicus! Hail, Pythionicus! Hail, Nero Apollo!"

## "WHAT AN ARTIST IS ABOUT TO DIE!"

Fresh dispatches from the revolted provinces of Gaul. Calling the Senate together, Nero briefly dismissed the conspiracy and consulted his ministers about a new organ played by water and other musical instruments.

Galba revolted from Nero on April 2, 68, and Otho, the former

FACADE OF ST. PAUL'S OUTSIDE THE WALLS OF ROME.

THE FLAVIAN THEATER.
Built by captive Jews after the destruction of Jerusalem on the site of Nero's Golden House.

husband of Poppaea, joined him. Nero was at dinner in the Golden House when the defection of the last legion was announced. He tore the letter; upset the table; dashed to the floor two wonderful cups, called Homeric, from the scenes on them; borrowed poison from Locusta and went to the Servilian Gardens; sent servants to Ostia to make ready a squadron of swift vessels for flight to Egypt; asked officers to go with him to escape; one of them dared sneer, "Is death so hard?"

INTERIOR OF CHURCH OF ST. PAUL WITHOUT THE WALLS.
Here the Apostle was buried.

Nero thought of resigning and supporting himself with his harp. He thought of getting support from the Parthian refugees. He thought of going to Gaul to meet the revolting armies unarmed and to conquer them with his tears. He thought of dressing in mourning, appearing barefooted and unshaven before the public, and imploring pardon for his crimes: if refused, he would beg to be made governor of Egypt. He went out to throw himself from the bridge into the Tiber, but his courage failed, and he came back. He called for the Pretorian guards; Tigellinus at their head had stolen his poison and stolen away. The German life-guard had

THE ENTRY OF TITUS INTO JERUSALEM.

PORTA DEL POPOLO. CHURCH OF SANTA MARIA DEL POPOLO.

THE ARCH OF CONSTANTINE.

also deserted. He rushed into the streets and knocked at the door of friends. None would take him in. He came back to his bedroom and called for the gladiator Speculus to kill him; Speculus was gone. He asked for a hiding-place. Phaon, Sporus, Epaphroditus, and a nameless fourth put the barefooted Nero on a horse to slink out of the Nomentana Gate to the freedman Phaon's villa four miles out on the Patinaria road. The lord of the world crept on all fours through the marsh and quenched his thirst with the stagnant water.

Inside, they put him on a couch and gave him some stale bread and tepid water. He ordered his grave dug and said, "What an artist is about to die!"

Seizing two daggers, he felt their points. He begged Sporus to kill him and wail for him. Hearing the horsemen come to arrest him, he recited from the Iliad: "Struck is the ear by the sound of the hoofs of the hurrying horses."

He feebly tried several times to push the dagger into his throat, but his nerve was gone. Then Epaphroditus helped and drove the dagger home. The soldiers burst in to seize him. "Too late! Is this your fidelity?"

THE EMPEROR CONSTANTINE THE GREAT.

In death his face had a frightful expression, and all fled in horror. June 9, 68 — the last of the Caesars!

The Senate had sentenced him to be beaten to death, dragged by the heels, and flung into the Tiber. Icelus, the freedman of Galba, permitted a decent funeral. Nero's faithful nurses, Claudia Ecloge and Alexandra, his mistress Acte, and three men raised $5,000, cremated the body, wrapped in a sheet of white woven with gold and used on his bed on New Year's night.

The ashes were placed in an urn of porphyry on an altar of Carrara in a tomb of Thracian marble at the burial-place of the family of the Domitii, on a spur of the Pincian Hill, to the right of Santa Maria del

A CHRISTIAN MOTHER STRENGTHENING HER DAUGHTER TO BE FAITHFUL UNTO DEATH.

LOUIS SAUZAY.

Popolo, where Pope Alexander VI was later buried, and where Luther lived for about four weeks.

The Pretorian guards made Galba Emperor in 68 and on January 15, 69, murdered him in the open Forum.

The new emperor was Otho, former husband of Poppaea. Defeated in battle, he leisurely and calmly slew himself after just eighty-eight days of empire.

SPOILS FROM THE TEMPLE AT JERUSALEM.
From the Arch of Titus.

The new emperor was Vitellius, "like to those unclean animals which, once gorged with food, think only of sleeping," says Tacitus. Civil war raged; 40,000 corpses in Rome; the Capitol in flames. The emperor sought shelter in a shack, was dragged the whole length of the Sacred Way, half naked, with a rope around his neck, jeered and jostled by the noble Romans, hacked to pieces, the quivering pieces cast into the Tiber.

*The executor of God's judgment over Jerusalem.* The new emperor was Vespasian, the conqueror of the Jews. His son Titus was "the darling and delight of mankind," who slew seven of Jerusalem's defenders with

FAITHFUL UNTO DEATH.     A. LELOIR.

seven arrows and took the city on the Sabbath, September 8, 70, on his daughter's birthday, when he was thirty and his father sixty. His arch at Rome tells his triumph to this very day.

Then the Temple worship at Jerusalem ended for all time.

"Behold, your house is left unto you desolate," Christ had said. Matt. 23, 38. And the Jews wail at the wall of wailing at Jerusalem.

Vespasian celebrated his victory over the Jews by striking medals with the legend *Judaea capta.* Hadrian forbade circumcision, placed a heathen colony in Jerusalem, called it Aelia Capitolina, on the foundations of the Temple he built a temple of Jupiter, and forbade the Jews to enter the city on pain of death. See Luke 19, 41.

The Caesars cruelly persecuted the Christians, but "the blood of the martyrs is the seed of the Church," and the Christians grew. Constantine saw what was coming. On his banner he placed the cross and in this sign conquered his pagan rival and became the first Christian emperor; his arch at Rome tells of his triumph to this day.

In 330 he passed under this arch from Rome to live at "New Rome," Constantinople.

Caligula brought over an obelisk from Egypt and set it up on the Vatican; it is now the sole and silent witness of the horrible tortures of the Christian martyrs in Nero's circus. But the victims became the victors — the Cross of Christ tops the obelisk and at the base an inscription reads: —

> Behold the cross of the Lord.
> Christ conquers:
> Christ reigns:
> Christ rules.
> Christ defend His people from every evil.

Also, we have read: —

> "Christ paid all our debts."

In 1586 the architect Domenico Fontana set it up in front of St. Peter's.

Marcus Aurelius celebrated his victory over the German Marcomanni on a splendid column in the Via Lata, or Broadway. Look up. Who stands on top? St. Paul. "At last Thou hast conquered, O Galilean!"

Paul had indeed no need to be ashamed of the Gospel of Christ, for by it he had turned the Roman world upside down.

## BY FAITH HE, BEING DEAD, YET SPEAKETH.
### Heb. 11, 4.

Aeneas brought the gods from conquered Troy to Rome and founded a mighty empire, and so Paul brought the true religion from conquered Jerusalem to Rome and planted the kingdom of God. He brought Christ from the East to the West, to Europe, and from there it was brought to the Western World, to America, where we enjoy the freedom of Christ in peace as it was never enjoyed before in all the history of the world.

> He who can part from country and from kin
>   And scorn delights and tread the thorny way,
> A heavenly crown through toil and pain to win;
>   He who, reviled, can tender love repay
>   And, buffeted, for bitter foes can pray;
> He who, upspringing at his Captain's call,
>   Fights the good fight, and when at last the day
> Of fiery trial comes, can nobly fall, —
>   Such were a saint — or more, and such the holy Paul.

He, too, came in the fulness of time. "He is the most vital and versatile character history knows. The hero of will and of thought, the leader in words and works. The deep and lofty thinker and at the same time the practical builder and gallant fighter; withal, the gentleman with the finest manners of any man upon record," in the opinion of Coleridge.

Adolphe Monod writes: "Should any one ask me to name the man who of all others has been the greatest benefactor of our race, I should say without hesitation, the Apostle Paul. His name is the type of activity the most endless and at the same time the most useful that history has cared to preserve."

The world's most important language is the Greek. The Greek of the New Testament is "the most important dialect in the literary history of the world," as Professor Moulton of Cambridge writes. In the New Testament, Paul's letters are veritable "tracts for the times," "written on the drumhead in the field of battle," written in a style "the most living, the most nervously sensitive, which the world has ever known," according to Dean Farrar. Look at the letters and see the gleaming rapier of his intellect flashing; put your ear to his letters and hear his heart throb with love for Christ and the Gentiles and the Jews.

Luther says the words of Paul are not dead words; they are living creatures and have hands and feet. And as was said of Luther's style, so it may be said of Paul's, it is a continual battle.

Millions and millions have thought Paul's thoughts after him and spoken his words after him. He is the "heart of the world," as Chrysostom called him, because, as Deissmann puts it, "Jesus is the One, Paul the first after the One, the first in the One."

Speaking of Paul's language, Mr. Ed Bevan says: "The preachers of the New Life, in breaking through the traditional literary conventions, . . . were not sinking to a lower level, even from a literary point of view, but rising to a higher." And Wilamovitz, the great Hellenist of Berlin, says: "That this Greek of his has no connection with any school or with any model, that it streams as best it may from the heart in an impetuous torrent, and yet is real Greek, . . . makes him a classic of Hellenism. Now at last one can again hear in Greek the utterance of an inner experience, fresh and living. It is only judging by very false and artificial standards that Paul can appear, as Bossuet represented him, a speaker destitute of power and charm, effective only by a transcendent miracle. Simply as eloquence or literature, First Corinthians 13 is superior to anything in Dio Chrysostom."

MEDALS STRUCK BY VESPASIAN TO CELEBRATE THE CAPTURE OF JERUSALEM.

Paul's letters are the earliest books of the New Testament, the beginning of Christian correspondence, an epoch in the history of the Church and of the world. Paul is the world's greatest letter-writer, and Chrysostom writes: "As I keep hearing the epistles of the blessed Paul read, and that twice every week, and often three or four times, I get roused and warmed with a desire at recognizing the voice so dear to me and seem to fancy him all but present to my sight and behold him conversing with me. But I grieve and am pained that all people do not know this man as they ought to know him." In our day Professor Peabody of Harvard writes: "If I had my life to live over again, I would be willing to devote the solid portion of my days to the study of the Pauline epistles. I should feel that in these alone there is work enough and joy enough for a lifelong scholarship."

RAFFAEL.
THE ARCHANGEL MICHAEL'S VICTORY OVER SATAN, OR PAUL'S VICTORY
OVER PAGANISM.

"Over the vast extent of the Roman Empire Paul everywhere projects his shadow," it has been truly said. Yes, and beyond the Roman Empire. Dean Stanley asks: "May we not believe, in a sense higher than Chrysostom ever dreamt of, that the pulses of that mighty heart are still the pulses of this world's life — still beat in these latter ages with greater force than ever?"

Yes, very emphatically, yes. Paul brought Christ from the East to the West, and since Luther freed Christ in Paul's letters, Christ has been brought to America, where the principles of Luther brought separation of Church and State into our Constitution, so that we can enjoy civil and religious liberty as never before in the history of the world.

# CHRONOLOGY OF THE ACTS OF THE APOSTLES.

| PERIOD | DATE, A. D. | ACTS | EVENTS | PLACE | CONTEMPORARY HISTORY, A. D. | Hastings' B. D. | Ramsay | Harnack | McGiffert | Zahn |
|---|---|---|---|---|---|---|---|---|---|---|
| JESUS, THE FOUNDATION OF THE CHURCH | B. C. 5 to A. D. 30, Apr. 30, Apr. May 18 | ......... 1, 1—12 | Life of Christ .................. Crucifixion .... Resurrection Days — 40 days, 10 appearances ... Ascension ........... | Palestine Jerusalem Galilee Near Bethany | Paul born B. C. 1 Augustus Caesar, 30 B. C. — 14 A. D. Tiberius, A. D. 14—37 Pontius Pilate, 26—36 Paul enters public life, A. D. 29, age 30 | | | | | |
| COMMISSION TO THE APOSTLES | 30 | 1, 8 | Commission to preach the Gospel and witness to Jesus, the Christ, unto all the world .... | Bethany | ...................... | 29—30 | 30 | 29 or 30 | 30 | 30 |
| THE POWER GIVEN | | 1, 13, 14 1, 15—26 2, 1—4 2, 5—13 | Waiting for the promise of the Father ......... Election of Matthias in place of Judas ........ Descent of the Holy Spirit ................. The gift of tongues ....................... | Jerusalem, in an upper room Jerusalem Jerusalem | Seneca, 4 B. C.—65 A. D. Essays and Tragedies | 29—30 | 30 | 29 or 30 | 30 | |
| I THE CHURCH AT JERUSALEM | | 2, 14—36 2, 37—41 2, 42—47 2, 44, 45 3, 1—10 3, 11—26 | Peter's address ........................... The first converts ... three thousand ....... Description of the early Church ............ The community of goods .................. The lame man healed in the Temple ......... Second address of Peter .................... | Jerusalem Temple courts | Gamaliel 30 B. C.—40 A. D. Philo Judaeus, 20 B. C. until after 40 A. D. | 29 or 30 | 30 | 29 or 30 | 30 | |
| Growth of the Church at Jerusalem. First church organization. Five or six years of undisturbed growth | 30 30 30 to 34 34 35 to 36 | 4, 1—22 4, 23—35 4, 36, 37 5, 1—11 5, 12—16 5, 17—42 6, 1—4 6, 5, 6 | The first persecution. Peter and John imprisoned. A fresh baptism of the Spirit ............... Barnabas and his gifts .................... Ananias and Sapphira .................... Signs and wonders. Healing the sick. Great increase in the number of disciples ...... Second persecution. Apostles imprisoned. Release. Rearrest. Address to the Sanhedrin ... A difficulty between Hebrews and Hellenists .... Deacons appointed to remedy the difficulty. The first church organization ............... | Jerusalem Jerusalem Jerusalem Jerusalem Jerusalem Jerusalem Jerusalem Jerusalem | | 30 to 35 | | | | |
| SUMMARY OF FIRST PERIOD | | 6, 7 | GREAT INCREASE IN NUMBERS ............ | Jerusalem | | | | | | |
| II BEGINNING OF OPPOSITION | 35 to 36 36 36 | 6, 8—15 7, 1—53 7, 54—60 | Stephen. Character, work, arrest. ........... Stephen's defense before the Sanhedrin ...... Stephen, the first Christian martyr .......... | Jerusalem Jerusalem Jerusalem | Pilate sent to Rome for trial A. D. 36 Vitellius takes his place as governor | 36 | 33 | 30 | 31 or 32 | |

NOTE. — The dates in the left-hand column are very nearly in accord with those of Mr. C. H. Turner in Dr. Hastings's *Dictionary of the Bible* and not far from the average of the leading authorities. Dates are also given from a number of leading scholars to show the variation of opinions, usually within narrow limits, and that we must be "content with what Harnack describes as relative rather than absolute chronology." The dates of secular events are derived originally from Tacitus, Josephus, and Eusebius; and these do not agree, although there are considerations, such as the different times of beginning the year, which may bring them closer together. But the dates are abundantly accurate for all practical purposes.

## CHRONOLOGY OF THE ACTS OF THE APOSTLES. — Continued.

| Period | Date, A.D. | Acts | Events | Place | Contemporary History, A.D. | Hastings B.D. | Ramsay | Harnack | McGiffert | Zahn | Clemen |
|---|---|---|---|---|---|---|---|---|---|---|---|
| **Gospel Extended to Samaria, Galilee, and Northern Syria, chiefly to Jews. Conversion of Paul.** | 36 | 8, 1—4 | A great persecution, extending the Gospel to | Samaria, Galilee, and Syria | | 36 | 33 | 30 | 31 or 32 | | |
| | 36 | 8, 5—24 | Philip the evangelist and Simon the magician | Samaria | Tiberius died Mar. 16, A.D. 37 | | | | | | |
| | 36 | 8, 25—40 | Philip and the Ethiopian Lord of the Treasury | Road to Gaza | | | | | | | |
| | 36 | 9, 1—19 | Paul of Tarsus converted | Near Damascus | Paul, age 37 | | | | | | |
| | 36 | 9, 20—22 | Paul preaching at Damascus | Damascus | | | | | | | |
| | 36—38 | 9, 23 | Paul in Arabia. Returns to Damascus | Arabia | | | | | | | |
| | | 9, 23—26 | Paul persecuted. Escapes in a basket over the wall | Damascus | | | | | | | |
| | 38—38 | 9, 27—29 | Paul comes to Jerusalem and preaches there | Jerusalem | Caligula, emperor, Mar. 16, 37, to Jan. 24, 41 | 38 | 35, 36 | 33 | 34, 35 | 38 | 30 |
| | 38—40 | 9, 30 | Paul in Cilicia and Syria several years till A.D. 42. | Cilicia, Tarsus, Syria | | | | | | 40 | 34 |
| **Summary of Second Period** | | 9, 31 | Rest from Persecution. Growth in Grace and Numbers | | | | | | | | |
| **III Church Extended to Antioch. Preparation for Receiving the Gentiles. First Gentile church. First Gentile convert** | 41 | 9, 32—35 | Peter cures Aeneas | Lydda | A.D. | | | | | | |
| | | 9, 36—42 | Dorcas restored to life | Joppa | | | | | | | |
| | | 10, 1—48 | Cornelius the Centurion converted. Peter's vision. Pentecost repeated | Caesarea | | | | | | | |
| | 38—41 | 11, 1—18 | Peter called to account for his part in it | Jerusalem | Claudius becomes emperor, Jan. 24, 41; continues till Oct. 13, 54 | | | | | | |
| | 42, 43 | 11, 19—21 | Church in Antioch founded among Gentiles | Antioch | Seneca in exile, 41—49 | | | | | | |
| | 42, 43 | 11, 22—24 | Barnabas comes to Antioch from Jerusalem | Antioch | | | | | | | |
| | 44—46 | 11, 25, 26 | Paul called to Antioch from Tarsus | Antioch | Romans in Britain, 43 | | | | | | |
| | 45, 46 | 11, 27—30 | Relief sent to Jerusalem by Barnabas and Saul | Palestine | The famine | 46 | 45, 46 | 45 | 44 | 43 | 42 to 43 |
| | 44, spring | 12, 1. 2 | Martyrdom of James | Jerusalem | Death of Herod Agrippa I at the games in Caesarea, aged 54 | | | | | 44 | |
| | 44, spring | 12, 3—18 | Imprisonment and deliverance of Peter | Jerusalem | | | | | | | |
| | 44 | 12, 19—23 | Death of Herod Agrippa I | Caesarea | | 44 | 44 | 44 | 44 | | |
| | Early summer 46 | 12, 24. 25 | Return of Paul and Barnabas with John Mark to | Antioch | Paul. Second visit to Jerusalem | | | | | | |
| **Summary of Third Period** | | 12, 24 | The Word of God Grew and Multiplied | | | | | | | | |
| **IV Gospel Extended to Gentiles. Missions in Asia Minor. Beginning of Paul's second missionary tour** | March, 47 to 49 | 13, 1—3 (Chaps.) 13, 14 | First foreign missionaries, Paul and Barnabas. First Missionary Journey | Antioch Asia Minor | London founded, 47 Expulsion of the Jews from Rome, 48 (?) | 47 to 49 | 47 to 50 | 48 to 51 | 45 to 47 | 50 to 51 | 43 to 47 |
| | | 13, 4—52 | Paul in Cyprus and Antioch of Pisidia. Success and persecution | Asia Minor | Paul, age 50 | | | | | | |
| | 49 | 14, 1—20 | Paul in Iconium, Lystra, Derbe | Asia Minor | | | | | | | |
| | 49 | 14, 21—25 | Revisiting the churches there formed | Antioch, in Syria | | | | | | | |
| | 50 | 14, 26—28 | Return to Antioch. Report to the home church | | | | | | | | |
| | 50 | 15, 1—35 | Council at Jerusalem. Early in 50 | Jerusalem | | 49 | 50 | 51 | 47 | 52 | 48 |
| | Spring, 50—52 | 15, 36—40 | Paul and Barnabas go on separate missions | Antioch | | | | | | | |
| | Spring, 50—52 | 15, 40. 41 | Paul, with Silas, begins his Second Missionary Tour | Asia Minor | | 49 to 52 | 50 to 53 | | 46 to 49 | 52 | 49 to 52 |
| | | 16, 1—4 | Paul revisits the churches of his first tour | Asia Minor | | | | | | | |
| **Summary of Fourth Period** | | 16, 5 | Churches Established in the Faith. Increasing Numbers | | | | | | | | |

## CHRONOLOGY OF THE ACTS OF THE APOSTLES. — *Continued.*

| | | | | | | | | | | |
|---|---|---|---|---|---|---|---|---|---|---|
| 50–52 | 16, 6–11 | Paul enters Europe | Macedonia | Caractacus defeated in Britain | Late in 50 | Late in 51 | Late in 52 | Late in 48 | Nov., 52 | |
| | 16, 12–40 | Paul at Philippi; Lydia; conversion of the jailer | Philippi | Expulsion of the Jews from Rome | | | | | May, 54 | |
| 51–52 | 17, 1–14 | Paul in Thessalonica and Berea | Macedonia | | | | | | | |
| | 17, 15–34 | Address on Mars Hill | Athens | | | | | | | |
| 51–52 | 18, 1–18 | Paul at Corinth. Crispus. *1. and 2. Thessalonians* | Corinth | Gallio, proconsul of Corinth | 52 | 53 | 54 | 50 | 54 | 53–59 |
| | 18, 18–22 | Returns home via Ephesus and Caesarea to | Antioch | Paul, age 52 | | | | | | |
| 52 | 18, 22 | Paul makes a brief visit to Jerusalem, his fourth(?) | Jerusalem(?) | | 52 to 56 | 53 to 57 | | 49 to 53 | 54 54 | |
| 53 | 18, 22, 23 | Paul spends some time in Antioch. *Galatians* | Syria | Nero, emperor, 54 to 68 | | | | | 55 | |
| | 18, 23 | Paul begins his Third Missionary Tour | Asia Minor | Birth of Tacitus, 55 | | | | | | |
| 53 | 18, 24–28 | Apollos at Ephesus | Asia Minor | St. Peter at Corinth, 55 or 56 | | | | | | |
| 53–56 | 19, 1–11 | Paul nearly three years at Ephesus. *1. Corinthians* | Ephesus | | | | | | | |
| | 19, 12–19 | Sceva, the exorcist. Burning the magic books | Ephesus | Felix, procurator, 52–59 | | | | | | |

**SUMMARY OF FIFTH PERIOD** 19, 20 MIGHTILY GREW THE WORD OF GOD AND PREVAILED

### VI

| | | | | | | | | | | |
|---|---|---|---|---|---|---|---|---|---|---|
| 57 | 19, 21–41 | The mob. Silver shrines of Diana | Ephesus | | | | | | | |
| | 20, 1–5 | Paul revisits Macedonia. *2. Corinthians* | Cities of Macedonia | | 55 | 56 | 53 | | 57 | |
| | | Paul three months in Greece. *Romans* | Greece | | | Dec., Jan., Feb., 57 | | | | |
| | 20, 6–12 | Paul at Troas. Eutychus restored to life | Troas | Paul, age 58 | | | | | | |
| | 20, 13–16 | Sails, via Assos, Mytilene, Samos, to | Miletus | | | | | | | |
| | 20, 17–38 | Address to the elders of Ephesus at | Miletus | | | | | | | |
| | 21, 1–10 | Journey to Jerusalem via Tyre (7 days), Caesarea (warning by Philip the evangelist) | Sea and land | | | | | | | |
| 57 | 21, 17–20 | Paul's reception at | Jerusalem | | 56 | 57 | 54 | 53 | Pente-cost, 58 | 59 |
| | 21, 21–31 | Paul's vow and the mob in the Temple | Jerusalem | | | | | | | |
| | 21, 31–40 | Rescue by the Roman general | Jerusalem | | | | | | | |
| | 22, 1–21 | Paul's address to the mob from the stairs | Jerusalem | | | | | | | |
| | 22, 22–30 | Paul a prisoner in Castle Antonia | Jerusalem | | | | | | | |
| | 23, 1–10 | Paul's defense in the castle hall | Jerusalem | | | | | | | |
| | 23, 11 | A vision of good cheer | Jerusalem | | | | | | | |
| | 23, 12–22 | The conspiracy against Paul's life | Jerusalem | | | | | | | |
| | 23, 23–35 | Paul sent secretly to Felix at | Caesarea | | | | | | | |
| June to June 58 and 59 | 24, 1–22 | Paul's trial before Felix | Caesarea | | | | | | | |
| 59 | 24, 23–27 | Paul in prison two years at | Caesarea | | | | | | | |
| 59 | 25, 1–9 | Paul accused to Festus, the new governor | Caesarea | Festus, procurator, 59 | written | | | | 60 | |
| 59 | 25, 10–12 | Paul's appeal to Caesar | Caesarea | *Luke's Gospel* probably | | | | | | |
| | 25, 13–27 | Festus consults with King Agrippa | Caesarea | by Suetonius in Britain | | | | | | |
| | 26, 1–32 | Paul's defense before Festus and his court | Caesarea | about 62 | | | | | | |
| Sept., 59 | 27, 1–44 | Paul's voyage and shipwreck | Mediterranean | | | | | | | |
| | 28, 1–10 | Paul rescued; his experience on the island of | Malta | | | | | | Sept., 60 | 59–61 |
| Spring, 60 | 28, 11–16 | Paul's journey from Malta to Rome | Italy | *Philippians* | 59 | | 57 | 55 | March, 61 | 61–62 |
| | 28, 15, 16 | Paul's reception at Rome | Rome | *Colossians* | | | | | | |
| | 28, 17–29 | Paul's conference with the Jews at Rome | Rome | *Ephesians* | | | | | | |
| 61–62 | 28, 30, 31 | Paul two years a prisoner in his own hired house | Rome | *Philemon* | 61 | | 59 | | | |
| | | Close of the history in the Acts | | Paul, age 61, 62 | | | | | | |

**SUMMARY OF SIXTH PERIOD** 28, 31 THE GOSPEL EXTENDED TO ROME

| | | | | | | | | | | |
|---|---|---|---|---|---|---|---|---|---|---|
| 62–68 | | Probable composition of *Acts* | Rome | | Before 80? | Before 80? | Before 80–90? | Before 81–96? | 63 | 62–64 |
| 63 | | Release | | | Yes 62 | Yes 59 | No 58 | | | |
| 63–66 | | Paul probably visited Macedonia, Greece, Ephesus, Spain. Burning of Rome, July 19, 64 | Europe | *1. Timothy* | | | | | | |
| 66 | | Second imprisonment of Paul | Rome | *Titus* | 65 | 65, 67 | 64 | 58 | 66, 67 | |
| 66 or 70 | | Martyrdom of Paul | Rome | *2. Timothy* | | | | | | |
| August, 70 | | Destruction of Jerusalem | | Martyrdom of St. Peter | | | | | | |

*Gospel Extended to Europe* — Second missionary journey continued into Europe. Third missionary journey

*Paul at Rome. The appeal to Caesar. The way by which Paul was brought to Rome*

*Gospel Extended to Rome*

# WORKS CONSULTED.

Abbott's, J., *Nero.*
Abbott's, L., *Paul.*
*Academy,* Vol. 42.
Adam's *Paul in Every-day Life.*
Aiton's *Paul and His Localities.*
Albrecht's *Paulus.*
Alexander's *Ethics of Paul.*
Alford's *Saul of Tarsus.*
Allen's, Katharine, *The Appian Way* in *Art and Archeology,* October, 1917.
Allen's *Missionary Methods of Paul.*
Allen and Grensted's *Intr. N.T. Books.*
*American Bible Repository,* Vol. 4.
*American Journal of Archeology,* Vol. 7.
Anderson's *Paulinism; Bibl. Rev.,* 1916.
Andrews's *Acts.*
Angus's *Environment Early Christianity.*
Arnold's *Paul and Protestantism.*
*Athenaeum,* 1902, II, 76.
Atkinson's *Paul.*
*Atlantic,* Vol. 68, p. 158.

Bacon's *Story of St. Paul; Making of N.T. Chronological Scheme of Acts; Harvard Theol. Review,* Apr., 1921.
Baldwin's *Men of N.T.*
*Baptist Quarterly,* Vols. 1 and 7.
Bartlet's *Acts; Apostolic Age; Char. and Comp. of Acts,* in *Bibl. World,* Vol. 19.
Baur's *Leben d. Ap. Paulus.*
Bernstorff's, And., Graf von, *Ap. Gesch.*
Berry's *Leah of Jerusalem.*
Besser's *Paulus; Ap. Gesch.*
*Bibliotheca Sacra,* Vols. 7, 9, 11, 35, 48, 52, 53, 55, 56, 59, 60.
Biggs's *Church's Task.*
Binney's *Paul.*
Bird's *Paul of Tarsus.*
Blunt's *Lect. Paul in Rome.*
Bonney's *Paul's Message,* in *Modern Sermons.*
*Book by Book.*
Bosworth's *Paul's Methods of Evangelization,* in *Bibl. World,* Vol. 22.
Bradley's *Have We Authentic Portraits of Paul? Bibl. World,* Vol. 9.
*Britannica.*

Brock's *Paul.*
Brown's *Paul's Thorn.*
Bruce's *Paul's Conception of Christianity.*
Bunsen's *Islam or True Christianity?*
Burton's *Paul; Records and Letters Ap. Age; Experiences of Saul,* in *Bibl. World,* Vol. 1.
Butler's *Paul in Rome.*

Cadbury's *Style and Lit. Meth. Luke.*
Campbell's *Paul the Mystic.*
Case's *Evol. Early Christianity.*
*Catholic Encyclopedia.*
Chase's *Credibility of Acts.*
*Christian Examiner,* Vols. 48, 51, 63, 69.
*Christian Literature,* Vol. 14.
*Christian Observer,* Vols. 10, 18, 39.
Clark's *Footsteps of Paul.*
Clarke's *Ideas of Paul.*
Clemen's *Paulus; Primitive Chr.*
Colbeck's *A Summer Cruise; A Track of Paul.*
Cone's *Paul; Ep. of Paul.*
*Congreg. Mag.,* Vols. 18, 20.
Conington's *Aeneid.*
Conybeare and Howson's *Paul.*
Couard's *Pred. Bekehrung Paulus'.*
Curtius's *Ephesos in Alt. u. Gegenwart; Athen, Korinth, Ephesos,* in *Gesam. Abhandl.*

Dawson's *Egypt and Syria.*
Deissmann's *Paul,* 2d ed.; *New Light from N.T.; Licht vom Osten; Rel. of Jesus and Faith of Paul.*
De La Flechere's *Portrait of Paul.*
Dill's *Roman Society.*
Dobschuetz's, Ernst, *Paulus: I. Seine weltgeschichtliche Bedeutung.* 1926.
Domaszewski's *Gesch. roem. Kaiser.*
Drummond's *Epistles of Paul.*
*Dublin Review,* Vol. 60.
*Dublin University Mag.,* Vols. 74, 76.
Dubowy's *Klemens v. Rom ueber d. Reise Pauli nach Spanien,* in Bardenhewer's *Bibl. Studien,* 19. Bd., Heft 3; Herder, 1914.

Duchesne's *Early Hist. Church.*
Duruy's *Greece; Rome.*

Eadie's *Paul.*
Edersheim's *Sketches of Jewish Social Life.*
Edmunson's *Church in Rome 1. Cent.*
*Encycl. Biblica.*
England's *Peter's Roman Episcopate,* in *Works,* Vol. 1.
Erdman's *Acts.*
Ernesti's *Ethik d. Paulus,* 3. Aufl.
Eucken's *Truth of Religion.*
Everett's *Gospel of Paul.*
*Expositor's Dict. Texts.*

Fairbairn's *Studies in Religion.*
Falkener's *Ephesus.*
Farrar's *Paul; Messages; Early Days.*
Faunce's *Paul before Agrippa,* in *Bibl. World,* Vol. 7.
Feine, *Der Apostel Paulus.*
Ferrero's *Women of the Caesars; Characters and Events of Roman History.*
Fisher's *Discussions, Paul.*
Foakes-Jackson's *Life of St. Paul.*
Forbes, S. Russell, *Footsteps of St. Paul in Rome.*
Ford's *SS. Peter and Paul Depicted.*
Formilli's, C. T. G., *The Stones of Italy.* 1927.
Fouard's *Paul; Last Years of Paul.*
Frazer's *Pausanias; Adonis, Attis, Osiris.*
Funcke's *Paulus zu Wasser u. zu Lande.*

Gardenhire's *Lux Crucis.*
Gardner's *Rel. Exp. Paul; Eph. Gospel.*
Gardner's, Alice, *Rome the Middle of the World.*
Garvie's *Studies of Paul and His Gospel.*
Gaunt's *Rome.*
Gebhardt's *Bleibt Ostern ein unbewegl. Fest? Daheim,* 3. Apr. 1920.
Gerok's *Von Jerusalem nach Rom.*
Gibbes's *Reflections on Paul.*
Gibbon's *Decline and Fall.*
Gilbert's *Acts; Students' Paul; Women in Public Worship,* in *Bibl. World,* Vol. 2.
*Good Words,* Vol. 31.
Gray's *Bibl. Encycl.*
Green's *Works,* Vol. 3.
Greenbough's *Mind of Christ in Paul.*
Greve's *Bekehrung Pauli.*
Gusman's *Pompeii.*

Hanson's *Paul.*
Hardy's *Studies in Roman History.*
Harnack's *Acts; Date of Acts; Luke the Physician; Expansion of Chr.*
Harris's *Four Lectures on the Western Text.*
Hastings's *Bible Dict.; Dict. Ap. Ch.*
Hauck's *R. E.*
Hausrath's *Paul; N. T. Times.*
Haweis's *Picture of Paul; Conquering Cross.*
Hayes's *Paul and His Epistles.*
Headlam's *St. Paul and Christianity.*
Hemsen's *Paulus.*
Hertzberg's *Gesch. d. roem. Kaiserreiches.*
Hicks's *Paul and Hellenism,* in *Studia Biblica.*
Hinck's *Paul's Mysticism,* in *Bibl. World,* Vol. 2.
Hort's *Sermons on Books of Bible.*
Horton's *Growth of N. T.*
Howson's *Companions of Paul; Metaphors of Paul.*
Hudelson's *Paul's Sufficiency,* in *Am. Bapt. Pulpit.*
Hutton's *Essays.*

*Independent,* Vol. 54, p. 2356.
Irons's *Christianity as Taught by Paul.*
Iverach's *Paul.*

Jackson's *Travels of Paul.*
Jacobus's *Notes on Acts.*
*Jewish Encycl.*
Johnston's *Private Life of Romans.*
Johnston's, C. N., *Paul and His Mission to the Roman Empire.*
Jones's *Paul the Hero; Paul the Orator; The N. T. in the 20. Cent.*
Jordan's *Philippian Gospel.*
Jowett's *Theol. Essays.*
Juelicher's *Paulus u. Jesus.*
Juvenal's *Satires.*

Kaemmel's *Rom u. d. Campagna.*
Keble's *Christian Year.*
Kent's *Work and Teachings of the Apostles; Bibl. Geog. and History.*
Knowling's *Testimony of Paul to Christ; Medical Language of Luke,* in *Bibl. World,* Vol. 20.
Knox's *Year with Paul.*
Koester's *Did Paul Model His Language after that of Demosthenes? Bibl. Sacra,* Vol. 2.

PAUL ON THE WAY TO ROME

Acts 28:15

Lake's *Earlier Epp. of Paul.*
Lanciani's *Golden Days; Pagan and Christian Rome; Destruction of Ancient Rome; New Tales of Old Rome; Forma Urbis Romae.*
La Piana's *Tombs of Peter and Paul Ad Catacumbas; Harv. Theol. Rev., Jan., 1921.*
Leacock's *Studies in Paul.*
Lees's *Paul and His Converts.*
Lewin's *Paul; Fasti Sacri.*
Liddon's *Lect. on Paul,* in *Essays and Addresses.*
Lightfoot's *Bibl. Essays; Dissert. Ap. Age.*
Ligon's *Paul the Apostle.*
Little's *Biog. and Lit. Studies.*
*London Quart. Rev.,* Vol. 34.
Lord's *Paul; Cleopatra.*
Luckock's *Footprints of the Apostles.*
Luke's *Acts.*
Luthardt's *Paul,* in *Christian Observer,* Oct., 1873.
Luzzi's *Struggle for Chr. Truth in Italy.*
Lyttelton's *Observ. Conv., Paul.*

Macduff's *Paul in Rome; Footsteps of Paul.*
Machen's *Jesus and Paul,* in *Princeton Bib. and Theol. Studies,* 1912; *Origin of Paul's Religion,* 1921.
M'Clymont's *N. T. Criticism.*
McGiffert's *Apostolic Age.*
Maclaren's *Acts; Paul's Prayers.*
McLachlam's *Luke.*
Macmillan's *Eastern Mediterranean; Macmillan's Mag.,* Vols. 14, 20.
Mackinlay's *Special Lucan Words; Bibl. Sac.,* Oct., 1920.
Magoun's *Paul's Phraseology and Roman Law,* in *Bibl. Sac.,* Vol. 52.
Martial's *Epigrams.*
Mason's *Spell of Southern Shores.*
Matheson's *Paul; Paul the Illuminated.*
Mathews's *Paul the Dauntless.*
Mathews's, S., *Social Teach. Paul,* in *Bibl. World,* Vols. 19, 20.
Mendenhall's *Plato and Paul.*
Menken's *Apostelgeschichte.*
Mentz's *Zusammenkunft d. Ap. in Jerus.,* in *Ztschr. N. T. Wiss.,* 18. Jahrg., Heft 3.
Merrill's *Essays in Early Christian History.*
*Metropolitan,* Vol. 4.
Meyer's, Arnold, *Jesus or Paul?*

Meyer's, H. A. W., *Commentary.*
Meyers's, F. B., *Paul.*
Miller's *Paul's Message for To-day.*
Miller's, Eliz., *Saul of Tarsus.* (Fiction.)
Moffatt's *Paul and Paulinism.*
Mommsen's *Roem. Provinzen.*
Monod's *Five Disc. on Paul.*
Moorehead's *Outline Studies Acts and Epistles.*
More's, Hannah, *Essays on Paul.*
Morgan's, G. C., *Living Messages.*
Morgan's, W., *Rel. and Theol. of Paul.*
Mueller's *Klass. Alt. Wiss.*
Mueller's, W. Max., *Tarshish,* in *Dict. Bible.*
Munzinger's *Paulus in Korinth.*
Muzzey's *Spiritual Heroes.*
Myers's *Paul.*

*National Mag.,* Vol. 3.
*National Review,* Vol. 1.
Naumann's *Paulus.*
*New Int. Encycl.*
Noble's *Disc. Philippians.*
Norris's *Key to Ep. of Paul.*

Orr's *Jesus and the Gospel; Faith of a Modern Christian.*

Paul's *Epistles.*
*Pauly-Wissowa Realenc. class. Alt.*
Peabody's *Ap. P. and Mod. Mind.*
Peloubet's *Notes,* 1897, 1909, 1916.
Pennell's *Pictures in Land of Temples.*
Pfleiderer's *Paulinism; Primitive Christianity; Influence of Paul.*
Phelps's *Paul as a Letter-writer,* in *Reading the Bible.*
Plumptre's *Paul in Asia Minor.*
*Presbyt. and Ref. Rev.,* Vol. 4.
Prideaux's *Cradle of Christianity.*
Princeton's *Bib. Studies, Paul.*
Pullan's *Books of N. T.*
Purves's *Apostolic Age.*

Ramsay's *Paul the Traveler; Early Church; Pauline Studies; Cities of Paul; Teaching of Paul; Pictures Ap. Church; Recent Discoveries; Luke the Physician; Letters to the Seven Churches; Histor. Com. on Galatians; Histor. Geog. Asia Minor; Tarsus,* in *Dict. Bible; Galatia,* in *Studia Biblica; Impressions of Turkey; Revolution Const. and Turkey.*

*Reformed Q. Rev.*, Vols. 38, 41.
Renan's *Paul; Apostles; Antichrist.*
Resker's *Paul's Illustrations.*
Robertson's *Epochs in Life of Paul; Gram. N. T. Greek; Luke the Historian; Paul the Interpreter of Christ.*
Robinson's, B. W., *Paul.*
Robinson's, Thomas, *Scripture Characters.*
Rockwell's *Latest Discussions on Peter and Paul in Rome,* in *Am. Jour. Theol.,* Jan., 1918.
Roemheld's *Durch Kampf zum Sieg.*
Ropes's *Apostolic Age.*
Rowland's *Paul's Ideal Church and People.*
Rydberg's *Roman Days.*

Sabatier's *Paul.*
Sadler's *Acts.*
Scherer's *Paul,* in *Four Princes.*
Schmiedel's *Did Paul Write Romans?* Hibbert J., Vol. 1.
Schneller's *Apostelfahrten; Paulus.*
Scott's *Pauline Epistles.*
Shahan's *Beginnings of Christianity.*
Sihler's *Cicero; Testimonium Animae; Failure of Classic Civilization; Stoicism and Christianity,* in *Bib. Rev.,* 1916, 1917; *From Augustus to Augustine.*
Sitterley's *Jerusalem to Rome.*
Smith's, David, *Paul.*
Smith's, Edwin, *Last Voyage of Paul,* in *Hom. Rev.,* Aug., 1919.
Smith's, James, *Voyage and Shipwreck of Paul,* 4th ed.
Smyth's *Story of Paul's Life and Letters.*
Soares's *Studies in Life of Paul.*
Speer's *Paul.*
Spence-Jones's *Early Christians in Rome.*
Stalker's *Paul.*
Steinmeyer's *Paulus u. d. Judentum; Paraklese d. Paulus a. d. Christenheit zu Rom.*
Stevens's *Messages of Paul; Theol. of Paul,* in *Bibl. World,* Vol. 3.
Still's *Paul on Trial.*
Stix's *Three Men of Judea.*
Stoeckhardt's *Roemerbrief; Epheserbrief.*
Stokes's *Acts.*
Stosch's *St. Paulus.*
Strong's *Pop. Lect. Books N. T.*
Suetonius's *Nero.*
*S. S. Times,* 1916.

Tacitus's *Annals.*
Talmage's *From Pyramids to Acropolis.*
Tarbell's *Guide,* 1909, 1916.
Taylor's, W. M., *Paul.*
Taylor's, D. H., *Paul.*
Thaddeus's, Victor, *Julius Caesar.* 1927.
*The Fifth Gospel,* by author of *Faith of a Christian.*
*Theol. Rev.,* Vol. 14.
Thirtle's *Who Wrote Hebrews?*
Tholuck's *Paul.*
Thomas's *Prayers of Paul; Acts.*
Torr's *Rhodes.*
Trollope's *Italy.*
Troupe's *Paul and the Mystery Religions.*
Tucker's *Life in Roman World.*

Upton's *Nero the Artist,* in *Musical Pastels.*
Upward's *Secrets of the Past.*

Van Dyke's *Many-sided Paul,* in *Outlook,* Vol. 61.
Vaughn's *Acts; Early Church.*
Vaux's *Asia Minor.*
Von Soden's *Early Hist. Chr. Ch.*
Vos's *Eschat. Aspect Pauline Conception of the Spirit,* in *Bibl. and Theol. Studies,* Princeton, 1912.

Walloth's *Oktavia.*
Warneck's, Joh., *Paulus im Licht d. heut. Heidenmission.*
Waterbury's *Paul,* in *Eloquent Preachers.*
Watkinson's *Moral Paradoxes of Paul.*
Weichardt's *Pompei vor d. Zerstoerung.*
Weinel's *Paulus.*
Weizsaecker's *N. T. Times.*
Wernle's *Begin. Christianity.*
Whyte's *Paul.*
Wilkinson's *Epic of Saul; Common Sense about Saul,* in *Daniel Webster.*
Willett and Campbell's *Teaching N. T.*
Williams's *Eras and Characters of History.*
Wise's *Paul and the Mystics,* in *Selected Writings.*
Wood's *Ephesus.*
Wood's *Life, Letters, and Religion of St. Paul.*
Woodsworth's *Acts; Greece.*
Wrede's *Paulus.*
Wright's *Cities of Paul; Master and Men.*

Zahn's *Introd. N. T.; Paulus,* in *R. E.; Das dritte Buch d. Lukas,* in *Neue kirchl. Ztschr,* 1917, 373—395.

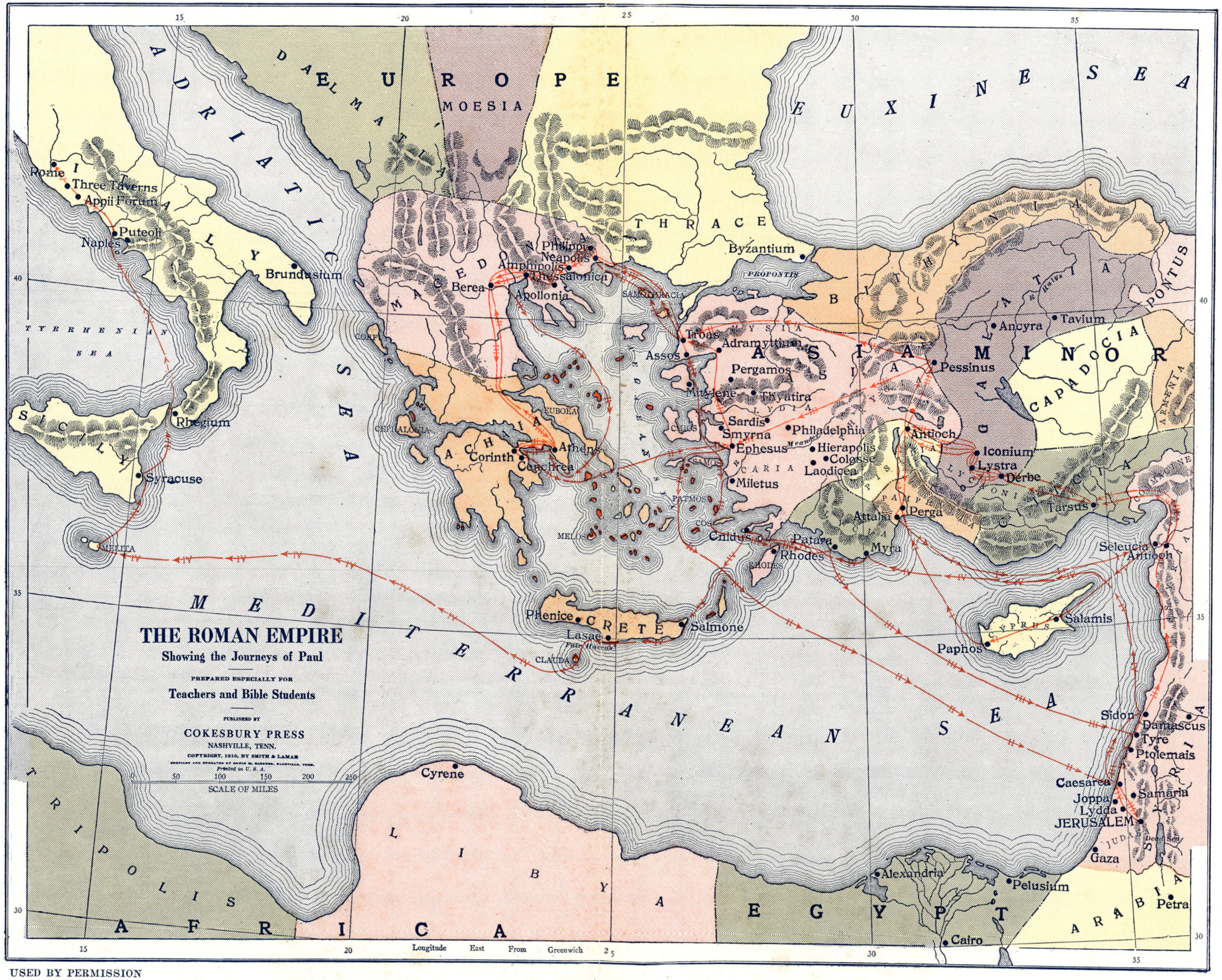


USED BY PERMISSION

## BY THE SAME AUTHOR.

### The Battle of the Bible with the "Bibles."

Cloth, 60 cts.

*Dr. Gerberding, U. L. C.* — "Unique and capital, surely *multum in parvo* [much in little]. To say that I read it with pleasure and profit expresses it mildly. Splendid, helpful book for mission-study."

*Lutheraner* — "Instructive booklet for those wishing to inform themselves about the other religions of the world."

*Lutheran Witness* — "This book supplies busy people, who can devote but little time to the study of false religions, a brief account of the essential teachings of each of these cults. And it is done in such a way that the truth of Christianity shines the brighter, the oftener it is placed upon the dark background of any heathen religion. It is surprising to find how much valuable information Dr. Dallmann has managed to get into these 66 pages."

*Walther League Messenger* — "We recommend this little volume most enthusiastically and hope that it will be widely distributed, especially among our young people."

*Homiletic Magazine* — "Salient facts are stated in a forceful way, and much valuable material is presented."

### Jesus — His Words and His Works.

195 halftones, and 2 maps of Palestine. IX and 481 pages. Size 7¾ × 10. Beautifully bound. Gilt top. Third edition. $4.00.

*Theol. Quartalschrift* — "A masterpiece; orthodox; gripping; fascinating; vivid; crisp. A precious gift of God, which Christendom ought to hail with joy and spread with zeal."

*Der Lutheraner* — "Earnest Bible readers will be delighted. Even the thoughtless will be spurred on to read and read on. Pithy, popular English. Sentences short; say much in few words; in their sureness of aim and hitting remind one of the crack of a repeating rifle. Above all, very interesting."

*Christian Herald, New York* — "A rarely beautiful book. Fascinating form, skilful manner; enjoyable and helpful to young and old."

*Theol. Quarterly* — "Some of the best that learning and art, piety and reverence, could produce. Will be read with unflagging interest and, what is more, with great spiritual profit."

### Martin Luther — His Life and His Labor for the Plain People.

143 illustrations, 300 pages. Cloth, $1.75. Second edition.

*After four hundred years:* —
"Surprises after surprises keep us awaiting other surprises." — "In parts sensational."

*After hundreds of lives of Luther:* —
"Quite different from any other. — Original. — Unique in purpose, arrangement, style, quotations, illustrations; so whimsical, so sarcastic, so utterly unusual, Dallmannesque. — Refreshing. — Breezy. Vivid. — Gripping. — Short and snappy. Splendid.—The reader, under the author's influence, does not have the impression that he is reading history; he imagines that he is entertained and educated by a captivating story-teller. — Most popular book of a very popular author. Written in the American tongue for the people living now. History more interesting than fiction. Yet scholars will enjoy it. The prettiest and most interesting book of the jubilee year."

### Luther's Catechism for Busy People.

43d edition. 15 cts.

### The Christian.

Third edition. 213 pages. Cloth, $1.25.

*Sunday-School Teachers' Quarterly* — "We welcome this beautiful gift edition both for its fine make-up and its valuable contents. In his own way, which has proved so popular, Dr. Dallmann paints the likenesses which ought to be found between Christ and the Christian."

*Theological Monthly* — "Not articles, not essays, not sketches, but Dallmannian presentations of great religious truths. . . . A *vade-mecum* of unusual merit."

*Homiletic Magazine* — "Christians will be enriched by a perusal of its lines, and even the man who does not yet know Christ must feel compelled to admit the Christian's high estate as it is delineated by the author."

# BY THE SAME AUTHOR.

*Concordia Junior Messenger*—"An inspiration and a help in leading every Christian to real service. Buy it. Read it again and again."

## The Lord's Prayer.

271 pages. $1.50.

*Professor Sommer*—"I have read many books on the Lord's Prayer, but this is the best of all."

*P. L., in Luth. Kirchenblatt* — "Every word in this prayer that is at all noteworthy is illuminated from all sides. The various discussions are short and terse, but they unfold a deep treasure of thought. The language is chaste and powerful."

## Follow Jesus.

300 pages. Cloth, $1.50.

*Theol. Quartalschrift* — "Typically American. Sound to the core. Thoroughly evangelical. Diction simple, yet varied. Brief and terse, plastic, ever concrete, seasoned with apt illustrations and examples, a refreshing directness. Popular in the good sense of the word. Never abstract, never tedious. Original everywhere."

## Portraits of Jesus.

Second edition. Cloth, 277 pages. $1.50.

*Der Lutheraner* — "Everybody can draw information, exhortation, and joy from these sermons with their doctrinal, yet crisp, terse, powerful sentences."

## Miles Coverdale.

The Translator of the First English Lutheran Hymn-book. Third edition. 55 illustrations, 164 pages. Cloth, 90 cts.

## John Wiclif.

"The Morning Star of the Reformation." Third edition. 79 pages, illustrated. Cloth, 50 cts.

## Robert Barnes.

Luther's English Friend. Third edition. 40 illustrations, 110 pages. Cloth, 50 cts.

## William Tyndale.

The Translator of the English New Testament. Third edition. 30 illustrations, 84 pages. Cloth, 35 cts.

## Patrick Hamilton.

The First Scotch Lutheran Martyr. Third edition. 16 illustrations, 61 pages. Cloth, 30 cts.

## John Hus.

The Bohemian Martyr. Second edition. 21 illustrations, 62 pages. Cloth, 30 cts.

## Paul Gerhardt.

The Sweet Singer and Staunch Confessor. Second edition. 76 pages, 12 illustrations. Cloth, 50 cts.

## Great Religious Americans.

Fourth edition. Illustrated, 88 pages, Cloth, 50 cts.

## The Titles of the Christians in the New Testament.

Cloth, 352 pages. $1.75.

*Theol. Quart., Wis.* — "Interesting, vivid, fascinating, beautiful."

*Pastor's Monthly, Ohio* — "Interesting and inspiring."

*Luth. Herald, Iowa* — "To select and to treat these titles was a happy thought. It offers us a new angle to old truths so dear to the heart of every believer. Dr. Dallmann's running comments are never tedious. What they may lack in profoundness, they more than make up by their readable form. The reviewer has placed this volume in the hands of a number of sick people of average intelligence. In each case the reaction was the same — praise and delight. The apt illustrations, simple diction, snappy style, and, above all, the soundly evangelical contents place this book among those few books written by Lutheran writers that will really be read by the average Lutheran Christian."

## Luther the Liberator.

Cloth, 87 pages, 30 cts.; 15 cts. by the 100. Fifth edition.

"Good reading for many who know no more about Luther than the mere name." — *Der Lutheraner.*

"Most complete collection of valuable quotations concerning Luther. — Especially valuable, classified under a very complete list of topics." — *American Lutheran Survey.*

[356]